Peer-to-Peer Video

Eli M. Noam • Lorenzo Maria Pupillo
Editors

Peer-to-Peer Video

The Economics, Policy, and Culture of Today's
New Mass Medium

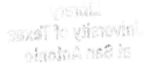
 Springer

Editors
Eli M. Noam
Columbia Institute for Tele-Information
Columbia Business School
3022 Broadway
New York, NY 10027
USA
noam@columbia.edu

Lorenzo Maria Pupillo
Telecom Italia
Corso d'Italia, 41
00198 Roma
Italy
lorenzo.pupillo@telecomitalia.it

ISBN: 978-0-387-76449-8   e-ISBN: 978-0-387-76450-4
DOI: 10.1007/978-0-387-76450-4

Library of Congress Control Number: 2008930764

Printed on acid-free paper

springer.com

To my mother Lotte, and to the memory of my father Ernst

on the one hundredth anniversary of his birth

– E.M.N.

To the memory of my mother Anna and my father Arrigo

– L.M.P.

Acknowledgments

The original impetus for this book came from a conference on Peer-to-Peer Video held at the Columbia Institute for Tele-Information. Since then, this topic started to be an area of permanent interest in the CITI research agenda, bringing together, as it does, video media, the Internet, and tele-communications networks, and transcending the national boundaries of traditional mass media. We would like to thank all of those who contributed chapters to this volume. Special thanks go to Darcy Gerbarg, a co-organizer of the original conference, to Giovanni Amendola for contributing to make this book possible, and to Giulia Mariotti for her excellent editorial assistance.

Introduction

Eli M. Noam and Lorenzo Maria Pupillo

For six decades, television was a relatively straightforward proposition: producers created programs; networks packaged and distributed them nationally; governments licensed the broadcast stations and cable operators that transmitted them, and viewers paid for them either through their attention to advertising, or through subscription payments and user charges. It was a system that was linear, unidirectional, and profitable. But now, the internet is changing all of this. With broadband internet becoming a fixture in the majority of households and its transmission rate growing, it has evolved from a text medium to a pictorial and audio medium, and now to a video medium.

Nowadays, media firms can make their video programs accessible to viewers anytime, anywhere. But this is just the beginning. The internet is not just another way of delivering the same content. It adds the dimensions of two-way communication, individualization, openness, distance insensitivity, searchability, and convergence with other media. On top of that, the cost and performance trend in electronics has made sophisticated equipment affordable to the masses. What this means is that numerous people can produce video programs and make them available to the world to watch, directly or via intermediaries. Thus the style of television and the content can become as varied as that of painting and literature; indeed, even more so since the breadth of variability is greater still for multimedia.

At the same time, the economic base of that new style of television is changing. While some content production might still be supported by advertising, subscription, or pay-per-view charges, a great part of it is created as a way of individual expression, not for a profit.

The move to individualized videos over the internet also carries major implications for traditional media companies such as broadcasters, cable and satellite operators, and production companies. Such a move will likewise be disruptive to the telecommunications networks which must face the challenge of distributing a hugely increased flow of bits, as well as upgrading, investing, and dealing with new competitive business models. Even more difficult will be the change with regards to the governmental process of regulation of electronic media. The creation and transition to new rules and regulations will inevitably be long, controversial, and confusing.

All this is happening right before our eyes. The pace of change is faster than that of any analysis. Yet, such an analysis is more necessary than ever for media companies, governments, and the public alike. It is not easy to conduct, given that the underlying facts keep changing. One of the ways to think about the future developments involving video is to fully understand the changes that have taken place in the – simpler – field of the audio, where music file sharing has been the reality for the past 10 years. That is a good starting point.

To deal with these issues is the aim of this book. It presents a collection of essays from some of the world's experts on internet policy and economics. These articles offer a broad set of analyses of the issues that policymakers, managers, and the public alike needs to deal with today. While there are a few articles on Peer-to-Peer[1] video that analyze specific issues in detail, there is a lack of literature that offers an accessible overview to a broad array of policy, technical, and economic issues. Our goal in putting together this material was to offer such an overview in a single volume. We cover a diverse set of topics (e.g., Economics of Peer-to-Peer, Implications of Video Peer-to-Peer on network usage, Peer-to-Peer and consumer behavior, Peer-to-Peer and user generated content, Policy issues) and perspectives (from industry and academia, and from the United States and Europe). The essays are grouped into three subsections: (1) Peer-to-Peer: Economics; (2) Peer-to-Peer: Market and Technology; and (3) Peer-to-Peer: Policy.

Part I – Peer-to-Peer: Economics

The essays in the first section set the stage for the basic understanding of the economics of Peer-to-Peer Video. In the first, "The Economics of User Generated Content and Peer-to-Peer: The Commons as the Enabler of Commerce," Eli Noam researches the reasons underlying the voluntary use by millions of people of community-based sharing arrangements, such as Peer-to-Peer file sharing. He explains that, although some media content companies view commons-type arrangements as an activity that disrupts markets, in reality a transaction-based economy is often based on the foundation of earlier sharing arrangements that create a base for usage. Therefore, the two systems are not much in conflict but rather stages of an evolutionary process. A sharing agreement is the foundation of transaction-based markets because it creates the conditions that make such transactions possible. Commons arrangements are part of a larger family of activities in which "grassroots" exist. For instance, in the early years of broadcasting, radio amateurs congregated in the airwaves, with no commercial broadcaster present. Later, a commercial broadcasting activity started – on the very basis of the amateur activity. Citizen Band radio users created a foundation for mobile telephony. More recently, the internet was started by the government outside the market, and then given life and structure by a non-profit and university-based community. Commercial internet activities followed. Applications like email and portals are other pertinent examples.

Noam's model starts with the observation that what all these examples have in common is that the participants in the activity derive a benefit from each other's participation, usually referred to as network effects. Total benefits grow with the number of users. Average costs decline with the number of users in high fixed cost, low marginal cost industries. When average costs are equal to average benefits, the point of critical mass, in terms of number of users, is reached and only beyond that point will commercial firms find it profitable to offer a service. Before the critical mass point is reached, no activity will take place, unless there is someone to support or subsidize the activity. This role can be played by the government, as in the early days of the internet, or by a business firm that underwrites the deficit for a while until the critical mass is reached. But there is also an important alternative: the community approach, when early users form a community. Added benefits are derived from an intense spirit of community and sharing. On the cost side, the community activity lowers costs by contributing voluntarist resources to the common endeavor, such as sharing content and computer resources. This enables community activities to start earlier than commercial ones. In time, however, the user base becomes large enough to face commercial entry. Although the community's role will decline, it is likely that it will move to the next new and innovative idea/product? Therefore, Eli Noam recommends that businesses and policy makers should take a positive stance towards these communities. In fact, media business firms should greatly value the community efforts that create the user base for their own subsequent expansion. Public policy should be oriented towards long term goals such as the development of broadband internet applications that can benefit the information economy as a whole.

W. Edward Steinmueller's essay, "Peer-to-Peer Media File Sharing: From Copyright Crisis to Market," points out that the conflict between copyright owners and internet users is creating a distinctive period in the history of internet that he calls the "copyright-crisis era". This crisis cannot exclusively be attributed to features of internet technologies such as Peer-to-Peer file sharing, but has more to do with the capabilities that the new technologies offer, such as the possibility offered to individuals to control their "media environment," i.e., the times and places in which they experience media. Therefore, copyrights not only constrain the way many users of information make use of recorded media, but they also force them into a position of passivity. These constraints ignore what is "technologically possible and socially desirable." However, the Peer-to-Peer's distribution of digital content unique "super copy machine" feature, does cause producers to have legitimate concerns about whether their existing business models will be able to survive. Prof. Steinmueller discusses the resulting tension that emerged in the opening years of the twenty-first century and how the changing users' needs and behaviors create new practices and institutions (rules, norms, and standards). He concludes that "if commercialized media downloading services will be capable of attracting users away from the underground, the result could well be a substantial growth of entry opportunities for new media of all kinds."

In the final essay in this section, "The Economics of Peer-to-Peer," Alain and Eric Bourdeau de Fontenay and Lorenzo Maria Pupillo consider Peer-to-Peer from the perspective of the commons. Although the "commons" have been mostly associated with publicly-held properties, the notion applies to all exchange regimes. Likewise, a new market like online music creates a commons jointly owned by consumers, hosting firms, record companies, and musicians. Good institutions and governance create incentives to achieve efficiency, while their neglect can result in a "tragedy of the commons." For example, music copyrights are a commons that have been disrupted by several subsequent innovations: the record, the radio, and, today, Peer-to-Peer. The authors suggest that this outcome can be avoided. It is conceivable that many of the members of these new Peer-to-Peer commons may be willing to shift to commercial Peer-to-Peer networks, as the commercial success of new services such as iTunes shows.

Viewing exchanges as a commons can improve regulation and business strategy, and can guide entrepreneurs in promoting new markets. For coordination to succeed, the rules and norms of this commons must encourage cooperative behavior. Markets are based on the presupposition that all players are opportunistic. This is not a generic requirement for a commons that recognizes diversity of attitudes among members of the society as a possibility. Interestingly, it is this diversity vis–à–vis opportunism that makes it possible to find governances that support efficient exchanges in the context of market failures. Consumers play a key role in facilitating the emergence of credible Peer-to-Peer content commercial services. Peer-to-Peer is transforming the content into a good that is, in and of itself, more attractive to consumers. However, the actual economic impact is still very sensitive to the strategies suppliers have been pursuing.

The rigidity of their position has contributed to the emergence of today's Peer-to-Peer networks creating an even greater chasm between copyright owners and consumers.

The owners of copyright content may point to their property rights. But the authors argue that they neglect the business dimension of those rights, and that a narrow and rigid interpretation effectively destroys the value of those property rights. It is not good business to enforce copyrights too narrowly. A property right cannot be arbitrarily imposed on society, since that society must find it reasonable in the long-run. It is this social and political dimension of property rights that is often neglected in discussions.

Looking at the extent to which Peer-to-Peer platforms have evolved technologically in response to institutional factors, the article concludes that the RIAA's victory over Napster and other networks such as Aimster, and its unwillingness to negotiate intermediate solutions, created strong incentives for entrepreneurs to favor the new generation of Peer-to-Peer networks. In that respect, it is not unreasonable to conclude that the copyright owners' strategy may have backfired, making it much harder to develop a Peer-to-Peer network that could meet reasonable industry demands while responding to customer demands that became apparent through Napster and similar networks.

Part II – Peer-to-Peer: Market and Technology

The seven essays in the second section focus on an array of issues related to the technological and market impacts of Peer-to-Peer developments. Kevin Werbach's paper throws some light on the implications of video Peer-to-Peer on network usage. Professor Werbach claims that "the tsunami is upon us," and video Peer-to-Peer would have a significant impact even if none of the files involved were subject to intellectual property protection. In fact, video Peer-to-Peer will have a much greater network impact than the largely music-dominated traffic. Already today, Peer-to-Peer file transfer represents an absolute majority of traffic on many networks, as high as 80% in some cases. This traffic is expected to grow for two reasons: enhanced technology and new applications. Peer-to-Peer technology has come a long way since Napster, and now swarming technology makes it possible to break up large files into small pieces, enabling quicker and more efficient file-downloading. On the other side of the equation – the demand – at least four primary classes of applications are likely to drive utilization of video Peer-to-Peer: sharing of pre-recorded video files, distribution of personal videos among families and friends, dissemination of "do it yourself" entertainment and news content, and monitoring and sensor applications. According to Professor Werbach, network operators can take several steps to respond to a growing flood of video Peer-to-Peer traffic. On one side they can put some restrictions on consumer behavior, also using deep packet inspection and blocking/filtering techniques. On the other side, they can take this opportunity to develop new revenue streams. The "if you can't beat'em, join 'em" strategy has already been put into place by many operators. He concludes that the question is when, not if, video Peer-to-Peer is here to stay.

The second and the third essay of this section bring the consumer behavior prospective into the Peer-to-Peer picture. John Carey's paper "Peer-to-Peer video file sharing: what can we learn from consumer behavior?" presents the results of a study of media habits conducted by the author among a core component of early adopters – 18- to 34-year olds – of Peer-to-Peer video. He claims that the place to start is not technology but lifestyle – where they live and the ways lifestyle affects media usage. Peer-to-Peer being predominantly unscheduled, it matches very well with the hectic and irregular schedules of these consumers. Furthermore, the Web is perceived by this group as a convenient and customizable tool that allows people to control content. Indeed, besides the established media companies, there are quite few early producers of Web videos: these include not only video bloggers, underground filmmakers, political activists, and amateur video photographers, but also businesses that create and share promotional content and institutions such as universities that create and share video courseware, distance learning materials, and video newsletters. The author concludes by asking whether the early users, applications, and devices will build towards a critical mass that can spread and lead to a greater range of users and applications. His answer is positive as long as a number of pieces come together: continued expansion of broadband in the homes; improved compression techniques to enhance video quality; interoperability among devices, and availability of high quality content and special interest video. Bringing video files into mobile environments is also likely to play an important role to this end.

Gali Einav's article "College Students: The Rationale for Peer-to-Peer Video File sharing" examines the reasons for video file sharing among students, shedding light on their attitudes towards the technology. Furthermore, it also inquires whether file sharing is a habit students will retain beyond college years. Students interviewed for this study claim that file sharing is "something they just do" because "other people around them do as well." The main reason students file share is not cost, but convenience – watching what they want when they want, using the PC instead of the TV set in their room. They see file sharing as a form of "quality control," to sample the content and be sure to pay for it only when they like it, and to promote new content to their friends. They like to share TV episodes previously viewed or missed and new movies releases. "As far as willingness to pay is concerned, Einav's paper claims that students are willing to pay for good, compelling content that they can keep indefinitely and without "annoying limitations." They are also willing to pay to secure their computers from viruses which can be transmitted through file sharing programs. The right range of prices for movies should be lower than a DVD rental, between three to five dollars per movies and between 99 cents and five dollars for TV shows.

The fourth essay of this section, the paper by Steven Rosenbaum "Peer-to-Peer and User Generated Content: Flash in the pan or the arrival of a new storytelling paradigm" offers an interesting prospective on the relationship between Peer-to-Peer and User Generated Content. The author claims that, despite the significant development of core technology to facilitate content creation and sharing, the real driver of user generated content is not technology but the community. Based on his own experience as CEO of companies, offering in the 1990s local and regional news magazine television, the author states that "people are far more interested in sharing their ideas with you than in commenting on the content created and distributed by mainstream media." Therefore, in the emergence of first-person storytelling, companies could provide assistance, help, tools, and framework, but people had to tell their own stories in their own way. According to Rosenbaum, "the impact of these changes will be profound and unparallel. The coming changes will reshape marketing, sociology, journalism, and politics."

The fifth essay by Sudip Bhattacharjee, Ram Gopal, James Marsden, and Rahul Telang, "A Survival Analysis of Albums on Ranking Charts," offers a quantitative assessment of the impact of technological innovation of MP3 and online file sharing on the music industry. Presenting a very innovative application to the music industry of the survival analysis methodology, the authors develop stochastic process models of the life cycles of music albums. The estimated models in the paper indicate a shift after the technological innovations of MP3 and online file sharing that occurred over the 1998–1999 period. The 2000–2002 period is characterized by a much shorter life cycle. This means that music as a digital good has been significantly affected by market changes brought about by easier information dissemination and access through new means such as file-sharing. The authors claim that "while overall album survival has decreased in the 2000–2002 period, the chances of survival increase dramatically after an album has survived the first week during this period. This indicates a pattern that the "good" albums survive more." In other words, easier sampling and information dissemination hurts only the lower quality albums. The authors conclude that the shorter shelf life of digital music calls for accelerated tactical and operational decision-making on behalf of music companies with regards to resource allocations, in order to improve their marketing and promotional efforts to target potential winners.

The chapter by Xu Cheng and Cameron Dale e Jiangchuan Liu, "Understanding the characteristics of Internet Short Video Sharing: YouTube as a Case Study," focuses on YouTube as a video sharing site and using traces crawled in a three-month period, presents an in-depth and systematic measurement study on the characteristics of YouTube videos. The authors claim that YouTube videos have noticeably different statistics compared to traditional streaming videos, ranging from length and access pattern, to their active lifespan, ratings and comments. This paper also looks closely at the social networking aspect of YouTube, as this is a key driving force toward its success. The authors find that the links to related videos generated by uploaders' choices form a small-world network. This suggests that the videos have strong correlations with each other, and creates opportunities for developing novel caching or Peer-to-Peer distribution schemes to efficiently deliver videos to end users.

The final chapter in this section is "Mobile distributing Consumer Media Venturing in YouTube" by Min Hang. It completes the analysis of the YouTube case by looking at the new venture the company by started delivering video content to mobile phones. In November 2006, YouTube announced that it would make a mobile phone debut, allying with Verizon Wireless. While its Youtube.com web site is free, YouTube's phone-based business will require a $15 a-month subscription to a Verizon Wireless service called VCast. The author in this paper presents the results of an empirical study conducted through interviews with the business director and editor of YouTube. She claims that for this business venturing, the "overall economics conditions" that include the "level of uncertainty, the specificity of investment, the level of agency costs" were relatively low, due to the huge market potential to develop mobile distributing business. Furthermore, the increasing popularity of YouTube brought positive brand benefits to the company's mobile services. The author suggests that the alliance with Verizon is only the first step of YouTube's mobile video business exploration.

Part III – Peer-to-Peer: Policy

The final section offers essays on three areas where Peer-to-Peer will have a significant policy impact.

In "Compulsory licensing vs. private negotiations in Peer-to-Peer sharing," Michael Botein and Edward Samuels focus on a proposal to use compulsory license to authorize and regulate Peer-to-Peer distribution of copyrighted works. While they are sympathetic with the goals of this proposal, they remain sceptical about the feasibility of implementing such a system because, considering the history of compulsory copyright licenses in a number of different settings, they conclude that compulsory licensing has not been successful in implementing policy goals. Instead, they suggest that privately negotiated contracts may be more efficient than governmental intervention.

In "Crouching Tiger, Hidden Dragon: Proxy Battles over Peer-to-Peer Movie Sharing," Viktor Mayer-Schönberger starts by claiming that "the genie – Peer-to-Peer technology – is out of the bottle" and the content industry, as we know it, seems beyond help because they fear that once the genie of Peer-to-Peer is out of the bottle it cannot be controlled. However, the author suggests that stopping Peer-to-Peer is neither the only nor necessarily the most effective chokepoint to interdict digital piracy. In fact, he shares the view that digital technology has facilitated (but not originated) the creation of a specific digital mindset, requiring from businesses a fundamental reevaluation of existing business models and value chains. Hollywood is not the first sector to be transformed by the consequences of the digital mindset. The music industry went through significant changes moving from the album as an arbitrary bundle of songs – the cornerstone of past success – to the individual high quality songs which can be downloaded at a reasonable price as an alternative to illegal Peer-to-Peer downloads. The author claims that the movie industry should be similarly innovative, following, for instance, the opposite direction: bundling content. With hard disk storage prices plummeting, a disk filled with 300 movies may turn to be the "next big thing" for the movie industry. Overall, the author suggests that when it comes to copyright, it is important to show that alternative mechanisms are conceivable, because fundamentally, "copyright is but a mechanism, a proxy to achieve a bigger goal."

In the final essay, "Peer-to-Peer network and the distribution in the EU," Andrea Gavosto and Bruno and Stefano Lamborghini offer an overview of the European development and diffusion of Peer-to-Peer, what Peer-to-Peer is used for, and what the reply of content providers is to the Peer-to-Peer challenge. They claim that the market is pushing for new business models for online content. Content publishers are seeking to bypass their traditional distributors and address customers directly. The authors present the regulatory approach to Peer-to-Peer in the European Union within the general legislation for copyright and related rights in the online environment, offering a detailed survey of Peer-to-Peer and the national legislation in France, Germany, UK, Spain, and Italy. Overall, they claim that while in Europe the online content market is expected to grow significantly in the coming years, business models remain uncertain. Furthermore, while the exploitation of intellectual property in digital form has required the existing legal framework protecting copyright to be amended, the legal status of Peer-to-Peer systems remains largely undefined. However, the authors suggest that the launch of content-industry backed Peer-to-Peer services will definitely help to increase the volume of authorized content on the internet.

How do these essays add up? Just like with video Peer-to-Peer, they are a glittering kaleidoscope, not a tightly focused telescope. But several themes can be discerned. One of them is the emergence of "peers" and of the "commons" – of community as an element in a mixed economic system, taking on an important role together with the private sector and the government. A community is more than non-governmental organization, because it is a voluntary association of autonomous individuals acting in decentralized collaboration. Such a community operates under different rules and incentives, and fully understanding it is vital for the future economic system more generally.

A second element is the vital role of intellectual property. Traditional rules cannot deal appropriately with the concept of sharing. Defensively, media companies circle the wagons and have laws enacted that try to stop the inevitable, and, consequently, create disdain for themselves and the rules that will come back to haunt them.

A third element is the generational change, with the new forms of video use as producer, consumer, and peer becoming prevalent among the key demographics of media creativity. Like new paradigms in science, the new way of television will prevail through its adoption by young generations. Their interaction is more vital than technology. Such interaction constantly finds new forms, such as over the emerging mobile broadband of cellular handsets.

A fourth element is the guidance that music file sharing provides to video Peer-to-Peer. It is the closest analogy to the internet video, just like radio was to television: the movie industry is learning how to deal with the phenomenon of online movie sharing faster than the recording industry.

The fifth element is the resigned look at the policy process, which does not look promising to any of the authors. Plainly it does not move at the rate of Moore's Law.

The sixth and last element is that the Peer-to-Peer process, while dynamic and unstable, is an expanding process: this might lead us to start considering whether indeed we are witnessing the emergence of a Peer-to-Peer economy.

What this means is that the new system will have to find its own way. With governments confused and the media industry in the defensive posture of profitable orthodoxy, the energy of change comes from its new-generation implementers and users. The rest will follow. But in the process, the entire form of economic activity will change to a more decentralized, project-oriented, freelancing, specialist-based form of economic activity – a Peer-to-Peer economy of networked and peered organizations. This trend is of huge significance, much larger even than the cultural and political impacts of a media Peer-to-Peer. In the past, too, information sector technology activities triggered wider economic changes. The printing press's movable type ushered in machinery of mass production. The electronic components of radios, telecommunications, and computing devices led to the digital revolution. With those fundamental changes in the economic system upon us, economic analysis must keep abreast and help enlighten and interpret this scenario. And such is one of the purposes of this volume.

Notes

1. Peer-to-Peer is essentially a communication structure in which individuals interact directly, without going through a centralized system or hierarchy. Users can share information, contribute to shared projects or transfer files.

References

OECD Information Technology Outlook 2004: Peer-to-Peer Networks in OECD Countries: http://www.oecd.org/dataoecd/55/57/32927686.pdf

Contents

Editors and Contributors

Editors

DR. ELI M. NOAM is Professor of Finance and Economics at the Columbia University Graduate School of Business and Director of the Columbia Institute for Tele-Information (CITI). Email: noam@columbia.edu

DR. LORENZO MARIA PUPILLO is an Executive Director in the Public Affairs Unit of Telecom Italia and Affiliated Researcher at Columbia Institute for Tele-Information. Email: lorenzo.pupillo@telecomitalia.it

Contributors

SUDIP BHATTACHARJEE is an Associate Professor and Ackerman Scholar in the Department of Operations and Information Management in the School of Business, University of Connecticut. Email: Sudip.Bhattacharjee@ business.uconn.edu

MICHAEL BOTEIN is Professor of Law and Director of the Media Center at New York Law School in New York City. Email: mbotein@nyls.edu

ALAIN BOURDEAU DE FONTENAY is a visiting scholar and Senior Affiliated Researcher with the Columbia Institute for Tele-Information (CITI), Columbia University. Email: fontenay@aol.com

ERIC BOURDEAU DE FONTENAY is founder and President of MusicDish LLC, magazine publisher and artist development/management. Email: ecfont@pipeline.com

JOHN CAREY is Professor of Communications and Media Industries at Fordham Business School. Email: johncarey@fordham.edu

XU CHENG is a graduate student and research assistant in the School of Computing Science at Simon Fraser University, British Columbia, Canada. Email: xuc@sfu.ca

CAMERON DALE is a graduate student in Computing Science at Simon Fraser University. Email: camerond@sfu.ca

GALI EINAV is the Director of Digital Technology Research at NBC Universal. Email: gali.einav@nbcuni.com

ANDREA GAVOSTO is Director of the Fondazione Giovanni Agnelli, formerly Chief Economist of Telecom Italia. Email: andrea.gavosto@fga.it

RAM D. GOPAL is GE Endowed Professor of Business in the Department of Operations and Information Management in the School of Business, University of Connecticut. Email: Ram.Gopal@business.uconn.edu

MIN HANG works for Tsinghua University, China and the Media Management and Transformation Center (MMTC) of Jönköping University, Sweden. Email: Min.Hang@ihh.hj.se

BRUNO LAMBORGHINI is Professor of Business Administration and Marketing at the Catholic University in Milan. Email: bruno.lamborghini@unicatt.it

STEFANO LAMBORGHINI is Senior Economist at Telecom Italia Strategy Unit. Email: stefano.lamborghini@telecomitalia.it

JIANGCHUAN LIU is Assistant Professor in the School of Computing Science, Simon Fraser University, British Columbia, Canada. Email: jcliu@cs.sfu.ca

JAMES R. MARSDEN is the Treibick Family Endowed Chair in e-Business and Board of Trustees Distinguished Professor. Email: Jim.Marsden@business.uconn.edu

STEVEN ROSENBAUM is the CEO of Magnify Networks. Email: steve@magnify.net

EDWARD SAMUELS is an intellectual property consultant in New York. Email: esamuels@edwardsamuels.com

VIKTOR MAYER-SCHÖNBERGER is Associate Professor of Public Policy at the John F. Kennedy School of Government, Harvard University. Email: Viktor_Mayer-Schoenberger@harvard.edu

W. EDWARD STEINMUELLER is Professor of Information and Communication Technology Policy at SPRU – Science and Technology Policy Research, University of Sussex. Email: w.e.steinmueller@sussex.ac.uk

RAHUL TELANG is an Assistant Professor of Information Systems and Management at the Heinz School, Carnegie Mellon University. Email: rtelang@andrew.cmu.edu

KEVIN WERBACH is an Assistant Professor of Legal Studies and Business Ethics at The Wharton School, University of Pennsylvania. Email: kevin@werbach.com

PART I – Peer-to-Peer: Economics

1

The Economics of User Generated Content and Peer-to-Peer: The Commons as the Enabler of Commerce

Eli M. Noam

Columbia University

Much public attention has accompanied the emergence of community-based sharing arrangements in high technology, such as music file sharing, open source software, and unlicensed spectrum applications. Academic attention has followed, though economists seem to have been slower in picking up on these developments than legal scholars. Even though the emergence of behavioral economics as a respectable analytical approach had raised questions on some basic assumption of economic rationality, the notion of sharing as an economic behavior smacked many economists as too close to socialism to be taken seriously as an efficient arrangement.

But why do these activities exist and why are they voluntarily used by millions? Normally, economists are the first to find an inherent efficiency in societal arrangements. But here, they found only inefficiency, whose explanation was often identified as government. The sharing behavior was explained either because of *too much* government – such as inadequate ability to trade spectrum and use it flexibly – or alternatively because of *not enough* government, with inadequate protection enforcement enabling a piracy of intellectual property. Commons-type arrangements, such as Peer-to-Peer file-sharing, are therefore viewed as an activity that disrupts markets. Instead of well-ordered transactions among buyers and sellers, the commons offers piracy that undermines legitimate prices, property, and investments. Thus, for orderly markets to exist, one needs to suppress such illegalities.

E.M. Noam and L.M. Pupillo (eds.), *Peer-to-Peer Video*, doi: 10.1007/978-0-387-76450-4_1,
© Springer Science + Business Media, LLC 2008

I will show the opposite: that a transactions-based economy is often based on the foundation of earlier sharing arrangements; that the two systems are not so much in conflict as they are phases that follow each other; and that a sharing arrangement is the foundation of transaction-based markets, because it creates the very conditions that enable such transactions.

Commons arrangements are part of a larger family of issues in which "grassroots" activities exist. In the early years of the broadcasting, radio amateurs congregated on the airwaves, with no commercial broadcaster around. David Sarnoff and RCA get the credit for starting broadcasting; but what they did was create a commercial broadcasting model on the base of a growing amateur activity.

In the 1970s, personal computers were built and discussed by a community of microcomputer builders, who succeeded in creating the challenge for IBM where RCA, GE, Siemens, and Bull had failed.

There was also the Citizens Band movement, which created millions of mobile communicators and sped up the development of cellular telephony. The internet was started by the government outside the market, and then given life and structure by a nonprofit university-based community.

And today, the use of wireless local area networks (WiFi) has similarly sprung from the grassroots, swept ahead of the licensing regime of the government, and advanced the provision of commercial broadband and longer-range WiMax.

Perhaps the main instance for a user community developing new things is science, where researchers have always shared knowledge and insights. And while there is a strongly developed ethic of recognition through priority credit, awards, and academic advancement, there are few elements of ownership and property, at least until recently. Indeed, basic scientific discoveries are not patentable. But the commercial development based on scientific advancement is encouraged.

Why do all of these arrangements exist? It cannot be said that they are necessarily more efficient in a static sense than a market-based system in which profit-maximizing firms compete with each other for business and customers, thereby pushing costs down and innovation up. There are costs of duplication and diseconomies of scale to an atomistic, non-proprietary system. Citizens' band radio with its babel over the air is an example. And incentives to some investment in innovation may be reduced.

And yet, the sharing movements are too frequent to lack an economic basis. Let us therefore analyze them with a simple model.

What our examples have in common is that the participants in the activity derive a benefit from each other's participation usually referred to as *positive externalities* or as *network effects*.

Assume a collaborative system of homogeneous n users, encountering costs and benefits.

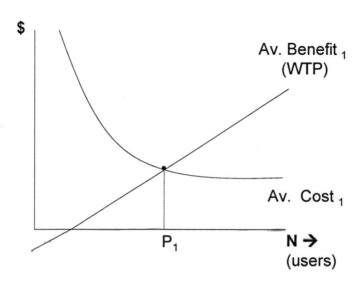

Graph 1.1

Total benefits grow with the number of users – the network effects.

We follow Metcalfe's Law defining total benefits as growing exponentially, bn^2-n, and with average benefits, hence, as $bn-b$. This is depicted in Graph 1.1 by the rising line. This average benefit would be a user's maximum willingness to pay. Total cost consists of fixed and variable costs. Unless marginal costs are rising strongly and/or are highly relative to fixed costs, average costs are declining with scale n. That average cost is also the minimum price that would cover costs.

To the right of the point of intersection P_1, average willingness to pay will be higher than average cost. It will be profitable for a firm to offer the service. That point is called the point of critical mass. But on the left of the point of critical mass, cost will be higher than willingness to pay. Therefore, this activity will not take place, unless there is someone to support and subsidize the activity until it reaches the size of a critical mass and becomes self-sustaining. Thus, there will be an under-investment in the activity.

How then does one get to the takeoff point if that is the goal? One way is for the government to step in and subsidize the early stages. One example is the early internet. Another example is the Minitel text terminal system in France.

A second way is to set a regulation of the activity, which would force an initial price below cost so that the takeoff point is shifted to the left, i.e., at a lower level. This would then be followed by a sustaining expansion, after which price regulation becomes unnecessary. This priming of the pump describes the traditional policy of universal service and rate setting in telecommunications.

A third way would be for a business firm to underwrite the deficit for a while until the critical mass is reached, and then profit from its earlier investment in that critical mass. The problem with this strategy is that if there is open entry and competition, such a user base would then be accessible by competitors, and thus the benefit would be shared, while the original investment would be borne only by the early provider. Hence, there will be an under-investment in initiating such activity. The incumbent firm will therefore try to preclude rivals from reaching the user base with its network externalities. For that reason, control over interconnection has been such a critical issue in telecommunications for over a century, and in cable TV for half a century. A firm is more likely to make the upfront investment in critical mass if there are substantial first-mover and scale advantages on the supply side so that subsequent rivals will have difficulties entering. In the extreme, a "natural monopoly" firm could be in such a position, and could then use its market power to charge users differentiated prices.

There is another reason for existing firms to under-invest in critical mass: they may already have an arrangement satisfactory to themselves in a related business activity, and which the firms do not want to destabilize. For example, Hollywood historically fought almost any new distribution technology, such as TV, cable TV, and the video cassette recorder. In each case, these new distribution technologies proved eventually to be a huge money maker for Hollywood. Why then the struggle? One should not dismiss this as merely a lack of vision on the part of Hollywood, although that played some role, too. But rather, it interfered with the carefully nurtured structure of distribution and its sequencing over a number of distribution channels. Neither Hollywood nor the music industries compete on price. They maintain above-competitive price levels through an oligopolistic industry structure, by a vertical integration of content production with distribution, and by product differentiation. Therefore, when a new technology of distribution emerges, as now with the broadband internet, the early potential benefits are outweighed by the destabilization to established profitable ways. In that sense, even the takeoff point P_1 might not be large enough if it is accompanied by offsetting losses (costs) in other distribution platforms. The average cost curve will be higher than before (Graph 1.2). The takeoff point for the oligopolistic industry will be P_2, where the user base has become large enough for its benefits to outweigh the lost business in the established forms of distribution (Graph 1.3).

The fourth alternative, and the one most overlooked, is the community approach. This means that the early users form a community with the aim of increasing benefits and externalities, and reducing costs.

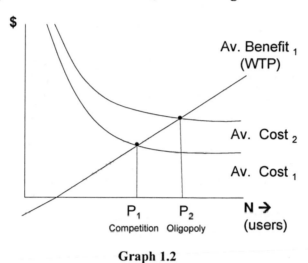

Graph 1.2

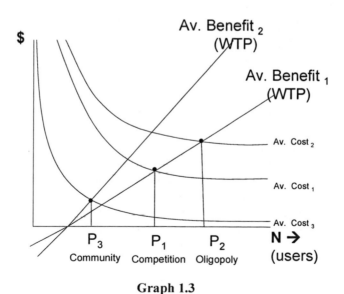

Graph 1.3

The benefit side is increased by an intense spirit of community and communication, such that each member adds more benefits to the others, and receives more from them, than would be the case without that spirit. It draws on various sources of utility such as being on the leading edge, sharing a new culture, or joining in breaking the stranglehold of powerful establishment. Hence, community building often is accompanied by a vilification of dominant firms and figures such as Hollywood, The Phone Company, IBM, or Bill Gates.

On the cost side, the community activity lowers costs by contributing voluntarist resources to the common endeavor – for example, a huge number of high-skilled program hours – and by sharing content and programs.

Together, these efforts push the critical mass point to the left, at P_3, to a smaller number of necessary participants. This point is the community takeoff point, in contrast with the market takeoff point P_1, or the oligopoly takeoff point P_2.

In some cases, the community takeoff will not lead to a self-sustained growth that will reach the commercially viable point P_1. The activity will remain community-based rather than commercial. Those situations are those, for example, of hobbyists clubs whose user benefits, user externalities, and user base are small.

But in other cases, the externalities and cost structure are such that the community takeoff leads to a community size that reaches the commercial takeoff point. At that point, business firms will enter.

Examples are, as mentioned, the commercial radio in the early 1920s, the commercial internet providers in the 1990s, Apple in downloading music and files, etc. The first to enter will tend to have no established business to lose, and hence it is likely to be firms from outside the established players. It is rarely clear when the takeoff point has been reached, so there will be trial and error entries. In providing video over the internet, the early commercial efforts went down in flames, mostly because of an insufficient base of broadband users at the time. Eventually, the number of users is large enough to sustain a commercial entrant, as the example of Apple's iTunes shows. Apple's entry demonstrates the existence of a fourth takeoff point P_4. We'll call P_4 the "complementarity takeoff point." Apple need not profit from its content download service iTunes as long as it enhances its hardware iPod sales, which it does. The music is the razor to the razorblade of the iPod. The same approach has led to the early dominance in radio by RCA (whose NBC network's function was to help sell RCA radios) and of the original BBC which was a joint venture of the British radio set manufacturers whose motivation was to sell radios (and keep cheap American receivers out of Britain) (Graph 1.4).

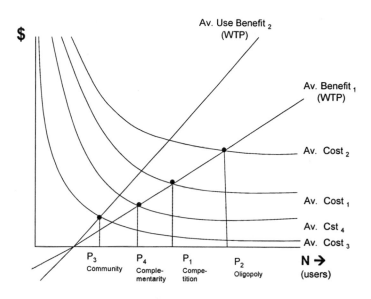

Graph 1.4

When the commercial entry takes place, it quickly, unavoidably, and unsentimentally pushes aside the community that made it all possible in the first place. The electronic common becomes the electronic metropolis. The community becomes marginalized. Some of its leaders cash in and commercialize. The commercial firms provide the investments to create user-friendly products that appeal to users beyond the original savvy community. Their often familiar brands reassure users. Their persistence is longer-lived than that of a voluntarism whose flame burns brighter in the beginning than when routine sets in. And their political influence is such that they are able to gain protective policies from government. In the end, markets assert themselves. Grassroots have created markets and network economies to scale, but then they are dismissed like pioneer stakeholders who settled the frontier ahead of the surveyors, land speculators, and developers.

Within the commercial model of operations, the center of gravity moves from P_4, the takeoff point of complementarity, to P_1, the takeoff point of competition, and then to P_2, the takeoff point oligopoly. The reason for the move to oligopoly is that competition will drive prices down to levels that will often be unsustainably low, given the high fixed costs and low marginal costs of content and its distribution. The solution, evident in most media industries, is to an oligopolistic market structure that maintains prices above marginal costs.

We can mourn this evolution from community to market and then to oligopoly as a commercial takeover. Or, we can celebrate it as part of a constant process of innovation, in which communal entrepreneurship and innovation play an important role, much more important than given credit for by the orthodox honoring of the individual entrepreneur and innovator (Graph 1.5).

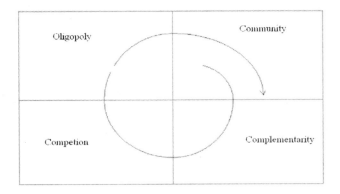

Graph 1.5

There is hence a logical flow from community to complementarity to competition to oligopoly. Nor is it likely to stop there, because the oligopoly will be challenged by innovators. When Joseph Schumpeter coined his ying-and-yang term of the "creative destruction of capitalism" he had mostly in mind the undermining of oligopoly by competitive innovators, P_1 or maybe P_4 challenging P_2. Not included was the challenge from community, P_3, which might provide the ingredients for the competitive challenge in the first place. Society lionizes the business-based disrupters as creative entrepreneurs, but ignores or even vilifies the community-based disrupters as pirates and squatters, taking a cue from those of the oligopolistic stage who want to protect themselves from challenge.

Once we recognize that there is a legitimate and useful role for community as an entrepreneurial element in the process of innovation, the question is what the business and policy implications are. By our analysis, even established media business firms should, if they take the long view, greatly value the community efforts that create the user base for their own subsequent expansion. Therefore, instead of fighting file sharing with all the tools at their disposal, they might actually embrace and support them in their formative stages, and let them lead to new business opportunities. In the media industry this was understood by Thomas Middelhoff, CEO of Bertelsmann, when he invested in Napster before being ousted. Similarly, Google acquired YouTube despite its content being often in violation of copyrights. And earlier, for home VCR – also facilitated by copyright violations – the overall gain to the content industry became in time much larger. But most media firms take a different view. For now, they see only short-term losses, not long term gains, or at least only long term gains that they must share with competitors.

But public policies need not be guided only by the same short term considerations. The gains go beyond entertainment media. Around the world, broadband internet is emerging. The United States does not have the same leadership role in broadband in that trend that it did for the narrowband internet. The problem is partly on the supply side, but also on the demand side. There is no clear killer app to entice people to sign up for broadband. Yet broadbanding all households would have enormous secondary benefits to the economy and to innovation, just as the internet did a few years ago. What might such a "killer app" be for broadband? It's pretty clear that entertainment content will be in that category. Thus, a sturdy, fair use rule that protects non-commercial applications would benefit not only users but also media firms, and the information economy as a whole. One must not suppress the community stage of innovation that can serve as the nutrient for the next link in the food chain.

And where is the next frontier for the community? Future Internet TV (IPTV) will not be to share movies one can get pretty cheaply in multiple other ways. Rather, it will be to create new forms and genres of communications based on a community's core strengths – creativity, energy, interactivity, and peership. This means new genres of interactive expression that we are only beginning to explore. While the one-way edited content will be dominant, the most interesting creative work will be that of shared and interactive content. We see the beginning in interactive games and in quirky user-generated content. The development of next generation content, and therefore of IPTV generally, are based on the initial ingredients of voluntarism to reduce costs and raise network externalities. It leads television media to evolve from the traditional system of "they TV" of the three dominant networks to the "me TV" of multichannel TV to the "we-TV" of next-generation interactive video. And as "we TV" grows and reaches more and more people, it will be embraced by commercial media firms. Another cycle begins. Another cycle from community to complementarity to competition to oligopoly. Another cycle from commons to commerce.[1]

Notes

1. Dr. Eli M. Noam is Professor of Finance and Economics at the Columbia University Graduate School of Business and Director of the Columbia Institute for Tele-Information. Email: noam@columbia.edu.

References

Alleman, J. and Noam, E., eds. *The New Investment Theory of Real Options and its Implication,* New York, NY: Kluwer Academic Publishers, 2000.

Antoniadis, P., Courcoubetis, C., and Mason, R. "Comparing Economic Incentives in Peer-to-Peer Networks." *Computer Networks*, 46, 2004, 133–146.

Asvanund, A., Clay, K.B., Krishnan, R., and Smith, M.D. "An Empirical Analysis of Network Externalities in Peer-to-Peer Music-Sharing Networks." *Information Systems Research*, 15 (2), 2004, 155–174.

Bardhan, P.K. and Ray, I. "Methodological Approaches to the Question of the Commons." *Economic Development and Cultural Change*, 54, 2006, 655–676.

Benkler, Y. *The Wealth of Networks,* New Haven, CT: Yale University Press, 2006.

Bhattacharjee, S., Gopal, R.D., and Lertwachara, J.R.K. "Consumer Search and Retailer Strategies in the Presence of Online Music Sharing." *Journal of Management Information Systems*, 2006.

Buragohain, C., Agrawal, D., and Suri, S. "A Game Theoretic Framework for Incentives in Peer-to-Peer Systems." Proceedings of the 3rd International Conference on Peer-to-Peer Computing, 2003.

Chandan, S. and Hogendorn, C. "The Bucket Brigade: Pricing and Network Externalities in Peer-to-Peer Communications Networks." Alexandria, VA.: Telecommunications Policy Research Conference, 27–29 October 2001.

Chen, M., Yang, G., Liu, X., and Zheng, W. "Prompting Cooperation Among Rational Participants in Peer-to-Peer Bulk File Sharing Environments." *Tsinghua Science And Technology*, 11 (1), 2006.

Chu, Y.-H., Chuang, J., and Zhang, H. "A Case of Taxation in Peer-to-Peer Streaming Broadcast," SIGCOM Workshops, Portland, OR, 30 August–3 September 2004.

Cunningham, B.M., Alexander, P.J., and Adilov, N. "Peer-to-Peer File Sharing Communities." *Information Economics and Policy*, 16 (2), 2004, 197–221.

Einhorn, M.A. and Rosenblatt, B. "Peer-to-Peer Networking and Digital Rights Management: How Market Tools Can Solve Copyright Problems." *Cato Institute Policy Analysis* No. 534, 2005, 1–20.

Fetscherin, M. and Zaugg, S. "Music Piracy on Peer-to-Peer Networks." IEEE International Conference on E-Technology, E-Commerce, and E-Services, 2004.

Jian, L. and MacKie-Mason, J. "Why Share in Peer-to-Peer Networks?" Proceedings of the ACM EC 2006 Workshop on the Economics of Networked Systems (NetEcon), 2006.

Liebowitz, S.J. "File Sharing: Creative Destruction or Just Plain Destruction." *The Journal of Law and Economics*, 49, 2006, 1–28.

Melville, N., Stevens, A., Plice, R.K., and Pavlov, O.V. "Unsolicited Commercial E-Mail: Empirical Analysis of a Digital Commons." *International Journal of Electronic Commerce*, 10 (4), 2006, 143–170.

Olson, M. *The Logic of Collective Action: Public Goods and the Theory of Groups.* Cambridge, MA: Harvard University Press, 1965.

Ostrom, E. "Collective Action and the Evolution of Social Norms." *The Journal of Economic Perspectives,* 14 (3), 2000, 137–158.

Steinmueller, W.E. "Virtual Communities and the New Economy." *Inside The Communication Revolution: Emerging Patterns of Social and Technical Interactions.* Oxford, UK: Oxford University Press, 2002.

Zentner, A. "Measuring the Effect of File Sharing on Music Purchases." *The Journal of Law and Economics*, 49, 2006, 63–90.

2

Peer-to-Peer Media File Sharing: From Copyright Crisis to Market?

W. Edward Steinmueller

University of Sussex

Introduction

"But if you copy a piece of software a thousand times, what is the cost? ... Infinitesimal ... this is a problem ... and it isn't just a problem of economics. We have a system of values, of *morality*, based on people competing with each other to copy things, at the lowest possible cost per unit. But when the cost, the object of all of this competition, effectively disappears, what happens to our system? Life gets very puzzling." (Jones 1998), p. 516 (emphasis as in original).

The use of Peer-to-Peer technologies for the exchange of digital information, including audio, text, and still and moving images presents both business and government policymakers with a profound dilemma. On the one hand, many copyright owners view Peer-to-Peer technologies as a new publishing medium that opens opportunities for new sources of revenue. On the other hand, copyright owners' customers are questioning why they should be prevented from or charged for using new technologies for acquiring, modifying, and exchanging information for entertainment, education, and cultural expression. In other words, the social convention of paying for a commodity whose marginal cost of reproduction is near zero has become increasingly frayed with the advance of technology.

Peer-to-Peer technologies have played a central role in improving the distribution of digital information and in facilitating copyright infringement. They provide means for improving the performance and functionality of the Internet as a storage and communication medium for a multiplicity of

E.M. Noam and L.M. Pupillo (eds.), *Peer-to-Peer Video*, doi: 10.1007/978-0-387-76450-4_2,
© Springer Science + Business Media, LLC 2008

applications – many of which have no direct relation to disputes over copyright. To alter these networks in ways that would protect intellectual property rights in the information exchanged over them would involve making major changes in the original architecture of the Internet, changes that might help create market power and ultimately a diminution in the value of the Internet as a medium for communication, (David 2001).

Current enforcement choices by copyright owners have created a legal quagmire of selective enforcement in which particular computer users are presented with large bills for copyright infringement and forced to choose between paying a settlement or attempting to defend their actions through litigation.[1] While there can be little doubt that many such users are, in fact, engaging in copyright infringement, there is far more doubt that their selection for civil prosecution represents a standard that is either fair or transparent.

Concerns about copyright protections being undercut by the advent of new technology are not new.[2] There are, however, qualitative differences between Internet applications such as Peer-to-Peer file sharing and earlier information reproduction and distribution technologies. Like the earlier technologies of plain paper copiers or magnetic tape recording, modern digital technologies provide a means to contravene property rights in information by facilitating the copying or "re-publication" of copyrighted materials. Unlike earlier copying technologies, however, the use of Internet-based technologies provides a means for large scale and global redistribution of the resulting copies. While there are additional distinctions (discussed below) between older copying and distribution technologies and those employing the Internet (including Peer-to-Peer file sharing technologies), it is the potential "volume" of illicit copies that might be distributed by Peer-to-Peer technologies that is of principal concern to copyright owners.

Rather than being confronted by a band of pirates who must invest in high volume reproduction technologies, create new (illicit) distribution channels, and promote the availability of their "products," copyright owners face a ready-made and "viral" or contagious form of infringement. Internet technologies provide the means to engage in high-volume copying, a global distribution channel supporting the distribution of copies, and a means to establish person-to-person communication networks either for distributing these copies or making their location known. Copyright owners' responses to this perceived threat include threatened legal action against individual users engaged in copyright infringement, and attacks and disruptions on centers or "nodes" of such activities on the Internet. These responses have the potential to discredit and disrupt progressive uses of the Internet for education, cultural expression, and recreation as well as its exploitation as a new platform for market development.

The conflict between copyright owners and Internet users is creating a distinctive period in the history of Internet development that we will call the "copyright-crisis era." This chapter pursues three complementary goals. The first is to provide a precise understanding of the influences that have produced the current "copyright crisis," especially those aspects of the crisis that are influenced by technologies and social institutions employed to protect copyright in digital media. The second is to outline how some of the influences creating the "crisis" are being resolved – e.g., by turning roadblocks into efficient tollbooths. The third is to examine how the means for resolving this crisis are likely to shape a "post-copyright-crisis era" whose outlines are just beginning to become clear. In this post-crisis era, Peer-to-Peer technologies will play a continuing role in the evolution of Internet architecture and new public and private "spaces" or "domains" are likely to co-exist in an uneasy complementary relationship with their use governed by new institutions (rules, norms, and standards).

The next section identifies the key technological influences that have established the nature of the copyright crisis. This copyright crisis is not due only to the features of Internet technologies such as Peer-to-Peer file sharing. The ways that individuals use collections of information is co-evolving with the technologies – the emergent uses for and interests that users have in the information that they generate, purchase, or otherwise acquire are influenced by the capabilities that new technologies offer and these capabilities influence technological development. Following is a section devoted to examining how these changing user needs and behaviors create new practices and institutions (rules, norms, and standards) that influence the nature of the copyright crisis era.

The subsequent section returns to the interests of the copyright owners, examining their efforts to preserve existing models and to devise new models of protection for copyrighted materials. A central focus of this section is the compromise between copyright owners and users responsible for the "new generation" of music downloading services such as iTunes, Rhapsody, and MusicMatch. The last section examines the technological and institutional (legal and social norm) changes that are emerging as we move into the post-copyright crisis era. It provides a vision of what this era might look like from both the copyright owners' and the users' per-spectives and concludes the discussion by highlighting some of the issues that are likely to remain unresolved.

The Role of Technology in the Copyright Crisis

The Internet provides a myriad of methods for the publishing, repro-duction, and exchange of information. Methods for recognizing and ignoring the provenance of information and for supporting or bypassing the control of information publishers or creators co-exist. The means for recognizing provenance and supporting publisher control are referred to as digital rights management (DRM) technologies. The goal of producers of DRM technologies is to create information storage and transmission domains in which copyright may be protected, most commonly by the use of encrypt-tion of media content so that only properly authorized "readers" or "players" can decode the information.

However, as with any other encryption system, once information has been decoded or "made clear" it may be captured and copied. Thus, for an encryption-based DRM management system to work, it must maintain control not only of decryption, but also how the user receives the infor-mation (e.g., a display, a sound reproduction, etc.), a goal that is at odds with the technical capabilities offered by the personal computer.[3] Moreover, the effort to retain control threatens to compromise many of the advantages of competition in computer software for playing media files, archiving their content according to users' preferences, editing files to users' tastes, or using media files on other "playback" devices that the user may own are either difficult to achieve or must be foregone entirely. As a consequence, DRM technologies have not been popular with users during the first 25 years of the personal computer era. The ways in which this unpopularity has been accommodated are considered in the section focus-ing on the evolution of producer strategies.

DRM has also historically seen as an encumbrance by the very people that would seem to have the most interest in employing it – information publishers. For example, music publishers distribute their products on compact discs (CDs) despite the fact that this medium of digital infor-mation recording can be used as a source of digital information for making flawless copies of the original.[4] Other schemes for preventing the copying of compact discs often create compatibility problems with the existing stock of hardware designed to play ordinary compact discs and ultimately have been only minor impediments for experienced users.

Traditionally, a primary goal of DRM was to prevent the creation of a decrypted version of information that could be transferred into the storage and distribution domains in which DRM is ignored.[5] This larger domain of services and applications in which the provenance and ownership of information is ignored is a basic feature of not only the personal computer, but also the Internet. Historically, the principle of maximizing the inter-operability of the Internet meant that the possibility of creating different "classes" of information with different rules as to how it might be exchanged was not addressed. A consequence is that the architecture of the Internet, as such, offers no tools for *blocking* copyright infringement.[6] It is unlikely that the architecture of the Internet will be re-engineered to provide such tools, and even more so because of the variety of DRM encryption technologies and standards that exist.

Those who choose to translate information from the information storage and distribution domains governed by DRM technologies to domains in which DRM is ignored do face some technological hurdles. This is particularly true for video media where the player may be closely linked to the display technology.[7] For audio media, however, a last resort (due to the reduction in fidelity of the signal), which always will exist, is simply to re-record the information as it is "sent" to the analogue output of the player or played through speakers. Technologies for overcoming DRM are specifically prohibited by the US Digital Millennium Copyright Act, but are generally available on the Internet. In general, DRM technologies should be viewed primarily as impediments to the average user's ability to translate information between DRM- and non-DRM-respecting storage and transmission domains.

Once a media file appears in the information storage and distribution domain without DRM encryption, it can be reproduced efficiently through the use of a multitude of applications as well as the basic file management techniques provided by computer operating systems. The information file can also be distributed using a myriad of techniques ranging from e-mail "attachments" to Peer-to-Peer file sharing arrangements. All such dis-tribution of copyrighted information is, from a legal viewpoint, copyright infringement. In terms of technology, however, there may be no difference between a "file" of information for which the original publisher is interested in maintaining control of copying and another "file" of information in which the original publisher has no such interest.

To the extent that users are capable of distinguishing a file that is likely to be "illicit" in the sense that distributing it to others almost certainly contravenes the copyright owners' interests, "self-policing" is a possible means to limit infringing behavior. The copyright owner must, however, rely on social institutions (rules, norms, and standards of behavior) rather than on technological "fixes" to solve the problem of illicit copying. Efforts continue to be made to influence these social institutions with the hope that users will eventually accept the formal rules and embrace new norms and standards of behavior that would prevent infringing behavior. So far these efforts have not had a significant effect on behavior – the volume of copyright infringement on the Internet remains large.[8]

Peer-to-Peer technologies have so far only been mentioned in passing as one of the means by which the re-distribution of information may be achieved using the Internet. This is because Peer-to-Peer technologies have tended to have more to do with the institutional nature of the copyright crisis than with technological innovation in information distribution. Peer-to-Peer technologies are a specific evolution of some of the oldest elements of the Internet architecture that were meant to permit processor and storage sharing in a computer network. Although Peer-to-Peer to technologies have been touted by some as "revolutionary," their basic principle of operation involving the distribution of files or file fragments over a network of mass storage devices is very similar to some of the earliest Internet applications involving the use of Gopher (invented at the University of Minnesota around 1991), a system for listing files available for download from computers distributed over the Internet.[9] In the context of the copyright crisis, the specific features of Peer-to-Peer file sharing have acted to diffuse or spread the responsibility for copyright infringement. Depending upon the point of view, these features may be viewed as a defect or a benefit of the technology. It may be most accurate to view them as a byproduct of the same approach to system design that governs the Internet more generally – services are designed to be as simple as possible and, thus, do not take account of issues of file provenance or ownership.

Peer-to-Peer file sharing may involve one of two practices. The first is "opening" a networked computer's storage system to allow other users to read (and copy) information on the understanding that others are providing a similar level of access. The second is the "opening" of a portion of a user's storage capacity to both reading and writing information by others with the understanding that the user will be able to store information on the storage systems of other users. The granting of these permissions creates "sub-networks" of exchange defined by a list of the Internet Protocol (IP) addresses of participating users, a subset of all of the IP addresses that define computers connected to the Internet. The choice of the method of "opening" has important implications. If the "opening" only allows other users to download files from a user's computer, the user faces a risk of being sued for copyright infringement if any of the files on their computer contain copyrighted information. When the user allows others to store information on his or her mass storage system (typically a hard disk drive), there is the further element of risk that others may store information that infringes copyright, that has malicious content (such as viruses) or that may be illegal in other ways (e.g., child pornography). To facilitate self-governance in such sub-networks, it is possible to block specific user IP addresses, although this may not offer an effective method of protection.

The final element defining a Peer-to-Peer file-sharing network is a scheme for locating the relevant files within the sub-network that a user may wish to receive or access. (This element is subject to very rapid on-going technological evolution and it is, therefore, inappropriate to describe in any detail the current arrangements.) In the specific history of music file sharing, the original architecture of Napster involved a centralized registry of file locations and this centralization made it possible to assign Napster with the responsibility for directory listings that pointed to copyright infringing material. Later generations of software defining Peer-to-Peer sub-networks have been based upon a decentralized "search" for files and it is this decentralization that has diffused or spread the responsibility for storing infringing files to all of the participants in a sub-network. When the user has "opened" his or her computer for "uploading" of files from other users, the user has little specific control over what files are stored on his or her computer. The fact that infringing files placed by others are there and may have little to do with a user's intent to infringe copyright, does not appear to provide a basis for defense against claims of copyright infringement.[10]

Where "uploading" of files in a Peer-to-Peer network is allowed, a copyright infringing file may appear in the sub-network and be replicated in a short period of time on many different computers – identifying the originating computer and hence the original user is thus very difficult if not impossible. The "state" of the sub-network at any moment in time with regard to which computers are storing which files is not recorded by any single computer, and this information is not required to be recorded – it can be entirely ephemeral so long as it is accurate at every instant in time. Ascertaining the entry of a new file would involve querying every computer in the sub-network simultaneously about the files available, which is, in general technologically infeasible. Thus, identifying the "origin" of a copyright infringing file is not generally feasible. It is, therefore, not possible to accurately assign responsibility for origination of copyright infringing files; the alternative is to pursue users that have such files, regardless of where they originated. The problem here is that legitimate uses of Peer-to-Peer file sharing involving "opening" to uploading are vulnerable to the risk that some uploaded files will be copyright infringing. Legal action against users with copyright infringing content has therefore, so far, focused on users retaining and providing access to large numbers of copyright infringing files, a situation that argues for intent to engage in copyright infringement.

In summary, the specific features defining Peer-to-Peer file sharing technologies are: (1) the elimination of a "central" source for information and decentralization of file storage and distribution within a sub-network of users each dedicating a portion of their mass storage to collective use (either by allowing access for downloading or for both uploading and downloading); and (2) the creation of a particular scheme for identifying the information that is collectively shared among users so that copies may be requested or transferred to other locations in the network. A byproduct of these two features is that the appearance and distribution of copyright infringing files is not easily "traceable." The same network may be used for exchange of information that has no proprietary "sponsors" and hence no DRM-related encryption, information that is encrypted using a particular type of DRM software and is only "readable" by having a suitable DRM-enabled player, and copyright infringing material distributed without DRM encryption.

As the above discussion demonstrates, Peer-to-Peer file sharing provides an effective means of distribution for files of information that is largely indifferent to issues of copyright interest. The system is equally effective in exchanging encrypted information files that must be "unlocked" with a DRM technology and files that are not locked and can be utilized by the appropriate software – in the case of media files, an appropriate "player." The system is also designed to create perfect copies – the binary content of a file distributed over this network remains unchanged and any particular copy is indistinguishable from any other copy of the same information. This feature of making "perfect copies" coupled with the automatic distribution of copies according to the demands of users allows unlimited duplication of information – a feature that is interpreted by copyright owners as unlimited capability for copyright infringement.

These capabilities are qualitatively different from earlier generations of copying technologies used to reproduce information content. Previous technologies from plain paper copy machines to magnetic tape recording (audio and video) shared two features. First, these technologies preserved a proximate relationship between the "original" and copies (multi-generation copies (copies of copies) involved degradation of the quality of reproduction) due to imperfections in the copying technologies. Second, copies remained "material" and thus could only be distributed through methods that were of similar efficiency to those used to distribute original content. The digital reproduction of information does not preserve proximity between the original and copies – copies and copies of copies are identical to the original. In addition, the distribution channel offered by Peer-to-Peer file sharing sub-networks of the Internet can be global in scope and involve an unlimited number of users.

This qualitatively new environment sets a new context for producer and user conflicts over the use of copyrighted information. On the one hand, existing or incumbent actors would like to preserve their rights and privileges in the new environment. On the other hand, new actors are providing technological options and capabilities that disrupt the existing distribution of rights and privileges. Policymakers are confronted with the need to restore balances established in a previous era, but in the process it is inevitable that all parties will take offence. For policy makers, who are accustomed either to nudging existing institutions toward some sort of accommodation or taking a centre stage role in making more dramatic changes in direction with substantial support from a cross-section of stakeholders, this is a no-win situation – hence the basis for characterizing the current era as one of crisis.

New Uses for Information, and the Copyright Crisis

The current copyright crisis is influenced in a fundamental way by tech-nological opportunity, but its nature and extent would be quite different if it was only about the acquisition of "pirated" copies of music and video recordings. To indicate the other influences at work, it is necessary to re-examine the uses of information and the relation of these uses to a "commodity based" model of information production and distribution. Several observations are needed to establish an alternative perspective on the relation of the "consumer" to media.

The history of media[11] development can be seen as involving several distinct trends – the proliferation of outlets by which media can be accessed, reductions in the cost of access, and increasing ability to "record" the media that individuals experience.[12] The last of these developments not only provides the point of origin for the copyright crisis, but operates with the first two to create expectations with regard to the ability of individuals to control their "media environment" – the times and places in which they experience media. The operation of markets as well as individual behavior has clearly demonstrated that people are interested in "programming" the time that they devote to experiencing media – they would like to be able to hear or see media of their choosing at the times and in the places of their choosing. Technologies that favor these developments generally appear to be accepted and many of these technologies involve the recording of media – either to "time shift" or to increase portability, i.e., making it possible to "place shift," media consumption.[13]

The wider implication of these developments is that individuals have been partially empowered with the ability to recapitulate past experience or accumulate experience by the repeated "viewing" or "hearing" of a particular "piece" of media. This is an abstract way of expressing a collection of related ideas – a particular piece of media or "title" may be appropriated as in "they're playing our song," associated with other life experiences as in "that was the summer we saw Casablanca together," or employed for a specific use as "when I am feeling a bit sad, I sing a few bars of 'Singing in the Rain'." All of these, as well as the many other ways in which individual lives are built in relation to media, indicate the larger contexts in which media are experienced not only once, but again in memory and with the possibility of supplementing that memory by the replay of the media. In this wider context, individuals are seeking to time and place shift their "re-consumption" of the media even in cases where they did not initially possess their "own" recorded copy of the media. From the copyright owner's perspective this is all quite desirable – for some media titles, persistent demand for new copies and copies in new formats will emerge. For the individual "consumers" of media, however, the value of the media is created by their own specific relationship to it – it is a value that is co-produced by the associations and the "instrument" of the listener/viewer, and the need to re-purchase the media may seem a lot like someone else owning their memories or life experience.

Neither of these observations is sufficient to suggest a fundamental rupture of the economic or legal relationship between individuals and media – the fact that the value of a commodity involves a measure of co-production with a user is not a basis for concluding that it should be freely available. The proprietors of holiday resorts would certainly not accept the view that because someone had once had an important life experience at their resort, they should be given a free room on a return visit. The distinction is that the technologies of media recording have demonstrated to individuals that had they taken the trouble to turn on the video recorder or the tape machine they would be able to re-experience an engaging experience with the media.[14] The influence of this knowledge, however, is powerful in shaping expectations about "scarcity" that, in general, legitimate market exchange – we pay for things that we understand require the time and efforts of others to produce (Mansell 1999).

It is this understanding of the legitimacy of market exchange in relation to both the co-production of value and to the efforts required by others that creates difficulties for the preservation of the current system of copyright. For example, one may engage in social relationships that involve meeting at the local pub to discuss world affairs. In doing this, individuals are recycling the content of copyrighted news stories or broadcasts as their own daily experience of world affairs is likely to be limited, perhaps reducing the collective demand for these and thereby damaging the economic interests of the copyright owners contributing this material. The extension of this model of "sharing" to the physical exchange of copyrighted material is not unusual – e.g., making copies of news stories for others. When this is done, copyright infringement has occurred. While the boundary between the two activities is clear in law, it may be obscure from the viewpoint of the individuals engaged in these activities.

The final observation to be made in relation to the evolution of users' experience concerns collective institutions such as libraries that acquire recorded media and make them available to the library's patrons, or used book stores that resell books and other recorded media no longer wanted by their original owners. The existence of libraries and used book stores can be seen by copyright owners as an incursion on their abilities to sell individual copies of recorded media to each consumer. Some individuals will borrow from the library rather than rent or purchase a copy. The resale of a "used copy" creates market competition for the copyright owner, reducing the price that they might be able to receive for new "original" copies. In general, these forms of collective sharing and market exchange of recorded media have been viewed as a socially appropriate "leakage" in the ability of the copyright owner to appropriate returns from sales of copies.

To summarize these observations, publishers of media often have an economic interest in maintaining control of individual copies of recorded media. This same economic interest has, however, led them to distribute copies of the media through a growing variety of channels and, in the process, provide access at declining costs in forms that are not effectively protected from copying or from being transferred from DRM-compliant to DRM-ignoring domains. Individuals in turn recognize that it is physically possible to retain copies of material they find of interest by using the proliferating array of technologies available for these purposes (ranging from plain paper copiers to video recorders). Moreover, the "ownership" of media is, from the individual's perspective, clouded by the fact that the value of media is "co-produced" by the individual's own experience of them. While from a legal and economic viewpoint, this "co-production" of value is ignored, the general acceptance of technologies that make it possible for an individual to control the time and place of media consumption indicate to the individual that he or she "owns" the copies in the sense of having physical control over their disposition. The existence of legal lines of demarcation between possible actions such as orally relating the content of a copyrighted news article and making a physical copy of it appear arbitrary and contrived to many individuals. This artificiality is further highlighted by the existence of libraries and used-bookstores from which original copies may be borrowed or purchased with no marginal benefit flowing to the copyright owner. In sum, from a user's viewpoint the "rules" make little sense other than being a way for copyright owners to extract money from the user.

For economists, these observations amount to an account of the consequences of the economics of information – its features of expansibility (ability to be reproduced at low or no cost) and non-rivalry (abilities of one person to use information without it affecting the ability or value of another using it) assure that any rule setting mechanisms of control and payment (other than for the first copy) will be contrived and artificial in comparison to goods and services that are not expansible and whose use involves rivalry, i.e., only one person at a time may use the good or service. Such rules are, however, needed to provide an incentive to invest in producing the first copy of the information – without them the price of the first copy would have to cover all of the costs of production – an untenable proposition.[15] In other words, recorded media are rather unique economic commodities that require unique rules for market exchange to occur. The observations above, however, also suggest a second important economic feature of media consumption that completes the re-examination of the relation of the use of media to the commodity system.

Using media recording and re-recording allows individuals to further their experience of media in ways that extend beyond shifting the time and location of their experience with it. Technologies for editing and combining recorded media are becoming more powerful and useful. For example, new and potentially valuable opportunities emerge as we proceed from plain paper copying where copies may be annotated with pen and ink to the use of optical character recognition in which "copies" can be processed as hypertext documents whose "annotations" may be links to other documents explaining terminology or expanding upon the exposition of the "copied" text. "Sampling" audio files and re-editing them to suit the preferences of the user began with magnetic tape recording, and with the digitization of recorded music ever more powerful techniques for modification have emerged. The excerpting of video images and the electronic processing of image files are only beginning to develop, but suggest numerous possibilities for "customizing" content according to individual interests, or for recombining content to satisfy individual preferences. All of these techniques are employable by the individual for his or her own use. As that which individuals add to the original becomes, in their own view, more significant, the desire to share and exchange with others grows, and the rules governing such exchange and sharing appear to individuals to be more capricious and arbitrary.

From the viewpoint of many users of information, it is not only that copyright arbitrarily constrains their use of recorded media, subjecting them to licensing arrangements that are opaque and fees that are arbitrary, it is that these rules force them into a position of passivity – their role is to serve as a receiver for recorded media and even where the media may be replayed for their own use an indefinite number of times, their exchange of this recorded media with others in ways that might allow independent viewing or modification of their content is viewed as a violation of the privileges and rights of the copyright owner. These constraints ignore what is technologically possible and socially desirable (at least for that part of society comprised of information users) in the use of recorded media and create an artificial scarcity in order to preserve the incentives for the initial creation of recorded media.

Evolution of Producer Strategies

Because Peer-to-Peer distribution of digital content including copyrighted materials, has the features of a "super copy machine" allowing thousands or millions of potential customers to exchange identical copies of copyrighted material with one another, producers do have legitimate concerns about whether their existing business models will be able to survive. At the same time, users' abilities to interact with one another in a common cultural space are limited to the extent that an important part of their cultural experience is based upon copyrighted information. One cannot directly share the experience of video, music, or other content despite the technological capabilities of doing so without being branded a "pirate" and facing legal sanctions. Predictably, this has led to a situation resembling a war or insurgency in which some users simply reject the legal rights of copyright owners and proceed to exchange what they want with whom they want because they have the capability to do so.

The resulting tension that emerged in the opening years of the twenty-first century was uncomfortable for all concerned. Producers found themselves in the position of having to take legal action against actual or potential customers. Users face legal risks in using the technological capabilities of the new communication medium, the Internet. Producers of Peer-to-Peer technologies had to negotiate with courts as to whether their technologies "facilitate" copyright infringement because of the uses made of these technologies. This situation was neither stable nor encouraging – it risked "poisoning" the Internet as a method of distributing digital content because users may come to disbelieve that it is a legitimate means of acquiring any type of content. In attempting to discourage copyright infringement, producers were generating bad publicity and ill-will concerning their existing rights while having very little impact on the volume of copyrighted information exchanged through Peer-to-Peer networks. Moreover, by discouraging the informal pirating activities of individuals, the activities of actual pirates – those making counterfeit copies of original media – may have been enhanced. There was a substantial possibility that an entire generation would reject the legitimacy of existing rules governing copyright protection.

Two very different defenses of the current copyright system appeared to prevail within the copyright industries. The first defense is essentially economic – copyright is an efficient incentive scheme for supporting investment in a variety of different products, many of which do not recover the costs of production and promotion. Without this incentive, producers argue that both the variety and quality of copyright material would be diminished. This argument is subject to rational assessment and is consistent with asking questions like, "would a convenience-based business model (one that competes with 'free' distribution that is less well organized and promoted) recover the costs of production and promotion costs in the media industry?" or "what are the long term consequences of widespread distribution of "free" content for the promotion of commodity sales (e.g., physical CDs and related merchandise) of a particular creator's work?"

The second defense is based upon a "natural rights" theory that publication, like performance, is an act of artistic creation and those that interfere with the absolute right to control reproduction are diminishing the creative artists and their agents, the publishers. Without contesting the moral or ethical validity of this defense, it is apparent that it is less amenable to rational analysis. Any alteration to copyright laws or any change in technology that produces negative effects for even one artist must be opposed – changes in the current system should provide higher standards of protection for the protection of the absolute rights of artists (and their publishers) to control the copying of their work.

Either argument confronts the real-world situation that users of copyrighted information are able and willing to share copies of copyrighted material using file transfer capabilities provided by the Internet including Peer-to-Peer and other methods (e.g., e-mail, ftp, etc.). Those who are making rational economic calculations will ask questions such as what will happen if we encourage or commission selective "pollution" of this "free distribution" system with corrupt files, or select a sample of infringers to be pursued with legal action (preferably with substantial publicity) in order to enhance the value of legitimate distribution. Those who maintain that copyright provides an absolute right to control reproduction will be willing to unleash entrepreneurial legal firms to "bounty hunt" infringers en masse and to attack all infrastructures supporting such infringement with all possible means.

In the first five years of the "copyright crisis" era (2001–2006), most publishers have limited themselves to the first of these strategies. This may only mean that the latter community, those in favor of absolute property rights, is willing to see if more modest measures are sufficient to curb the behavior they see as undesirable. It may also reflect concerns that more aggressive actions will not be supported by the litigation system, which must hear those cases that are not settled after threats of legal action, and that will eventually receive complaints based on claims of "denial of service" or other legal remedies for practices aimed at disrupting file sharing networks. The most complete "cycle" of the conflict between copyright owners and the users of information has occurred in the case of online music file sharing and the history of this case provides some insights into likely outcomes with other digital media.

In the case of music file sharing, the principal technology employed is the MP3 technical standard for recording audio files with music content developed by Fraunhoffer Gesellschaft, a public research laboratory in Germany.[16] Fraunhoffer developed the MP3 technology according to the technical challenge of creating a technical standard for music compression (a smaller number file size than the original) that would preserve as much of the perceived audio fidelity of the original recording as possible. The use of this technology for copyright infringement has been facilitated by "conversion" software that makes it possible to copy or "rip" original content from a purchased CD into an MP3 file. The dramatic reduction in file size provided by the MP3 format facilitates the exchange of MP3 files over the Internet and has been the basis for a burgeoning market in portable "players" able to store hours of musical entertainment (a technology facilitating "place shifting"). Copyright owners have been unwilling to sell MP3 files directly to users because of the widespread exchange of such files.

Several different strategies have been developed to resolve this apparent impasse and the current state of the market involves rapid growth of "music downloading" services with different approaches to DRM. The most interesting of these services from the perspective of balancing producer and user interests is the development of Apple Computer's iTunes music distribution service. iTunes is neither the first nor likely the last scheme for distributing digital content protected by a DRM system and dedicated "players" that respect the DRM system. iTunes does, however, have two distinguishing features. The first is that it is linked to a successful (at present, approximately 45% market share) portable music player, the iPod, which supports a DRM format proprietary to Apple Computer, and second, it can also be used to make MP3 copies by a somewhat convoluted method.[17] Major recording companies as well as smaller independent labels have been willing to provide content to iTunes despite the potential leakage into the "pirate" domain of this content. In this case, copyright owners have demonstrated a willingness to participate in a new business model that provides only a *partial* or "weak" DRM protection for content.

The technology developed by Apple Computer is based on a bet that the convenience and functionality of staying within the rules will prevail – that customers will elect to purchase their "master" copies from iTunes (and hence indirectly from the recording industry) rather than acquiring them through direct exchange with other computer users. In effect, Apple Computer is offering high quality music files that can be removed from DRM only by suffering "quality loss" and following an elaborate procedure for making DRM-independent copies of the recording relative to the results that the user could obtain by purchasing a copy of the original disk.[18]

A business model similar to iTunes has been employed by others such as Rhapsody, a company whose original model was based on a "streaming" service (music chosen by the user is played on an on-demand basis with no "downloading" or saving of the file). Rhapsody has made it possible for users to "burn" copies of certain songs to compact disks. In Rhapsody's explanation to users about what they can subsequently do with the recorded copy, the similarity of online and physical acquisition is explained:

> Question: "Once I burn CDs using Rhapsody, can I make copies of them?" Answer: "The same legal conditions apply to CDs burned using rhapsody as any music CD you would purchase at a retail store. CDs burned using our service may be copied solely for personal use of the subscriber. You may not make copies for others."[19]

Other music downloading services, such as those offered by MusicMatch or Walmart, are based upon Microsoft's digital media player technology, which retains DRM control, requiring the user to employ DRM-compliant players.[20] Among the companies offering such services is Napster. Napster was the original leader in Peer-to-Peer file sharing whose service was closed by court order because it employed a centralized server to locate copies of files users were willing to share and therefore could be assigned blame for the fact that many of the files users made available were copyright-infringing. The "new Napster" model is based upon the strong protection model offered by Microsoft's Windows media player technology and the DRM-compliant WMA (windows media audio) format.[21]

The iTunes business model as well as the recording industry's willingness to participate in this market, indicate a possible resolution to the copyright crisis period in Internet media exchange. The key elements of this model are: 1) the development of DRM compliant models for distribution of original content; 2) the provision of a popular DRM compliant player platform that provides users with a means to meet their desires for time and place shifting of media consumption; and 3) the ability to create (at some inconvenience) copies of the media for other purposes (some of which may constitute copyright infringement). With respect to the third element, the iTunes model (as implemented by iTunes and Rhapsody) is competing with the "strong" DRM model based on the use of Windows WMA format. WMA format files may be "locked" permanently, preventing many users from transforming files into other formats (such as MP3), and therefore require the purchase of WMA-compliant players. A market test that is now underway in the music download business is whether the iTunes model will prevail over the strong DRM of retail models based upon WMA and Windows media player and preliminary results indicate that the iTunes model is preferred.

A principal question about the extensibility of this "limited intellectual property rights (IPR) protection" model is whether the second element, the creation of a popular DRM compliant player platform, is essential. The main contribution of the existence of a DRM compliant player platform is that instead of "forcing" users into a particular pattern of behavior this business model "channels" or "shapes" their behavior by making it more convenient and straightforward to stay within the boundaries of DRM than to stray from these boundaries.[22] Rhapsody's on-demand service can be seen as an online DRM-compliant player combined with a complementary download service providing greater portability. The absence of a player platform (either of the physical iTunes/iPod or virtual Rhapsody type) might well encourage users to exploit the third feature of the model to exchange media content with one another rather than acquiring it from the distributor. Widespread behavior of this sort would "unravel" the incentives for media publishers to provide their content to such distribution services because of unacceptable revenue leakages. The result of such an unraveling would be to shift the advantage towards the Microsoft Windows media player and WMA alternative.

A historical case provides some indication of the resistance that DRM can provoke. A common standard for transportable video files is DivX, such as those downloaded from Peer-to-Peer networks in contravention of copyright. DivX is a compression standard that ironically was developed to support a business model employing DRM-compliant player platforms to compete with conventional DVD rentals. DivX-encoded DVD video media could be distributed in a "self-destruct" format so that after a number of playbacks the DRM compliant player would no longer work for the media.[23] Despite the apparent advantages of not having to make a return trip to the rental outlet, user resistance to this player led to a campaign against the player and appears to have delayed motion picture studio willingness to license films for distribution of DivX-encoded DVDs. The result was a withdrawal of the player platform from the market. The DivX compression standard did, however, remain in active use and software for converting conventional DVDs into DivX compressed files has become a major standard for online distribution of copyright infringing video content. Even after compression, however, the Internet distribution of video media represents a technical challenge due to the size of files that is easing as consumer broadband capacity increases.

One means of addressing the issue of network capacity may be the home entertainment network in which networked personal computers or other devices based on transient storage of media files are used to "order and acquire" media for future playback. If the user is willing to order in advance, downloading times of hours are not a fundamental problem (although the resulting flow of information of this sort over networks may create its own problems).

To summarize this discussion, the experience with the distribution of DRM compliant music, text, and video media files has produced a notable success in the case of iTunes, which employs a "limited IPR protection" model. The iTunes model is reproducible. Rhapsody, which is primarily a library subscription service for "streaming" or "play on demand" music, offers a similar "limited protection" sale of content, but only for a portion of its total library. With iTunes, the development of a DRM compliant player technology to "channel" users' behavior away from copyright infringing use of the media appears to be an important feature in garnering music publisher support for content. At the same time, however, the iTunes model does not provide a "hard barrier" preventing users from making copies of music for various purposes including infringement of copyright when they distribute content to others. The iTunes model is in active competition with the Windows media player and the related WMA format which is a "strong" DRM system, preventing the conversion of files into the DRM-indifferent domain (e.g., by the creation of MP3 files).

In the case of video and film media where strong DRM prevails, as in the case of the DivX player, the technology has not been very popular with users and, in the case of DivX, provoked active campaigning by users against the technology. Whether similar issues will emerge with HD TV DVDs remains to be seen.

In the cases of iTunes and Rhapsody, publishers have clearly accepted a model that compromises between *absolute* protection of copyright and user acceptance. With slight variations, it seems possible to extend this model to other media. This appears to be the path that is now leading out of the current copyright crisis era – nonetheless, it leaves several questions about the nature of the post-crisis era to be addressed, the subject of the next (concluding) section.

The Post-Copyright-Crisis Era

The preceding discussion has a very important limitation. It does not consider the effects on the variety and nature of media that will be made available or will come into existence as the consequence of a passing of the "crisis" struggle over copyrighted content. If a business model of partial protection of copyright content becomes the prevailing standard there are a series of implications for the existing "packaging" of media, the opportunities for entry in media publishing by both artists and publishers, and the nature of the "underground" in which copyright infringement continues to be practiced by some users.

This section considers these implications in order to provide a vision of the post-copyright-crisis era that is somewhat brighter than the scenario in which the crisis might be prolonged indefinitely, sustained by the continued existence of a large copyright-infringing underground and the relentless pursuit of these infringers by a growing and largely self-financing (from settlements and litigation awards) tribe of lawyers representing copyright owners' interests.

The co-existence of different channels for the distribution of media suggests, and perhaps even requires, a degree of product differentiation. One method for establishing this differentiation for physical media is the "packaging" in which media is contained. Contemporary packaging reflects the evolution of past technologies. For example, the markets for compact disc collections of up to 74 minutes of musical content ("albums") co-exist with other markets such as "singles" and compilations. The "album" compact disc roughly corresponds to the previous technology of LP (long play) vinyl records while the heritage of the single recording extends to the origins of recorded music.[24]

The CD, like its predecessor, provides the LP recording with a significant amount of "value added" in the form of "liner notes" and other information about the recording while "singles" (vinyl or CD) have only very basic packaging.[25] Many of the informational or artistic qualities of this packaging can, in principle, be reproduced in the online distribution system but, in doing so, it is information, rather than the form and aesthetics of the package, that is reproduced.[26] It seems likely that, for the foreseeable future, distribution of physical musical recordings will continue, not only because of the "value added" by packaging, but because of the portability and amenities in shelving and organizing personal collections of musical media in a physical format.

Similar practices are employed in the case of video media, although the size of the "single" market, e.g., a single one-hour television program, initially appeared to be smaller. This has changed with the "packaging" concept of the "season" of episodes, a collection of DVDs providing an entire year of a particular television series. The DVD packaging format is often based upon "additional features" of potential interest to viewers such as documentary footage on the making of the film, interviews with the director or actors, and scenes that were not included in the final version. All of these features are part of the packaging that adds value to the physical distribution of media.

These observations about media packaging indicate that there are a variety of possible "formats" for online distribution. If the markets for online musical and video media content grow, they will support more diversified and specialized offerings. What can be said at this stage about such markets is that the online market for music appears to be focused more on individual "songs" than on albums (the online market for classical music recording has not yet developed strongly) and this initial focus may prove to be persistent as the market expands simply because listening habits have, in recent years, become more focused on a stream of singles than on the playing of entire albums.[27]

The flexibility in formatting provided by online distribution has a number of implications for the production of media content. At present, the economics of physical media promotion and distribution make it highly desirable to focus on "hits" that will sell tens of thousands more copies than the average recording. Hits or "blockbusters" offer important economies of scale in promotion and important advantages in competing for shelf space in the physical media outlets where such shelf space is very limited (e.g., retail stores in which recorded music is only one department that must compete with other products for shelf space). There are some corresponding features in the online environment – the "home page" and various "departments" of an online media store will have limited space for display advertising with the likelihood that "best selling" media will be highlighted.

Once the user begins to interactively state preferences and search for material, however, the "shelf space" for storing media offerings has no inherent limits. Moreover, because a successful online media service will draw upon a national or global audience the contents of the media library can be viewed and accessed by far more people than any single retail outlet (as the market grows, the number of users accessing the online store is likely to exceed the number of customers at even the largest outlets of retail chains for music and video). Finally, it becomes possible to create new "intermediaries" including the artists themselves, providing a guide to discography and other outlets for recorded work.

The very large library capacity of online stores raises an important empirical question about how concentrated demand will be. What share of sales will be accounted for by the top 1,000 or 10,000 offerings? At what size will an addition to the library attract zero customers? There is little evidence as yet on which to assess this issue. An interesting example involves Rhapsody, the on-demand music streaming service discussed earlier. In the case of Rhapsody, users purchase a subscription to the entire library, any entry of which can be played on demand and the amount played is limited only by the user's available time.[28] In a recent examination of the issue of user demand in the new environment that appeared in *Wired* magazine (Anderson 2004), and subsequently as a book (Anderson 2006), showed that the drop off in interest in additional listings was unexpectedly small. *Every* entry in Rhapsody is being played by some user, and this trend in "consumption" was keeping up with the very rapid pace at which new content was being added to Rhapsody.[29] This suggests that the size of the "store" in the online environment combined with the diversity of the audience may support a great deal more diversity than is currently present in media industries.

This finding implies the interesting possibility that the online market for media may lead to greater diversification of media content, creating markets for more artists and publishers than the current physical distribution system supports. Moreover, the same capacity suggests the possibility of additional or "variant" offerings of "hit" recordings, the creation of alternative versions of the same movie, and a much greater variety of media content from all kinds of producers.

This diversification of user demand also would raise the value of the music distribution services as providing guides to content including interactive processes for suggesting new media related to the previous choices of the user, ability to search for additional work by the same artist or involving some of the same artists as previous work, and the possibility of a much larger collection of "complementary" media related to artist, venue, content of the media, history of the recording or composition, etc.

All of these possibilities are extensions of the "centralized" server model that has been employed by iTunes, Rhapsody, and other similar music distribution services. Extending this model to the Peer-to-Peer environment is relatively straightforward and offers further possibilities for the spread of the limited protection model of media distribution. Like the earlier Napster, the centralized file server can be used as a means to locate content on Peer-to-Peer networks with the distinction that the centralized file server will only be available for the location of DRM compliant material, the path now being followed by the reborn Napster as well as KaZaA following its capitulation to similar litigation.

Peer-to-Peer networks may still be used for other models of information access including infringement, but the nature of the competition between DRM-compliant and DRM-indifferent content is quite distinct – the "copyright advantage" becomes the ability to provide centralized information resources with regard to the availability of content that is distributed in the Peer-to-Peer network and excludes DRM-indifferent content.

This pushes DRM-indifferent content to a more marginal position – exchanging infringing copies among networks of friends resembles the older practice of lending recordings to others to make copies, rather than "re-publishing" the record for an unlimited number of users. It will still be possible to find infringing copies of the "hits" distributed on Peer-to-Peer networks using other means of indexing and there are likely to be continuing conflicts as publishers take legal actions against services and users. Whether these actions, which have cumulatively been targeted at thousands of users, will serve their stated purpose of "educating" users or will fuel a growing "underground" of file exchanging remains to be seen.[30]

If commercialized media downloading services are capable of attracting users away from the underground, the result could well be a substantial growth in entry opportunities for new media of all kinds. It is likely that the commercial model will continue to support the concentration of revenues in the "top hits," and the business model of investing in their production and promotion. The extent of this concentration may, however, be significantly reduced as users diversify their media acquisition behavior and larger amounts of content are made available. In part, the reduction in concentration may be a consequence of greater spending on a more diverse collection of media – a preference for variety. In part, the reduction in concentration is likely to come from a modest reduction in the revenues from the biggest hits as consumers opt for greater variety.

This generally optimistic scenario remains clouded by the prospects for a continued struggle between the producers and users of copyrighted information. While the agencies of copyright owners may regard prosecuting thousands of file sharers as an educational lesson – those thousands as well as the tens or even hundreds of thousands who actively or tacitly support greater balance between copyright owners and the users of information constitute the onset of an even broader conflict whose ultimate resolution could be a dramatic restructuring of copyright owner privilege.

At one extreme, a relatively small change in the law for remedying copyright infringement to limit actions against those who do not personally profit from infringement, would substantially alter the balance between producer and user rights in copyright information. A less confiscatory approach would be to impose a tax on the use of the network or the producers of hardware that is non-DRM compliant and the distribution of this tax to copyright owners. For those who advocate a "natural rights" theory of copyright, either of these proposals would be heretical, amounting to the confiscation of property – for those who see copyright as an arbitrary rule governing the allocation of rents from the state grant of monopoly to copyright owners, such responses might well appear to be in the social interest.[31]

Notes

1. The "selectivity" of the enforcement has not yet failed to meet the requirements of US criminal law where it is not only necessary to demonstrate that the authorities have chosen to prosecute one party rather than others similarly situated, but also that the prosecuted party is a member of some group or class of individuals (e.g., the offence of being of Chinese ethnicity while operating a laundry in a wooden building, a landmark decision in the US Supreme Court's definition of the selective prosecution defense, 118 U.S. 356 Yick Wo v. Hopkins, http://www.law.cornell.edu/supct/html/historics/USSC_CR_0118_0356_ZS.html Accessed 2 September 2006).
2. Facetiously, it is tempting to suggest that the relevant category of persons being pursued is "relatively naïve users," those who do not take the precaution of obscuring their identities before infringing on copyright.
3. Resolving conflicts between publishers and "re-publishers" was, along with the aim of suppressing heretical texts, a principal goal of the first copyright laws (see David 1993) One of the first studies to consider the problems of copyright protection in the digital era reviewed the history of earlier electronic copying technologies (see Office of Technology Assessment 1986).
4. Concisely, there are many points on the paths that data follows in the personal computer that can be used to divert data streams to mass storage – hence, copying the signal when it becomes "clear" of encryption. This possibility is being limited in two ways. First, the US Digital Millennium Copyright Act (US Public Law No. 105-304, 112 Stat. 2860 (Oct. 28, 1998)) and the relatives of this Act in other countries have criminalized the production and sale of hardware and software technologies for achieving such diversions. Second, the creation of DTCP (digital transmission content protection), a DRM technology, and its embedding in HDTV display devices makes it possible to send an encrypted signal to the display device, eliminating the possibility of signal diversion.
5. This is a consequence of the standards adopted for players and recorders, which do not incorporate encryption. Consumer electronics CD recorders make two concessions to DRM. They accept only a particular type of recordable CD, the "music recordable CD" which is recognizable due to the setting of a "disk application flag" during the manufacturer of the disk. The recorder also sets a flag on the data of the recorded disk indicating that it is a copy and most recorders will not record *from* a disk that has had this flag set, barring copies of copies.
6. Other methods that are sometimes referred to as DRM techniques may be employed to trace the provenance of a particular recording with the aim of creating evidence of infringing copies rather than blocking the copying of information.
7. Other DRM technologies, such as "watermarking" that do not actually block copying can be employed to detect and trace copyright infringement.

8. See footnote 3 on HDTV display devices. However, the technique which is analogous to the re-recording of audio material is the videotaping of the display, a technique that at present is used to create source material for "pirated" film releases.

9. Liebowitz 2006.

10. While Gopher is a "client-server" application, the assumed asymmetry between "clients" and "servers" have eroded over time, obscuring the legitimacy of this distinction. On the original specification of the Gopher protocol see RFC 1436, http://www.cse.ohio-state.edu/cgi-bin/rfc/rfc1436.html, Last Accessed 3 September 2006.

11. Electronic Frontier Foundation, http://www.eff.org/IP/Peer-to-Peer/howto-notgetsued.php, last accessed 3 September 2006.

12. In this chapter, rather than repeating the term "digital media" the term media is employed to refer to all forms of information that might be shared with others and that might be recorded digitally. Thus, printed books can be "scanned" as digital images and are media in this definition. This definition includes information that is not ordinarily considered as media – e.g., personal communications such as e-mail messages.

13. The term "experience" is used along with the term "consume" in what follows. The latter term suggests a commodity relationship that does not necessarily apply to all forms of media – e.g., a family photo album shared on the Internet. Experience is therefore used in more general contexts while "consume" is used in those contexts where the publisher of the information is likely to be seeking an audience of "customers" or "readers" who may directly or indirectly (e.g., through advertising support) be a source of revenue.

14. Technologies that do not ordinarily involve time or place shifting, but still involve some user control of the "programming" of media consumption include video media rental, pay per view television and video on demand.

15. Of course this is not always an option; consider viewing a film in a cinema. Although the cinema film cannot, strictly speaking, be "shared" with others, the continuum of talking about the subject of the film, describing the plot, showing excerpts of the film, and acquiring a video recording of the film are all approximations of having seen the film.

16. The "effectiveness" of copyright protection is in relation to the principle alternative – providing a collective payment from society to information producers. For some types of information, e.g., scientific results, it has been possible to create a governance system that regulates the size and influences the nature of initiatives undertaken. For recorded media it is generally believed to be infeasible or undesirable to take a collective decision as to the amount of media that it is desirable to produce or to direct the activities of those who create recorded media with a few exceptions (e.g., certain forms of pornography).

17. The MP3 technical standard employs acoustic science to achieve a higher standard of fidelity to human perception of musical recording and is therefore most useful for content of this type. For many users, the perceived loss of audio quality of an MP3 file is small or insignificant, making a compressed file equivalent to the original.
18. IPod market share from Canalys (http://www.canalys.com/pr/2005/r2005091.htm, accessed 5 September 2006). It is possible to use iTunes to record ("burn") a standard audio disc that can be "ripped" or stored in standard files that can, in turn, be converted in to MP3 files using other software, effectively moving the music from the DRM-compliant to the DRM-indifferent domain. Note, however, that the first step produces an audio file that is technically inferior to a copy that might be made from a compact disc manufactured by the copyright owner.
19. The AAC (Advanced Audio Coding) file compression format offered by Apple Computer is somewhat higher quality than the most commonly used settings for MP3 files. The MP3 format does, however, offer higher quality formats that exceed the quality offered by iTunes' ability to record AAC files to MP3 disks. To employ these higher quality settings requires a higher quality original or a "master" copy such as a commercially distributed compact disk. It is important to note, however, that only a small proportion of the population can consistently identify the difference between the original and an AAC version of a musical recording.
20. Rhapsody, FAQ Section, http://www.listen.com/faq.jsp?sect=answer, last Accessed 3 September 2006.
21. The Websites for MusicMatch and Walmart's music downloading services are reachable from their home pages, http://www.walmart.com/ and http://www.musicmatch.com/, last Accessed 3 September 2006.
22. Napster, http://www.napster.com/, last Accessed 3 September 2006.
23. Apple has extended the iTunes business model to other media including audio books and videos. The principles identified above have been applied in each case although, in the case of video, users may have to use specialized equipment and software to transfer content to some devices.
24. The following account draws upon Mansell and Steinmueller (2000), pp. 322–323). The term DivX is not an acronym; it is derived from the company's name that invented it (DivX Networks, Inc.) Confusingly, DivX (Digital Video Express) is the name this company employed for their limited play business model that employed DivX-encoded DVDs of film and a player platform for these DVDs.
25. For example, wax cylinder recordings were of individual compositions.
26. There is a problem of circularity here as the lower investment in "liner notes" and other features of the single influences the size of the market for this format as well as being a consequence of the smaller size of the market. A purely economic explanation is probably less convincing than the historical explanation that the promotion of LP recordings required additional "value added" to justify the higher unit price of such recordings as compared to earlier formats.

27. Abilities to pursue these strategies are and will continue to be supported by the copyright on such content, which can be used to pursue organized attempts by others to copy this information. The emergence of alternative "liner notes" and guides that do not infringe copyright can be expected as the size of the digital market grows.
28. More cynically, many would observe that the contents of many albums are "filler" for a few songs that are outstanding. Whether this is true, or continues to be true, when there is a level competitive playing field between albums and singles remains to be seen.
29. As noted earlier, Rhapsody is also following the emerging business model allowing users to record their own copies of an offering. This service is priced per item.
30. A possible criticism of this conclusion is that the marginal cost of playing an additional recording on Rhapsody is zero due to the fixed charge subscription nature of the service. However, this argument ignores the opportunity cost of user time – unless actual demand for these "fringe" recordings exist, users should be allocating their time to recordings for which they have a defined preference. Users may be exploring what their preferences are, but this is both consistent with their behavior and with the implications of the analysis and is a behavior that has an opportunity cost.
31. Borland 2004.

References

Anderson, C. *The Long Tail. Wired.* 12.10: 170–177, 2004.
Anderson, C. *The Long Tail: How Endless Choice is Creating Unlimited Demand.* New York: Random House Business Books, 2006.
Borland, J. "RIAA Files New Round of Peer-to-Peer Lawsuits." C-Net News, 2004.
David, P.A. "Intellectual Property Institutions and the Panda's Thumb: Patents, Copyrights, and Trade Secrets in Economic Theory and History." *Global Dimensions of Intellectual Property Rights in Science and Technology.* M. Wallerstein, M. Mogee, and R. Schoen, eds. Washington, DC: National Academy Press, 1993.
David, P.A. "The Evolving Accidental Information Super-Highway." *Oxford Review of Economic Policy*, 17 (2, June 1), 2001, 159–187.
Jones, G. "La Cenerentola." *The Mammoth Book of Best New SF 12.* G. Dozois, ed. London: Robinson, 1998, 510–524.
Liebowitz, S.J. "File Sharing: Creative Destruction or Just Plain Destruction?" *Journal of Law and Economics*, XLIX (April), 2006, 1–28.
Mansell, R. "New Media Competition and Access: The Scarcity–Abundance Dialectic." *New Media & Society*, 1 (2), 1999, 155–182.

Mansell, R. and Steinmueller, W.E. *Mobilizing the Information Society: Strategies for Growth and Opportunity*. London: Oxford University Press, 2000.

Office of Technology Assessment. *Intellectual Property Rights in an Age of Electronics and Information*. Washington, DC: Office of Technology Assessment, US Congress, Government Printing Office, OTA-CIT-302, April, 1986.

3

The Economics of Peer-to-Peer

Alain Bourdeau de Fontenay[1], Eric Bourdeau de Fontenay[2],
Lorenzo Maria Pupillo[3]

[1]*Columbia University*
[2]*MusicDish LCC*
[3]*Telecom Italia*

Introduction

Peer-to-Peer networks boast three characteristics that make them unique. First, they are layered networks conceived and operating in a similar fashion to the Internet. Second, they are completely decentralized, making servers of individual computers at the Peer-to-Peer layer, and acting in the way an ISP acts at the Internet IP layer. Finally, Peer-to-Peer networks are made up of the resources that individual members make available when they use their Peer-to-Peer networks.[1] These networks, which were initially used by individuals to share and download content, including a significant amount of copyright material such as music, are now increasingly used for downloading games, videos, and software.[2]

In this paper, we focus on the economics of Peer-to-Peer in terms of the impact that Peer-to-Peer innovation is having on the content sector, especially on copyrighted material, and on how the latter has in turn influenced Peer-to-Peer networks. Peer-to-Peer technology makes a server of end-users. In addition, while Peer-to-Peer network service providers may retain some control over their own networks, this control is effectively restricted to the Peer-to-Peer layer as a pure transport and file-sharing layer, and is independent of the content that is shared, at least in the post-Napster era.

In this paper, we study Peer-to-Peer from the perspective of the "commons."[3] Since Hardin's study (1998) it is best to distinguish between "managed" and "unmanaged" commons. Currently, all Peer-to-Peer networks are "unmanaged" at file-sharing level, which means that the commercial links between individual members of existing Peer-to-Peer communities

E.M. Noam and L.M. Pupillo (eds.), *Peer-to-Peer Video*, doi: 10.1007/978-0-387-76450-4_3,
© Springer Science + Business Media, LLC 2008

and the owners of the copyright material that is being shared have now completely disappeared. Furthermore, institutions that clarify the scope of fair use in everyday practice have not yet been created.

At the same time, experimental economics suggests that this outcome does not automatically create a "tragedy of the commons."[4] As the commercial success of new services such as iTunes shows, it is conceivable that many members of those new Peer-to-Peer commons may be willing to shift to commercial Peer-to-Peer networks that incorporate reasonable payments to artists, thus reflecting the expanded use of copyrighted material. The above is also suggested by the willingness of individual users to participate in voluntary programs such as SETI.

However, these experimental results also suggest that the current practice may be becoming routine-like, i.e., that the window of opportunity for that kind of solution may shut in the near future, with consumers increasingly reluctant to diverge from the routines they are developing.

The willingness of members of Peer-to-Peer communities to contribute with access and computer resources to the community is another commons Peer-to-Peer is creating.

Today's Peer-to-Peer file sharing makes it simple for individuals and their downloaded Peer-to-Peer software to search for, share, and download files from other users on the same Peer-to-Peer system. While a few years have elapsed since court decisions in the USA essentially eliminated Peer-to-Peer networks such as Napster and Aimster, many of the lessons that are relevant to a Peer-to-Peer economic analysis can still be traced back to those two cases.[5]

In 2001, The Economist observed that, "[t]he most important lesson of Napster is that people are willing to open their computers to, and share files with, complete strangers – as long as they see value in doing so. In the process, they have shown how really large computer networks can be created rapidly through the piecemeal contribution of millions of individual PCs, each of which functions as a server as well as client" (The Economist 2001).[6]

Over the years, the content sector has evolved into the industry we know today. It is, at present, a complex and, generally, highly concentrated sector that is characterized by a range of content types, the major elements of which are the video entertainment and music sectors as well as, increasingly, the gaming one. Through time, the sector has been characterized by the growing role of intermediation and the impact of technology on the ability to produce, access, copy and store content, as well as share and consume it. Technological innovation has revolutionized more than just the ability to access, transform, and consume content. It has redefined the very meaning of access, by copying and storing, sharing, and consuming.[7]

Peer-to-Peer is a new enough activity the alternative object of which that can be associated with the sector's economic analysis needs to be clarified. With the gradual emergence of the Peer-to-Peer institutional setting, the economics of Peer-to-Peer are moving from the economic analysis of the transition process to the economic analysis of Peer-to-Peer as an established communication and processing architecture.

At one end of the spectrum, we could consider the Peer-to-Peer sector in terms of conventional questions such as the demand for content and the role of free-riding. At the other end, economic analysis can help better understand the evolution of the institutional environment. It might help to understand the economic implications of competing frameworks within which Peer-to-Peer might operate.

The kind of questions involved relate to subject matters such as the extent and meaning of copyrights ownership. The Napster court and Aimster cases as well as, more recently, the Ninth Circuit Court's Decision, are all elements of the trial and error process through which society is identifying the context within which Peer-to-Peer will largely be able to operate.

What is the economics of Peer-to-Peer? Everything suggests that Peer-to-Peer's role is of growing significance for the content sector. There is no doubt that this is particularly true for video Peer-to-Peer. After all, this is the fastest growing segment of Peer-to-Peer, which is itself one of the fastest growing sectors in the digital economy. In addition, while the courts have been addressing Peer-to-Peer issues since the Napster Decision, the process is far from being complete: discussions on Peer-to-Peer economics in terms of a stable institutional setting are yet to take place.

The specificity of Peer-to-Peer networks and their historical setting today raise questions about the applicability of many conventional economic tools. This has led us to select an analytical methodology that pays far more attention to the institutions that are developing with the growth of Peer-to-Peer, and to the economic forces that contribute to shape the same institutions. Conventional economic tools generally presume that stability and maturity are characteristics of the sectors that are under study. On the other hand, the process through which institutions take shape is a complex one involving not only economics but also a wide range of other factors.

Nevertheless, it is important to evaluate the economic forces at play in this process, in order to understand the type of scenario that is likely to emerge and the changes it can bring about as new stakeholders compete to set up in the new environment.

One of the main reasons why the understanding of the dynamics that shapes the transformation of the content sector into a mature Peer-to-Peer environment is so important, especially for those who believe in an optimal spontaneous order, is that the outcome is not predetermined as a unique "optimal" solution. In fact, our hope is that studies such as this one will help improve and streamline the process through which Peer-to-Peer could become established efficiently.

Our analysis helps us focus on intermediation, the functionality that is most affected by Peer-to-Peer, in the emergence of stable and predictable Peer-to-Peer institutions. Indeed, through time, today's aggregators have built – and now use – intermediation to their advantage. Thus, aggregators have transformed their role from one of mere intermediation into one of ownership and brokerage. Such new functions have exacerbated the incumbency dimension of their position and, with it, the inherent tension that emerges between extracting more rents from existing assets, and developing new assets with new artists.

Our analysis incorporates the rather unique characteristics of economics of the arts and performance.[8] These dimensions force us to make a distinction between live performances by artists and musical reproductions enabled by technology, in the same way that theater can be differentiated from cinema, or movie-making from movie-viewing.

The stakeholders involved are not simply the aggregators. As one would expect in a time of change, many other stakeholders are jockeying for a role in the emerging environment. Some, like the players from the computer and software sectors, are obvious, as are those who, like Gnutella, are gaining a growing stake in the emerging Peer-to-Peer distribution sector. Less obvious are new intermediaries such as BigChampagne, who are developing new data-gathering techniques to support marketing and other analyses of the sector, and companies such as Tag It, who use their knowledge of the new media to find new ways to help artists take advantage of the media and make themselves known.

One of our conclusions is that Peer-to-Peer, together with other technological changes, may be creating a growing wedge between the objectives of artists, especially new artists, and today's legacy intermediaries. Such an outcome may make the development of sufficiently fast alternatives to existing Peer-to-Peer networks more difficult.

Technology may spark a transformation in the access and consumption of content, but the process is more complex as society's response to the technological change takes the form of legislation and/or regulations. The process through which these changes emerge in turn transforms the technology. Once again, Napster illustrates this process in the context of the music industry. For instance, once the Napster decision was announced, the RIAA's response, which was nothing more than its long-run strategy to refuse to negotiate compromises (whether justified or not) created in practice (and quite predictably) a demand for further technological advances that could bypass Napster's flaws.

The paper is organized in seven sections. After the introduction, we provide a descriptive overview of the Peer-to-Peer sector in the recording, video, games, and TV industries. The section following defines the economic characteristics of Peer-to-Peer and considers how Peer-to-Peer relates to content. It emphasizes that, with Peer-to-Peer, content owners have, for the first time, lost all channels that link them directly or indirectly to consumers. This analysis helps us identify what makes Peer-to-Peer so different from previous innovations. The subsequent section uses the concept of the commons first formulated by Hardin (1968) to describe the characteristics of Peer-to-Peer and to identify their "unmanaged" dimension at the file-sharing level. It describes how Peer-to-Peer technology is changing the economic institutions. After that, we consider the most likely consumer response to the emergence of Peer-to-Peer and to the failure of the content sector in facilitating the development of credible Peer-to-Peer commercial services, and, subsequently, we highlight the extent to which Peer-to-Peer platforms have evolved technologically in response to institutional factors. We state that the conventional assumption of exogenous technology that economists continue to make in industrial organization is, at best, misleading. In the last section we draw our conclusions.

The Peer-to-Peer Sector

Overview

According to the OECD Information Technology Outlook 2006,[9] the number of simultaneous Peer-to-Peer users (people who are jointly connected at any given moment) in March 2006 was close to 11.5 million, up from 7.3 million in March 2003. Comparing the growth of Peer-to-Peer users of the popular fast-track networks such as KaZaA with all other Networks (such as eDonkey, eMule, Torrents), two messages emerge: the decline of the number of users of the fast-track networks from the peak of October 2003 and the parallel growth of the number of users of all monitored networks. While the former is attributed by OECD analysts primarily to an increase in lawsuits against users of Peer-to-Peer networks, and to the rise of successful commercial music downloading services such as Apple iTunes, the latter suggests a migration of Peer-to-Peer users to networks that attract less attention from the music industry and related lawsuits.

In terms of geographical distribution of Peer-to-Peer users, the OECD report shows that the United States account for 66%, Germany for 5%, France for 3.5%, and Canada for 3.2%. Weighing the data by population,

Luxemburg seems to be the country with the greatest number of Peer-to-Peer simultaneous users (12% of the population), followed by Iceland, Finland, Norway Ireland, and the United States. On average, 1% of the OECD population is logged on to a Peer-to-Peer network (four times the value of 2003).

The case for displacement, i.e., the migration of Peer-to-Peer users from the Fast Track network to new ones, can also be made by looking at the volume of data exchanged on Peer-to-Peer networks. Each day the equivalent of roughly 3 billion songs or 5 million movies zip between computers, and Internet users around the globe freely exchange a staggering 10 petabytes of data, much of which in the form of copyright protected songs, movies, software, and video games.[10]

Peer-to-Peer is also becoming the largest consumer of data on ISP networks, significantly outweighing web traffic and costing an average per year of $598 million globally, according to Cachelogic, a UK network equipment producer.[11]

The OECD report, using BigChampagne data, also states that the majority of files traded are audio files. However, video and other files, including software, make up 35% of total files exchanged and their share is on the rise due to higher availability of bandwidth and new DVD and CD burning technologies.

The geographical distribution of these data reveals that the increase in the downloading of larger video and other files is particularly relevant in Europe. Germany has the highest share of video files downloaded via fast-track networks (about 40% of the total), followed by Italy (37%), Belgium (33%), Norway (31%), Canada (30%), and the United Kingdom (29%). According to the OECD analysts, this is partly due to the broad diffusion in Europe of the Peer-to-Peer technology (eDonkey), which is particularly useful for sharing large files (600 MB or more), while in the USA most users rely on Fast Track, which is better suited for sharing smaller files.

The Economic Impact of Peer-to-Peer file sharing

Copyright issues, network costs, and also the commercial opportunities connected to Peer-to-Peer technologies related to new applications of legal file-sharing call for an evaluation of the economic effects of file-sharing.

As far as intellectual property is concerned, the initiatives of the recording industry are motivated by the legitimate objective of protecting their intellectual property. However, as mentioned in Krishnan et al. (2003a), "this legitimate effort [.] can, in some cases, collide with the interests and rights of entrepreneurs attempting to develop novel information sharing networks, individuals exercising fair use rights associated with legitimately purchased materials, and network operators seeking to protect the privacy of their users." Furthermore, copyright holders, besides threatening users with fines and lawsuits for illegal sharing, are defining new strategies such as inundating Peer-to-Peer systems with "spoof" files in order to increase Peer-to-Peer users' cost for searching and finding the music they are interested in.

The network costs that ISPs face to provide Peer-to-Peer network services to their users is becoming an increasingly important issue for the huge consumption of scarce bandwidth and the large transit fees that are currently borne by ISPs to provide such services. In order to optimize Peer-to-Peer networks and cope with rising costs, beside the reduction of the quality of services for Peer-to-Peer services, or more drastic decisions such as the shutdown of Peer-to-Peer networks, some researchers such as Asvanund et al. (2003a,b) suggest the creation of clubs in Peer-to-Peer networks based on common interests or network location proximity.

The issue we wish to focus on in this section is how much of an impact do Peer-to-Peer networks actually have on the sales of associated information products. We will start with the recording industry and then move on to the movie industry.

The Recording Industry

The sales of music CDs have fallen considerably over the last few years. The record industry has claimed that this decline is due to file-sharing. The first question that we need to address is: is there a clear theoretical prediction for such a phenomenon? The causality between file-sharing and record sales is not clear. On the one hand, there is a possibility of a substitution effect between CDs and downloaded files, with a negative impact on sales. On the other hand, there is a debate among economists on the results on the sales of what is called the *sampling effect*, i.e., the possibility of learning from file-sharing about music users would not otherwise be exposed to.

Oberholzer and Strump (2004)[12] claim that "File sharing lowers the price of music, which draws in low-evaluation individuals who would otherwise not have purchased albums. That is, file sharing primarily serves to increase total music consumption." Liebowitz (2004) claims that, contrary to the common belief of a positive effect on sales, the effects from sampling are more subtle and tend to lead to a decrease in sales in the CD market.[13] It follows that there is no clear theoretical prediction on the effect of file-sharing on CD sales. However, when we turn to empirical evidence, the uncertainty does not seem to disappear.

The two above-mentioned studies also include empirical results.[14] As these papers follow very different methodological approaches, they can be considered particularly relevant for the investigation of these issues. Liebowitz (2004) states that the file-sharing explanation for the decline of CD sales in the 1999–2003 period is so compelling that only extremely powerful empirical evidence of the contrary would allow this belief to be ruled out. Therefore, he examines other possible explanations for the decline of record sales (price and income changes; changes in substitute/complementary markets, such as DVDs; changes in the quality of the music; and changes in the supply of music). The study concludes that, because the alternative explanations do not appear capable of explaining the sharp decrease in national record sales of CDs, the file-sharing hypothesis must be embraced.[15]

The paper by Oberholzer and Strump (2004) to some extent complements Liebowitz's aggregate analysis. Indeed, it uses micro data – i.e., the album sales and the actual downloads of albums based on data collected by OpenNap (a centralized Peer-to-Peer network) and uses it to create a large and representative sample in which individuals are generally unaware that their actions are being recorded.[16] The data on sales are taken primarily from Nielsen SoundScan and from other sources.

The above analysis shows that there is no relationship between the number of downloads of a particular album and the actual sales of the album itself – i.e., file-sharing does not reduce record sales. Furthermore, most people who shared files appear to be individuals who would not have bought the albums that they downloaded and the more popular CDs seem to benefit from file-sharing.[17]

All the above-mentioned studies suffer from various imperfections and do not offer strong evidence in one direction or another. This has definitely to do with the fact that the analysis of file-sharing is still in its initial phase. Therefore, the lack of strong evidence convinces us to avoid using these results for policy prescriptions. Furthermore, this lack of evidence can be considered as an opportunity to shift the focus from non-commercial file-sharing to the business potential that Peer-to-Peer applications may have with regard to the digital delivery of services for new business models and the legal digital distribution of music and other applications (Peer-to-Peer is not equal to music sharing!).

The Movie Industry

Movies have been available through online rentals for quite some time. But downloading movies is a comparatively new phenomenon. Movies-download work in two ways. One is file-swapping and free downloads as in the case of music. Some people gain access to a sneak preview of the movie, copy it, process it and put it up on the World Wide Web where it can be downloaded through networks such as KaZaA.

The other way is offered, as an experiment, by Hollywood film companies for public downloading. However, the movie must be viewed within 24 hours; indeed, after 24 hours the file self-destructs. Furthermore, only old successful films or second-rate new releases are put on offer.

How big is this phenomenon? According to Cachelogic, the exchange of films and software is booming and the vast majority of Peer-to-Peer traffic is made up of files larger than 100 MB. "Many of these are likely to be copies of films, with Cachelogic reporting that 30% of Peer-to-Peer traffic for one ISP was all from a single 600 MB file, which they suspect was a copy of a major film that had just been released."[18]

A report from Britain's Informa Media Group stated that selling films across the Internet could develop into an industry worth over $800 million a year by 2010, but would be worth more than $1.3 billion if it were not for illegal downloads. Despite the growth of downloads, the study estimated that sales of hard copies of DVDs and videos will remain by far the largest category of film sales: $2.62 billion in 2010, up from $804 million in 2003. These data show that although the movie downloading is becoming a fast-growing phenomenon and is already harming the movie industry, the "big bite" from revenues will only come 5 years from now.[19]

There are differences in technologies and consumers' behavior that can shape the history of movie downloads differently from the music one. Currently, watching a movie downloaded off the Internet usually means waiting far longer than for an MP3 file to download, as well as accepting lower quality. But with broadband connections, as speed increases, so do the quality and quantity of films available. Compression formats like DivX continue to improve, thus enabling the exchange of higher-quality movies. This offers more opportunities to the movie industry to set up legal downloading services that can satisfy the customers' need to avoid the downloading of poor quality films which could contain viruses.

How does downloading affect the social experience of "going out to the movies"? Can legal downloading help in testing customers' preferences, reducing marketing costs? And what about customers' repeated viewing habits? Is not this behavior different from listening to music and does it not generate different incentives for downloading?

All these issues call for Peer-to-Peer technologies to be embraced by the movie industry.

Peer-to-Peer and Games[20]

A totally different approach from that of the Music Industry has been followed by the games industry. Games publishers are actually working with Peer-to-Peer networks to sell legal copies of their products alongside the illicit copies. Trymedia, an anti-piracy software firm, offers about 300 legitimate games on Peer-to-Peer networks and has experienced 20 million downloads in 18 months. The global market for legally downloaded games is currently estimated at $150 million per year, and the figure is poised to double each year.

Peer-to-Peer is seen as a sales channel for games. Companies such as Trymedia, Softwrap, and Macromedia are offering games publishers software that stops games from being copied or limits access to them for a trial period. Therefore, demo versions of the games can be played before buying the product. Peer-to-Peer networks enable the enhancement of the "viral sharing of content between friends" that has always been the biggest promoter for software content. Trymedia's Zicherman says: "If you can convert 5% of users into legitimate buyers, then you'll be ahead." Converting pirates to sales is their goal!

Peer-to-Peer and TV[21]

Atzio technology announced recently the availability of the company's Peer-to-Peer television technology which enables internet television. Atzio's legitimate Peer-to-Peer platform is designed to offer subscribers movies and television shows that can be ordered and downloaded for viewing at their own convenience. With Atzio's distribution model, when a video is released by a content provider, it is packaged for internet distribution, protected by digital rights management technology, and added to the content producer's online catalog.

The company's Peer-to-Peer television technology works by splitting large video files into several digital "chunks." Each chunk is distributed to peers. Each peer then transmits its chunk to another, using a portion of the upstream bandwidth available to each peer. This technology can satisfactorily complement the offering of television networks, studios, and independent content providers.

The Economic Characteristics of Peer-to-Peer

To study the economics of Peer-to-Peer, the way in which Peer-to-Peer relates to content should be taken into consideration. More specifically, the very nature of artistic content, and how technology has impacted the ways artists deliver their content to the public, should be analyzed. In this section, we study the ways content through the ages has become easier and easier to reproduce. While Peer-to-Peer may not be the last step in this trend, nevertheless, it, breaks with the past because content owners, for the first time, have effectively lost all channels that link them directly or indirectly to the consumers.

With today's Peer-to-Peer services, consumers do not have to go through a store or the Internet to purchase a record or an online service. In addition, the Peer-to-Peer network service provider's business model is to attract as many users as possible in order to justify advertising revenues. What is even more dramatic for content owners is that today's Peer-to-Peer platforms, over which file transfers take place, are economically viable and formally independent of content.

This is because the Peer-to-Peer network service provider's business is a transport platform over which file-sharing takes place through consumers' own initiative. Such a service takes place at a layer below content, i.e., the Peer-to-Peer sector's organization has no element that would naturally link it to the content sector the way television and radio stations do in their broadcasting business.

In a Peer-to-Peer environment, the Peer-to-Peer community that corresponds to a given Peer-to-Peer network becomes the entity that consumes the content that individuals, independent of the community, may have purchased or pirated on a personal basis. While the content, initially, is what individuals have purchased or obtained in other ways, once an individual becomes a member of a Peer-to-Peer community, even of an ephemeral one, that content potentially becomes the community's content.

Economics relates to the exchange of goods and services between individuals. The generic exchange of goods and services is defined here as a "commons."[22] Commons are beneficial to society as a whole because they provide the institutional framework for all economic exchanges, hence for trade. Trade makes it possible for people to specialize in different sectors, hence in general to carry out the tasks they are best at, as described by the division of labor.[23] The result is greater wealth within the society. This is achieved not only by the greater efficiency with which labor is utilized, but also through the increased diversity of goods and services people produce.

Trade is an inherent activity of any society, no matter how isolated it might be. In the most isolated society, trade means the exchange of goods and services within that society. Such a form of trade may not be perceived by the community's members as trade. Whatever it may be, trade consists of activities that are typically governed by strict rules and protocols facilitated by routines.

Trade is unlikely to take on more complex forms as long as such communities remain sufficiently small that there is no need for accounting and record keeping. Some of the activities of those societies involve the arts and entertainment, which are integrated within the society through an informal form of exchange and labor specialization that is also governed by laws and protocols.

As societies become larger and develop in the form of multiple communities, trade begins to involve exchanges between growing numbers of individuals belonging more and more often to distinct communities.

As societies grow, there is a parallel need to develop some form of content that is seen as essential to the societies themselves. Typically, the content all societies appear to value above all is their individual history, the history of "the people," as with the Inuits. At this stage, as history becomes complex and involves too many elements for individuals – even the elders – to remember, societies may select one of their members, typically one of the most gifted, to become people's history.

In some parts of Africa, that person is the grillot. The grillot develops unique skills to keep the complex record of the society's history and is rewarded by gifts and various forms of payments that are also governed by laws and protocols. As demonstrated by the grillot, content does not travel in the same way as physical goods and services, and trade in content remains within the boundaries of individual societies or "people."

In due course, often through the creation of empires, trade and content become so complex that people eventually develop art, sculpture, and, at some stage, writing. This step transforms the availability of content among people because it can now be reproduced. Historically, this step was controlled by the religious and, at times, by the political authorities. This meant that those responsible for content within the society had ways to be paid for their work.

However, the way artists and entertainers were paid in the past already encompassed the great discrepancies we observe today. Suffice it to compare artists such as the three Limbourg brothers and the masterpieces they created for the Duc de Berry with popular entertainers such as Hugo's Notre Dame de Paris' Esmeralda.

Gutenberg transformed the reproduction process and made content accessible to an even larger population. The invention of photography, and, subsequently, the phonograph and movie in the nineteenth century further transformed access to content and the works of artists. Around that period, the copyright protection of the works artists produced became increasingly widespread.

Although the process afforded some protection to the artists, it also gave them the responsibility of making sure they could collect the payments, a task that could turn out to be a challenge, as demonstrated by Dickens' experience when he visited the United States.

The radio was the next major transformation in the way individuals could access content. With radio, individuals could listen to music and other forms of content without a direct transaction with the artists or their intermediaries. Copyrights were covered in many places by a flat tax; elsewhere, as advertisers paid to have access to radio listeners, providing a way to pay for whatever copyright fees had been negotiated.

From an economic perspective, radio transformed the relationship between artists and entertainers on one hand and listeners on the other by eliminating the commercial transaction that gave the public access to the artists' work. Effectively, with radio and, eventually, the television, society was returning to a form of commons that dominated ancient societies.[24]

While the process was different from the ancient times, radio stations were privately owned, artists and entertainers had recourse to have their rights recognized as individual stations, just as individual commons, were centrally managed. They had an owner who was responsible for using copyrighted material for commercial ends, i.e., someone from whom they could collect copyright fees.

The media commodity has the unique characteristic that copyright owners keep the property rights over the artists' work by effectively transferring a license to customers to view and listen to the material.[25] That license is becoming increasingly imprecise with the increased flexibility technology allows people to enjoy, hence to consume, the artists' works. This has led to the introduction of the concept of "fair use" that details the terms of the license, i.e., how individuals are entitled to consume the copyright material.

With radio and television, artists found that technology was restricting their ability to select the pricing model of their choice, and that they lost the possibility of charging each individual for listening and/or viewing their creation. However, the change in pricing, where the link between the price customers pay and the specificity of consumption becomes less and less precise, is a general trend, and not a specific characteristic of the media sector. The trend reflects the greater number of ways customer demands can be met; consequently, the need to find new pricing structures that simplify the processing tasks of consumers arises.

Internet radio and, in time, Internet television further expand the extent of the population that can be reached by the technology. That population, now, is the global population of Internet users. Nevertheless, Internet radio and television leave one dimension unchanged, the community of users. That community is still organized in a centralized manner since it depends on a single entity; the Internet station owner. With Internet radio and television, even with its global reach, artists do not lose the recourse to a single owner.

Peer-to-Peer changes this situation. While there may be, initially, a single platform, the Peer-to-Peer community emerges totally decentralized with each member free to act as they wish. As those communities are open, i.e., anyone can join simply by downloading the software, and as the network is made by the Peer-to-Peer community members' contribution to that particular community, for example, KaZaA, the community that emerges is totally decentralized and has no governance.[26]

Pure Peer-to-Peer creates what Hardin (1998) defined as "unmanaged" communities. A priori, "unmanaged" communities, i.e., communities that have no governance, should not be sustainable. After all, those are the communities that contribute to the "tragedy of the commons."[27]

However, the challenge Peer-to-Peer creates cannot simply be reduced to a "tragedy of the commons." A closer look at modern communities points to their complexity. Communities are typically multidimensional, and managed communities deal with some dimensions and leave community members free in terms of other dimensions. For instance, while some religious communities specify foods that members are not allowed to eat, they do not specify how other foods are to be eaten, and nothing prevents a community member becoming sick following an eating binge.

This is the situation that the content industry faces with Peer-to-Peer today. That community has become increasingly layered, with its governance restricted to a subset of layers; layers that have nothing to do with the content sector. A Peer-to-Peer network service provider such as eDonkey can only survive if its members as a group provide enough capacity for the network to function.

Should a community's sustainability be threatened, economists and others are developing algorithms that would create incentives for a particular community's members to contribute access and computing resources.[28]

Such activities at the layer where community members provide resources to sustain the network do not address the copyright issue. In other words, the sustainability of Peer-to-Peer networks, regardless of the governance under which they are managed, act at a layer that is independent of the exchange of content.

Peer-to-Peer and the Disruption and Changes in Economic Institutions

Peer-to-Peer and the Commons

The way individual members of Peer-to-Peer networks interact with their network has a double "free riding" and "non-excludability" dimension. In other words, it brings us to one of the most basic market failures that Hardin in 1968 called the "tragedy of the commons," a status that had already been detailed by economists.[29] Hardin's use of the expression "commons" was intentional. It was calculated to highlight a specific market failure, the instability of an economic environment where those two characteristics coexist.

In this section of the paper we consider this failure as well as other sources of market failures. We also consider the ambiguities of the copyright owners with respect to the numerous information asymmetries that are found in the sector as well as an additional market failure at the level of transaction costs. This leads us to adopt an analytical framework that is broader than the conventional market setting, the commons. The rationale is to find solutions to those market failures that are efficient, if not optimal.

The purchase of movies or music from, say, a store, is a transaction. In 1967, when Demsetz began to develop the theory of property rights, he wrote that "[w]hen a transaction is completed in the marketplace, two bundles of property rights are exchanged." He added that "it is the value of the rights that determines the value of what is exchanged." While strictly speaking correct, Demsetz's description illustrates what is for most consumers an inherent ambiguity, namely the actual property rights individuals purchase when they buy a CD or download music through iTunes.

For most people, buying music that way is not essentially different from buying new clothes or buying a picture to decorate a room. In practice, this is related to the concept of usufruct, the right to dispose off something we own, as we want. This is one of the three dimensions of private property, together with excludability and alienability. In most situations, societies recognize those rights but impose limitations on them.

Copyright illustrates the complexity of property rights and the limitations it imposes on those three dimensions of private property. The owner of copyright material has complete control over it as long as the work is not made publicly available. This means in practice that the owner holds the rights of usufruct, alienability, and exclusivity.

The same owner's commercialization of the works through, say, digital copies, creates a unique situation to the extent that, through commercialization, the owner transfers to the customers who purchase online reproductions of the work some rights. In other words, in contrast to the sharing of a copyright work through Peer-to-Peer, where individuals possess a work that they do not own, in the case of a commercial transaction, they own rights (which we will associate here, for simplicity, with a license to use the work).

Carruthers and Ariovich (2004) have observed recently that "what separates ownership from mere possession is the fact that others recognize ownership." However, here even the terminology of ownership leaves ambiguities, and society imposes restrictions on the ways individuals are entitled to use the copyright material.

The so-called "license" a customer purchases has a number of characteristics, some of which need to be highlighted. First, the individual is not generally aware of all the limitations that are associated with the particular purchased reproduction; Second, copyright owners do not make an effort to spell out, at the time of the sale, the restrictions associated with the transfer of the work's reproduction. We can infer from the marketing approach that copyright owners are not generally concerned with the way individuals use such reproductions. Logically, this would reflect the fear copyright owners have that detailing the actual terms and conditions as specified in the legislation would negatively impact sales, and hence the owner's profits. This also means that there are some discrepancies between de jure and de facto terms and conditions for the use of reproduced copyright material.

De facto, the commercialization of reproduced copyright material differs in a number of ways from the economic concept of the market. For instance, there is significant information asymmetry between the buyer and the seller in terms of the content and the copyrights' terms and conditions. Similarly, the buyer typically has only partial knowledge of the purchased material. On the other side of the coin, it is generally extremely costly for the copyright owner, barring clear abuses, to know how the material will be used in practice; thus, the buyer has room to free-ride, say, by sharing the work with friends.

Beyond that, we have seen that it is in the interest of the copyright owner to keep many questions ambiguous because there are situations when he may benefit from significant externalities by leaving considerable leeway for the way customers actually use the material. For instance, by allowing de facto consumers to share the material, the supplier is often able to mitigate one of the information asymmetries identified below.

There are also practical reasons for keeping the enforcement sufficiently vague. Even if a strict enforcement were not to have a dampening effect on demand, i.e., because the demand elasticity is zero, the cost of monitoring and enforcement would make the process commercially unsustainable. The transaction costs would simply be too high. Effectively, the commercialization process, together with legislation, provides a benchmark that serves as a rough reference for the way people effectively use their license.

As an analogy one could think of speed limits. While there may be few cars that abide by the speed limit, this does not imply that the speed limit is not an effective tool for controlling the speed at which people drive.

At the same time, the copyright owner faces the danger of suffering from rivalry since the direct impact (evidently, not necessarily the net effect) of sharing lowers his revenues. We have shown through examples that some of the dimensions that characterize the commercial exchange do contribute to inefficiencies within the market process, including some that result in a market failure. We conclude that it is useful to set the problem within the more general context of the commons.

This status quo is periodically shaken by new technologies, as illustrated by the Betamax decision regarding the ability of making copies of copyright material for private use. Each time, however, it seems that the industry needs to find a new equilibrium. In the case of the Betamax decision, this was facilitated by an eventual balance between the increased ability to access, copy, and often share content on one hand, and the increased demand for easier and friendlier access to copyright content that new technologies had created.

Today, Peer-to-Peer would seem to have shattered that equilibrium in a fundamental manner. In the past, individuals' ability to reproduce copyright material was limited, as was their ability to share it. Today, with Peer-to-Peer, the community of people with whom content may be shared is global. A Peer-to-Peer network gives individual members of the particular Peer-to-Peer community – for example, Gnutella, the ability to digitally store a film or any other form of digital copyright material in such a way that all members are capable of accessing it.

This means that such a work becomes available for all members to download. Effectively, it becomes a public good within that particular Peer-to-Peer community. To fully appreciate the implication of Peer-to-Peer, we cannot look at the community as isolated, but need to consider simultaneously the community of artists and entertainers who produced the material. In addition, we need also to look at the network of intermediaries that facilitates access to the material. This perspective is necessary since those who actually own the property rights over the copyright material have not participated in the creation and management of such networks.

From such an economic perspective, the ability to download those works has the direct effect of lowering revenues for recorded sales. Even though the indirect effect may more than compensate for the direct loss in revenue, this assumption is much more hypothetical than in the pre-Peer-to-Peer days.

Today's Peer-to-Peer networks have created, as we noted earlier, "unmanaged" commons at the level of copyright material, i.e., commons that are potentially similar to those described by Hardin in his 1968 paper. Hardin's commons refer to a specific period in the history of the commons, i.e., when – in the late eighteenth and early nineteenth centuries – they started to be converted through enclosures into private properties.

As Hardin recognized, those commons had existed for centuries, far longer than today's capitalistic system. Hardin attributed the collapse of the commons to the emergence of rivalry associated with population growth. Such an assertion is not supported by a historical analysis to the extent that the commons were never treated by society as an "unmanaged" free good.

Commons were typically a sophisticated social system that dealt with the allocation of resources. Occasionally, such a system also dealt with other dimensions such as social welfare in the form of assistance to lower-income individuals. Those objectives were typically achieved through constraints on the access and usage of the commons that reflected the needs and social status of the various members of the community. Membership in the commons and the associated rights reflected the diversity of the local population and of its economic status. Baumol (1971) describes such a commons in his analysis of entertainment in ancient Athens.

When one considers the commons and the communities relative to which they are defined, membership means both the ability to benefit from the communal system, i.e., the commons, and the need, in general, to contribute resources to that system or to face some rationing system when consuming what the commons produce, or both.[30] That was also true in the historical commons with many tasks required to maintain the commons allocated through customs and other systems.

The main difference between the historical commons and today's Peer-to-Peer network communities is that, historically, i.e., throughout the Middle Ages, the commons underwent an evolution which enabled the institutions, customs and routines that appear to be generally sustainable and efficient today were developed over the years. With reference to the commons Hardin studied in 1968, had land not become scarce, there would not have been a need for them at all – therefore, the phenomenon should be studied from that particular perspective.[31] The original determinants of the commons had to be based on more conventional economic forces and only through time did complementary factors such as customs and religion emerge, thereby increasing the efficiency of the institution by further lowering transaction costs.

Opportunism, Altruism, and the Efficiency of the Commons

In this section, we study the process through which the commons often achieve efficient solutions in spite of market failures. Those processes are not always necessary to achieve efficiency, nevertheless they highlight results from experimental analysis that have consistently been neglected by economists in favor of assuming pure utility and profit maximization without adequate room for efficient group behavior.

Following Hardin's contribution, the commons has become a generic term that is rarely adequately defined. Free-riding is an inherent problem with the commons as long as all agents act independently and cannot credibly signal to one another that they commit not to act opportunistically.

This is the kind of opportunism that Ostrom (2000) called "rational egoism." This is why the economic literature has assumed away the question. For instance, the commons that is most prominent in economic activities is the government, and economists take the government, in terms of its most elementary functions of providing services to ensure trade, as given. Where economists consider market solutions that internalize some of the government functions, they effectively exclude the prisoner's dilemma, i.e., the danger of opportunistic behavior, without providing an analytical structure that is able to model such an environment.[32]

Observations of everyday life demonstrate the inadequacies of building economic analysis exclusively upon rational, opportunistic, profit/utility maximizing economic agents. Such observations are corroborated by experimental results that show that the temptation to free-ride is universal but that it coexists with the ability and willingness of people to cooperate to their mutual benefits.[33] That literature strongly supports the view that people tend to be willing to undertake actions that can be beneficial to the collective as a whole through private, individual steps and without assurance of reciprocity.

The commons are defined as the generic environment within which economic activities take place and markets are best studied as embedded within the commons, essentially, as subsets that emerge once a conventional economic framework is imposed: "[C]ommons... include all economic exchanges, whether market-based, based upon central-planning allocations, or other arrangements that could be government and/or community-based."[34] Markets are based on the presumption that all players are opportunistic.[35] This is not a generic requirement for the commons that accept a diversity of attitudes among members of the society as a possibility.

Interestingly, it is that diversity vis–à–vis opportunism that makes it possible to find governances that support efficient exchange in the context of market failures. Hardin's (1998) terminology of "unmanaged" commons highlights the limitations of markets since, by definition, markets correspond to Hardin's "unmanaged" commons.

The commons, just as much as the markets that are embedded within them, are not static concepts. Rather, they are dynamic concepts that evolve through time in manners that are closely associated with property rights.[36] Numerous forces bring about changes. For instance, if we consider the restaurant sector, it is easy to observe the way eating habits have evolved in many places, given the growing number of people who choose to go out, i.e., who choose the market place, to eat.

Peer-to-Peer is one of the factors that contribute to those changes. For instance, the demand Peer-to-Peer networks make upon commercial activities that take place outside the marketplace is such that it challenges well-established, customary boundaries. Those activities include the participation of any Peer-to-Peer community in the form of making resources available to all, in an independent fashion of conventional commercial relationships.

The English landed gentry's success in redefining their property rights was its ability to do away with the historical commons through the enclosure and to translate the change into a system of private property.

We have seen that Peer-to-Peer is best studied in a context that is broader than conventional market analysis, namely the context of the commons. That perspective provides us both with concerns and hopes. Our concerns reflect the "unmanaged" nature of the various Peer-to-Peer commons at the level of copyright material, a concern that is particularly serious since it need not imply that the Peer-to-Peer infrastructure itself is unmanaged, and, even if it were unmanaged, that it is unsustainable.

The more positive note derives from the characteristics of individuals acting in what they perceive as a commons. If artists were able to bypass the attitude of many of the intermediaries, they may well encourage the emergence of an economically viable commons that would also support their own creative efforts.

Disruption in the Institutions

From the very beginning, the unprecedented success of Napster, and the RIAA's judicial challenges erased any doubts about the stresses Peer-to-Peer as an innovation was already imposing upon the institutions of the time. Many determinants contribute to shaping the process of adjusting existing institutions to achieve compatibility with the Peer-to-Peer innovation.

Many of these determinants are of an economic nature and can be studied to gain a better understanding of the way conditions evolve in response to Peer-to-Peer. It is fundamental to understand those economic dimensions if we have to analyze how Peer-to-Peer creates pressure on institutions to evolve and to infer from those changes what is happening to the sector.

We can illustrate the process by looking at how Peer-to-Peer changes the way consumers increasingly perceive access to, and use of, content. Peer-to-Peer raises some questions about some of the dimensions of existing implicit licenses under which people are entitled to use copyrighted material. For instance, the Betamax decision never considered the implications of someone placing a piece of work, for example, a movie, in their own open computer space the way some individuals often play music from their car/apartment in such a way that it is shared by the whole street.

The other lesson relates to the emergence of new possibilities, namely the ability to access almost any kind of content through file-sharing within a Peer-to-Peer community. Such a possibility offers an expanded range of options for consumers, and, consequently, the reference to residual rights regarding the customers' licenses. However, this possibility provides us with information only on what consumers can do, not on what they will actually do with it, and does not inform us about how today's implicit license may restrict what consumers are permitted to do; finally, it does not provide information about what that may mean for artists.

Artists may find it easier to carry out many of the steps themselves, e.g., to publicize and commercialize their works or to call upon new intermediaries. How much easier this will prove probably depends more on technologies that are complementary to Peer-to-Peer than on Peer-to-Peer itself. Hence, to what extent Peer-to-Peer might simplify the tasks that are currently carried out by intermediaries will remain an open question until we begin to appreciate how Peer-to-Peer is affecting intermediation, something that will only come through time as artists gain more experience with the ways Peer-to-Peer makes up for many of the existing services that intermediaries – such as content owners – provide.

Those changes do not address the "unmanaged" nature of the commons Peer-to-Peer creates at the level of copyright material. Those changes are also unlikely to affect all artists in the same measure. For instance, it is reasonable to assume that Peer-to-Peer will lower marketing costs for some artists, or equivalently, increase their reach. It is also reasonable to assume that those artists who use the major content aggregators today to market their works will be better protected from conflict of interests by aggregators. At the same time, it may be that artists, who vie for the top chart, and consequently, depend upon exceptional and costly marketing campaigns and know-how, may not see much change at the intermediation level; when one considers how competitive artists are, that may prove to be the majority.

This is the process through which residual rights associated with the licenses that specify how content can be used and shared are created and evaluated by stakeholders. Once the residual rights are allocated, they regulate what the stakeholders are entitled to and determine how they will fare in a Peer-to-Peer environment. Some of the court decisions help clarify the entitlement of the various stakeholders, i.e., consumers, Peer-to-Peer network service providers, artists and producers, and, evidently, the owners of copyrighted material.

Coase (1960) specifies the relativistic nature of the process, i.e., the extent to which, in the present situation, the balance between the copyright owners' property rights and the consumers' *de facto* licenses are specified in a social context in terms of the limitations society (as well as private communities) imposes on the use of those rights.

In most cases, Peer-to-Peer is a disruptive technology, even though there are exceptions. For instance, the recent court decision through which the Betamax principles were applied to Peer-to-Peer illustrates a degree of continuity. However, on the whole, the experience gained with Peer-to-Peer suggests something far more disruptive. To start with, today, consumers are still in a sort of no-man's-land regarding the way they can benefit from Peer-to-Peer. Consumers also have the option of ignoring Peer-to-Peer and the way it transforms the concept of access to content for individuals.

The alternative for those same individuals is to access content through new Peer-to-Peer services such as KaZaA and Gnutella, or even eDonkey, for instance. The first option means that consumers have to forego new ways to consume content even though there is ample evidence that this would force them to forego options that enhance their utility. The second option means on the other hand a significant level of uncertainty about what would be considered reasonable and, beyond that, the legitimacy of their actions and, in the long run, their legality.

The institutional perspective we have developed here goes a long way in helping us to look at the many conflicts that have arisen since the emergence of Peer-to-Peer from an economic perspective.[37] Conflicts such as the numerous court battles RIAA mounted against various stakeholders are playing an essential role in helping clarify the institutions that will support Peer-to-Peer. The perspective also reflects the predictable response by an incumbent to an innovative threat. Most institutions are likely to evolve in response to Peer-to-Peer. Some may disappear while new ones may emerge.

Peer-to-Peer is transforming the content industry, not so much at the production level as at the intermediation level. For instance, consumers still have to find out what is the reasonable use and sharing of content within a Peer-to-Peer community. Other legal issues such as the redefinition of consumers' implicit licenses where the residual rights of different parties overlap – as illustrated by the legality of the RIAA invading Peer-to-Peer systems – may not rely as heavily on the body of legal precedents.

Institutions are complemented by governances which are largely controlled by entrepreneurs and others who create Peer-to-Peer communities.[38] Those governances generally take the form of unwritten contracts that regulate the way members (even if they link up only once to the network) and the community leader(s) act within that community.

However, our previous analysis showed that in the post-Napster Peer-to-Peer networks, Peer-to-Peer network service providers' ability to create governance is restricted to the Peer-to-Peer network layer. It is not clear whether those providers could create governances at the copyright content layer level. Such governances could make them vulnerable to legal actions by industry organizations such as MPA and RIAA.

In addition, even if they could do, the potential membership perception and response to such governances and the fact that for the last 5 years consumers have had access to Peer-to-Peer networks that had no governance at the content level, effectively restrict future options. Those conditions imply severe limitations to the range of existing governances for those who create communities.

The other side of the coin is that some entrepreneurs are stimulated to respond to the needs of artists to become innovative and introduce new governance concepts with a view to bypass those challenges. Such entrepreneurs could become able to offer a far superior service to existing Peer-to-Peer networks, to the extent that they could manage the information about, and the access to, copyright material in a far more user-friendly way.

The interdependence between those emerging governances and established stakeholders can be illustrated by the response of the RIAA to Peer-to-Peer and the response of the technology to the RIAA's strategy.

As we will see below, today copyright holders are typically intermediaries who transform the raw content product into something consumers know about and might be willing to pay for. In other words, their function is the added value they provide to the original work of the artists. That added-value component can be significant.

However, the role of intermediation in the content sector is not different to the role of intermediation in other sectors of the economy. Inter-mediation is a function that evolves rapidly in response to technological changes such as Peer-to-Peer, to the extent that such technological changes make a substantial portion of the intermediation added-value services obsolete.

It is evidently in the interest of copyright owners, inasmuch as they are intermediaries, ceteris paribus, to take steps to prevent the drop in value of their past investments in intermediation. This is no different from the attitude horse-drawn carriage owners embraced when they were threatened by newer technologies such as the automobile industry. In the market, such ability is limited both by demand considerations and by new artists' ability in bypassing the old intermediation process.

While the narrow incentive of the content sector is predictable, the strategies followed may not be. There are reasons to believe that the strategies pursued by the content intermediaries have been backfiring. Krim (2004) documents how the activities of the RIAA, such as the way they went after Napster, resulted in a substantial shift in the categories of governance that entrepreneurs select. RIAA's attacks on Napster created strong incentives in the emerging Peer-to-Peer network sector to favor highly decentralized systems such as Gnutella that appeared to be immune, and were eventually so ruled by the courts, to the RIAA's legal attacks.

Institutions and customs are not rigid and unchanging. While they affect economic activities, they also evolve in response to those activities. The emergence of Napster pressured RIAA, and through it, various institutions. As Betamax before, Napster challenged existing paradigms that were conceived for an environment that did not know innovations such as Peer-to-Peer.

The process through which institutions evolve is one in which conflicting forces seek, hopefully, to bring about a social welfare solution. Coase's (1960) social cost analysis provides a benchmark to consider innovations such as Peer-to-Peer and how institutions could adjust to further social welfare. However, it is an analysis that is set in a narrow framework of laws and regulations and we know today that issues such as those raised by Coase are typically addressed at least in part through a more informal and complex set of rules that includes different cultures, customs, and routines. Laws and regulations as well as customs and practices are some of the dimensions that provide a framework within which economic activities take place. Those are institutions which, whether formal or informal, inevitably shape the way commerce takes place.

Consumers

Introduction

In this section, we consider the likely consumer response to the emergence of Peer-to-Peer as well as to the failure of the content sector to facilitate the development of credible Peer-to-Peer content commercial services. We then treat the characteristics of content services and the ways Peer-to-Peer changes them. Those changes would seem to be fundamental inasmuch as they create a major discontinuity and make the extrapolation from the former environment problematic.

We show that, from the consumer perspective, Peer-to-Peer is transforming the content into a good that is, in and of itself, more attractive to consumers. However, the actual economic impact is still very sensitive to the strategies suppliers have been pursuing. Our best guess is that the rigidity of their position has contributed to the emergence of today's Peer-to-Peer networks, thus creating an even greater chasm between copyright owners on one hand and consumers on the other. The damage to the suppliers' long-term interests may be even greater as the lack of a solution that is satisfactory both to consumers and to the copyright owners may result in the consumers institutionalizing the present Peer-to-Peer file-sharing environment.

Consumers who would have been more ready to support fostering pay services have not received the support from copyright owners that they needed. As it is, results from experimental analysis suggest that those consumers may give up and accept today's free bypass services such as KaZaA or eDonkey.

The owners of copyright content may point to their property rights. They may point to piracy in the USA through the downloading and exchanging of popular music and increasingly of videos, but such an attitude has two fundamental flaws. Firstly, they neglect the business dimension of those rights, namely, that their narrow and rigid interpretation effectively destroys the value of those property rights. It is not good business to enforce copyrights too narrowly.

Secondly, they overlook the most essential dimension of property rights. A property right, if it is not to be imposed by sheer power and ruthless fiat, but rather if it is to be a factor within a democratic society, cannot be arbitrarily imposed on that society. Rather, it must reflect the society's acceptance of the granting of power that the society's recognition of ownership de facto implies. This means that the society must find them reasonable in the long run.

It is that social and political dimensions of property rights that is so often neglected and overlooked in discussions. Narrow approaches to property rights, as expressed, for instance, in Einhorn and Rosenblatt (2004), take those dimensions for granted. Yet Coase (1960) observes that "the rights of a land-owner are not unlimited... This does not come about simply because of Government regulation. It would be equally true under the common law. In fact it would be true under any system of law." Coase's analysis, here, is generic. It is not restricted to the specific case of a land-owner.

Consumer Demand and the Commons

Consumers are involved in the process that will determine a mature Peer-to-Peer environment just as much as members of the industry. Their involvement, with the exception of a very small minority, is not a direct one in which they formulate a strategy in order to shape Peer-to-Peer to best meet their needs. It is, nevertheless, just as powerful an involvement as that of other actors because of the number of those involved and the signal it conveys to other stakeholders. In many ways, the involvement of consumers is the most important of all to the extent that the sector cannot exist and survive without their participation.

Consumers impact the solution that needs to emerge to the extent that they express their dissatisfaction, directly in the market, through political means or other social strategies, or through a combination of those strategies.

To understand how consumers tend to influence the system, one can use an analogy with an object consumers are familiar with, namely, cars. Innovations and technological changes have made cars significantly safer. Roads and highways have also improved. This means that safety as well as speed has increased while the number of cars on the highway has also increased without negatively affecting safety. These trends explain the governments' decisions, in the USA, to allow higher speed on highways.

However, for argument's sake, let's imagine that some interest group that is opposed to this change were to change the speed limit and lower it, for example, to 25 mph everywhere, including on major highways; such a prohibition could be seen as a benchmark. We can easily guess the medium to long-term impact such a new policy might have. It may be that for a while there would be limited support for such a measure, and that the threat of receiving a ticket might be sufficient for the police to enforce it. However, such a speed limit is inconsistent with today's cars and driving habits. Hence, it is reasonable to assume that, progressively, more and more people would begin to drive at a higher speed. This would complicate the enforcement task of the police to such an extent that it may actually become impossible.[39]

At that stage, a government would essentially have two courses of action open. It could acknowledge the increasingly dominant trend toward higher speed by allocating fewer and fewer resources to its enforcement, and/or change the law.

Recently, the Belgium Communications Minister attacked Peer-to-Peer. At the end of his speech, in response to questions, he asserted that he was not allocating any resources to address the Peer-to-Peer issue. Alternatively, a government could impose more and more severe sanctions. However, this latter option is unlikely to be chosen because of the impact it may have on the public support. The above analogy underlines the effective power of consumers, even if their power is indirect. It also highlights the extent to which the solutions toward which courts and regulators evolve are bound to reflect, among various determinants, consumers' attitudes, which can be assumed to be endogenous.

To the extent that our analogy has its merits, it has serious implications for the way the content industry is likely to organize itself in a Peer-to-Peer sector. Krim (2004) provides a substantial amount of evidence on the unwillingness of content stakeholders to negotiate a solution that would recognize the demands of other players, including equipment vendors. The present analysis suggests that such a hard-line strategy is most likely to backfire on the content sector, or at least, on today's major players.

We have already indicated that it is reasonable to conclude that the RIAA's hard-line stand, even after the victory over Napster, has contributed to the success of new Peer-to-Peer networks that are largely immune to the RIAA's legal activities. We have also concluded that solutions that do not meet consumer expectations are unlikely to be sustainable. This is not just due to the further negative impact it would have on demand, and, consequently, on Peer-to-Peer profits, but also due to the failure by the industry to acknowledge the expectations Peer-to-Peer has created among consumers.

Those factors should be reinforced by what one would reasonably expect from consumers. Experimental economics does not support the view that the RIAA and others in the sector have expressed, i.e., that consumers who access Peer-to-Peer through networks such as KaZaA would not pay for Peer-to-Peer services even if reasonable services were offered.[40] The market response to iTunes also contradicts the content sector's position – even though iTunes offers a much narrower range of services than KaZaA. In other words, empirical observation confirms what experimental economics suggests.

Everyday observation provides plenty of evidence that the content sector has taken a rigid position in the last decade or more when negotiating with other stakeholders; such a result is confirmed by Krim (2004). This has meant that it has stalled efforts to develop strategies that acknowledge the emergence of Peer-to-Peer. Given the consumer response to that innovation, this also means that the content sector has undermined the emergence of Peer-to-Peer commercial solutions.

There is now extensive experimental literature that has identified key segmentations in communities in general regarding the willingness of subsets of the population of communities to allocate their own, personal, scarce resources to social tasks that do not benefit them directly and that may never benefit them individually.[41]

The experimental literature also considers the social dynamics among the members of communities where members differ in terms of their willingness to contribute, at least initially, to the social welfare. Depending on the external conditions, i.e., on the response members receive from outside the community, those who are willing to look for a social solution may be able to win others over to their view. That way the community may be able to create a sustainable commons with broad support from the members of the community.

That same literature shows that, where the outside world is not supportive, social dynamics may eventually discourage those who are looking for a social solution. At that stage, those will begin to join those who are looking exclusively for their own selfish good and the community is likely to become the kind of "unmanaged" community Hardin described in 1968.

The latter outcome would pose a serious problem for copyright owners since it would mean that members of society in general would begin to take for granted the piracy Carruthers and Ariovich (2004) observe.

The Content Commodity

Some innovations do not really change the nature of the commodity itself but simply lower the cost of production and little else. Innovations generally change the commodity that is offered to consumers on the market. Sometimes, innovations transform the commodity to such an extent that any extrapolation from the commodity in the pre-innovation phase to describe the new commodity does not make sense. This appears to be the case with Peer-to-Peer, where consumers who have experienced content delivered through such networks are unwilling to go back to the old access methods.

In the video environment sector, the previous assertion might be somewhat premature. Nevertheless, features such as the instantaneous availability of an exhaustive video catalog in the major networks that rely exclusively upon their members for content availability, are very important. At least in a sector such as the music industry, consumers appear to respond to the availability of that feature. In this respect, it is certainly a characteristic that needs to be incorporated in business models.

The attractiveness of the complete catalog may sound surprising when one observes that most consumers listen almost exclusively to a small number of hit records that typically comes from the selection made by the major labels. It may be that the option to listen to any piece of music at any time is nevertheless important to consumers even if it is rarely used. It may also be that the availability of music from independent artists, videos from different producers, and, potentially, from producers worldwide is valued highly by consumers. Inasmuch as this characteristic facilitates access to content apart from the most requested by the public, it may be viewed as threatening by those who control it. Yet, it may help contribute to increase the overall demand that may benefit even those who do not provide that expanded content.

Peer-to-Peer's ability to allow artists to bypass copyright owners may pose a more serious threat to established content owners. However, even that issue is full of ambiguities inasmuch as most artists, directors and producers will still need someone to advise consumers regarding what they are likely to want to look for at the major labels, as was illustrated in MP3.com.

The change in the commodity seems to follow closely what users are able to consume – for example, a video – with minimal time and geographic constraints. The information consumers have about their options is another dimension that affects the sector's growth. These options also affect the product that users consume. All in all, these changes should make the product more attractive to consumers, and, consequently, lead to an increase in overall demand. However, the business problem may not be that simple. Today, those who own content are major players with major stakes in the sector and substantial market and political power. In addition, they are likely to be those most affected by the changes Peer-to-Peer is bringing about.

Peer-to-Peer Innovation, Technology, and Business Strategies

The Technology: Exogenous or Endogenous?

In this section, we consider the extent to which Peer-to-Peer platforms have evolved technologically in response to institutional factors. It is not possible to assert unambiguously how the Peer-to-Peer fight has transformed Peer-to-Peer technology. After all, we cannot observe and compare multiple parallel technological paths. Nevertheless, adopting a "best guess" criterion, the conclusion is that the RIAA's victory over Napster and other networks such as Aimster, together with its unwillingness to negotiate intermediate solutions,[42] created strong incentives for entrepreneurs to favor a new generation of Peer-to-Peer networks.

That new generation was conceived to eliminate the technological elements, such as the centralized catalog, that had led to the demise of the first generation of Peer-to-Peer networks in Courts. In that respect, it is not unreasonable to conclude that the copyright owners' strategy may have largely backfired making it that much harder to develop a Peer-to-Peer network that could meet reasonable industry demands while responding to customer demands that became apparent through Napster and other cases. In addition, such policies by copyright aggregators have led Peer-to-Peer network operators to take a layered approach with respect to file transfer in order to build business models that are also immune to challenges by copyright owners.

Individuals, especially economists, have a tendency to vest technology with unique powers. That force means that technology is largely conceived as the external and exogenous instrument of change. This perspective implies a world largely static in the absence of technology. We would like to challenge this concept of change in our environment, a concept that imposes an artificial, *ex ante* dichotomy between technology and institutions.

It is a natural reflex in today's society to look at technology as an inherent and independent force that is continuously shaping, reshaping, and transforming the environment within which we live. However, this formulation is essentially passive, leaving us to "passively accept" what happens around us. In this vision, technology happens outside our influence and is independent of our economic activities; it also imposes on us an inherently dynamic force that takes us out of our routines. This is the cornerstone of most industrial organizations and, to the extent that it is not a crucial dimension of our analysis, it is a very elegant manner to simplify the analysis.

However, in this paper, technology and its impact on the sector is not the sole factor that needs to be studied. It is equally likely that the technology path depends on the institutions – especially on the response of the copyright owners to the technology itself. In this respect, the conventional assumption of exogenous technology that economists continue to make in industrial organization is at best misleading.[43] Such a perspective does not even address the time dimension of technological change or the interdependence of technologies and innovations.

From the perspective of technology, innovations challenge consumers, entrepreneurs, venture capitalists, and others and inspire them to do things in new ways. For economists, this reflects nothing more than the constant tension that is naturally felt between the need to innovate and create new paths and the need to protect and draw benefits from the assets that past innovations continue to convey to us.[44] A key dimension within this tension is the distribution of asset ownership among the stakeholders. A natural analogy consists in comparing a population of young and old people. It is safe to assume that younger people will not have accumulated a significant quantity of assets, in contrast to older people, i.e., that they have less sunk capital to protect. Subsequently, given the emergence of an innovation that effectively undermines the value of existing assets, the younger people will seize the innovation to build up their assets while the older generation can be expected to take steps to defend the existing technology.

In a Peer-to-Peer environment, the paradigm relates to those who are in a position to achieve a breakthrough by thrusting their new talents and approaches towards arts and entertainment on the market. The paradigm contrasts with the attitude of those who have already branded their product and whose focus is to consolidate that brand, i.e., the works for which they are already known. Established artists, such as Picasso, who continue to break new ground even after they are established are unusual. The norm would rather be established artists such as Salvador Dali.

In the same vein, Peer-to-Peer innovation came from young people, especially when considering Napster's Sean. The opposition to Peer-to-Peer has all the decorum of the established order. No one has painted the transition from the new path-breaking youth to the established older person in a more brilliant style than Jacques Brel with "les Bourgeois."[45]

Peer-to-Peer appears to many as the instrument today's new entrant uses to challenge what has become today's establishment. As in most of these innovations, established stakeholders create a picture of Barbarians at the gates when talking about the onslaught of new artists. Few have the vision of Leonard Bernstein who, when talking about Janice Joplin, noted that before he could not imagine someone making art from yelling but that he had learned that he had been wrong.

Those responses are there again in the Napster and Aimster challenges. Those were painted "ex post" as nothing more than steps taken by "con-artists" whose only goal was to cheat the owners of copyright material from their revenue requirements, to use an established expression in the regulated industries such as telephony.

It is not the object of this paper to identify the precise motives of the stakeholders enacting the Peer-to-Peer saga, nor to judge between the merits of the entrants versus those of the legacy. The objective is rather to understand those inherent tensions that naturally emerge between the two groups and the economic forces that buttress them and, finally, to understand how those groups often use technology as ammunition in this battle.

Intermediation and the Historical Ownership of Copyrights

In the first instance, the cost of the inputs can only be lowered by decreasing the earnings of the artists and such earnings, as Baumol had noted in 1965, are already exceptionally low when compared to those of others in the society. In principle, this could be contrasted by increasing the audience for whom the artists perform. However, Baumol (1971) suggests that this is unlikely to happen. He also adds that, to the extent that there is a trend, it would be the other way round, i.e., with audiences that do not increase proportionately with the overall population, and that often decrease.

We conclude that the content equation that impacts the sector as well as the digitalization of the content and its distribution, as with Peer-to-Peer, contains one element that cannot be reduced any further, regardless of technological changes. The division of labor does not apply to the contribution of artists any more than it applies to many people in the medical profession. This technological and organizational characteristic is unique to artists and performers and to a few others such as medical doctors. This has meant and will continue to mean low pay and low earnings as already documented by Baumol (1965).

Artists are nevertheless able to reach through the reproduction of their work and, in recent years, through their digitalization, ever larger audiences, a process that has not stopped since Guttenberg and the printing press. The process is not just a matter of reproduction, but it also involves other functions that may entail tasks such as billing, production, and financing.

That process in economics is called "intermediation" and it involves intermediaries who facilitate the task of artists in such areas as billing, reproduction, and distribution. The point of differentiating the artists' works from the contribution of intermediaries is that innovation and technological change are the factors that are constantly transforming the intermediation process. This means that intermediaries need fewer and fewer resources and incur in less and less costs to provide services to artists.

The intermediation process is essentially different from the process through which artists create and perform. Throughout history, technology – together with the division of labor – has transformed intermediation, eliminating an increasing number of tasks that mediators used to perform. While the division of labor cannot be applied to artists and their creative process as we know it today, it does apply to intermediaries as it applies to any other sector of the economy. This means that, through innovation and with an ever-growing market, it has been possible to decrease the human labor input, and, consequently, reduce costs.

The consumers' response has been to increase consumption of entertainment and works of art. The technological process tends to be straightforward for consumers. Consumers are very leery of complexities. The same does not hold true for the supply side. On the supply side, innovation and its realization through technological change can be ruthless, with little regard for even the best-run businesses, as Christensen (2000) demonstrated so effectively.

Peer-to-Peer continues the trend that has dominated the sector and is reinforcing the transformation of the sector brought about by the convergence of digitalization and telecommunications.

Peer-to-Peer has demonstrated its capacity to build a bridge between individual artists and their public. What the sector has yet to develop is an approach that meets at the same time the needs of artists and those of their public. The complexity of the task results from a number of factors, over most of which artists have little control.

For instance, as noted above, innovations such as Peer-to-Peer impact artists and intermediaries in completely different ways. There will probably always be a role for intermediaries but that role is shrinking and shifting at the same time. This means that legacy intermediaries such as the aggregators need to redefine themselves, a step that is almost impossible for established firms.

The technological changes have a major impact on intermediation and its *raison d'être*. The reason for that is that intermediation emerged largely in response to the way technology was transforming the general public's access to the creative works of artists. The outcome is that intermediatries have been the most vocal stakeholders in this technological process.

Their ability to gain a disproportionate amount of attention in the fight to know which stakeholder gets what as technology disrupts the environment within which content is consumed has been greatly helped by their ability to aggregate existing copyrights among a small number of very large players.

Copyrighted commodities have unique characteristics relative to conventional economic analysis. A further analogy can help us understand better the economic meaning of those characteristics. Perfect competition in a partial equilibrium context, as it is conventionally presented,[46] is a zero-profit environment where any deviation from the equilibrium is instantly corrected through arbitrage. Instantaneous adjustment means that all transaction costs are reflected in the vertical organization of relevant sets of activities. It is the internal organization of multiple activities that establishes the possibility that some vertically integrated firms may emerge in a competitive environment.[47]

It is important to stress that we are still in the widget economics' paradigm. The optimality of this model is built on conditions such as the instantaneous identification of arbitrage opportunities by all parties. Evidently, it is not just the identification of arbitrage opportunities that is instantaneous. The stakeholders all respond instantaneously, which means that they never extract any rents from arbitrage. One of the dimensions of the constraints on the system is the fact that all such processes basically happen independent of time in such a way that economic decisions and strategies have no duration.

This is also the framework that is commonly used to study the economy of copyrights.[48] In this framework, there is no room for court cases such as Napster and venture capitalists never end up in front of a court since this would be irrational in a world of perfect knowledge. The law is perfectly known and judges, just like entrepreneurs and other actors, are automats with unchangeable, efficient decisions. Perfect competition means, as Sengupta (2001) reminds us, a world where "[p]erfect institutional order… is fully predictable behavior [resulting in the] complete absence of individual freedom."

An alternative to the neoclassical framework is the modeling approach proposed by the Austrian School. In that world, economic actors are not automats and the outcome of their actions is not pre-determined. Thierer (1994) observes that "[c]ompetition… is a dynamic process of constant entrepreneurial adjustment to market signals. The market is never at rest; today's monopoly could be tomorrow's competitive market…" This model is essentially different from the model of perfect competition used to study widgets. Here, we lose the idea that competition could ever be perfect.

In this Austrian world, economists have to rely on a different concept to achieve competitive efficiency, namely, the spontaneous order.[49] At the same time, they are unable to establish the efficiency of the outcome, either in the short or long-run. The outcome is based on a belief: "… [E]conomists with allegiance to the Austrian School of economics, such as

Dominick T. Armentano (1990), F.A. Hayek (1948), and Israel M. Kirzner (1973), believe that not only are answers to the questions about natural monopoly wrong, the questions themselves are improperly formulated."[50]

Whichever way we may choose to model the way stakeholders interact with one another – be it neoclassical, Austrian, or other – the idiosyncratic dimension of art and entertainment works is the cornerstone of the analysis of the copyrights market. Yet, at the same time, this is also the characteristic that is the most ignored by economists. The sector cannot be reduced to the economic activities defined in terms of a stock comparable to the stock of power plants in the public utilities sector or the stock of air routes in the air transportation sector.

At the same time, it is just as misleading to reduce the dimensions of the sector's economic activities to the study of flows, the way one would treat most industrial sectors, for example, the computer sector. Such simplifications may be adequate in some limited circumstances when the objective is to study specific problems that can be safely treated from a partial equilibrium perspective. For instance, the label may be carrying market studies to explore how best to classify – for positioning and commercialization purposes – and then to present an artist such as, for example, Melissa Auf der Maur.[51] However, such simplifications are certainly not appropriate for policy purposes in the context of Peer-to-Peer.

An artist, for example, a singer like Melissa Auf der Maur, produces the antithesis of the "widget" commodity. Each work is "hand-crafted." Artists such as Auf der Maur, create and develop their pieces and then rework them until they are satisfied with the quality of the work to be released. It is a process that has more in common with the wine maker who spends whatever time it takes to develop and transform the juice of grapes into a wine with depth and bouquet.

In the same manner, Auf der Maur, like so many artists, puts her time and energy in months of work to become what she believes is her creation, what she wants others to hear. She crafts each song, each album, individually, one at a time, taking her time as required in a similar fashion to the way artisans worked in the past.

It is in this context that one must look at the contribution of the aggregators. The glamorous image they like to convey is the image of "l'enfant terrible," an image that conveys the idea that they work extremely hard to search for, discover, and transform blockbuster artists in such a way that the public will worship them. The image suggests the high risk inherent to their job as aggregators – i.e., the need, the time, and the expense of going through hundreds and thousands of artists so that they can discover "the Beatles," the artists and their work – to show the world how essential their role is.

Their role is not all that glamorous. Through consolidation they have gained the ability to manage huge portfolios of artists. Given the size of the library already in existence, and given the continuous flow of additions, aggregators are able to benefit from a demand for intermediation that organizes and processes information to the extent that it makes the decisions by potential customers, i.e., it actually lowers transaction costs.[52]

That type of strategy has enabled them to use their size to shield themselves effectively from many of the risks of failure that individual artists and small intermediates would face. The outcome is their ability to gain control over a significant share of copyrighted material. In the same process, they begin to act as an insurance company. The strategy also creates a pool to artists who may hate the process and who may dream to "make it" without the aggregators, but who also dream to be able to sign in as members of that select group the aggregators manage. It is their market concentration and their ability to integrate those various intermediation functions that largely protect them from competition.

Their most visible role, at least from the perspective of the outside observer, is to intermediate between the artists and the public. They organize the works of artists, pushing some and keeping many behind, preparing a select menu of products for consumers, the way many restaurants develop special menus. To return to the example of Auf de Maur, they position her work within categories of music content.

The above is a process that makes it easier, by lowering the transaction costs for the general public, for people to get a sense of the kind of music Auf der Maur produces, and whether or not they may be interested in exploring her work further. Given the inability of individual consumers to sample and evaluate all the music that is available today, this step will generally streamline the search process. It is a process that facilitates linking Auf der Maur with those who are likely to be interested in her music. It is also a process that can help steer away those who are unlikely to consider such music because, for example, they are exclusively interested in country music.

Today's economic studies largely ignore the complex market structure within which intermediation takes place; hence, they ignore the determinants of economic efficiency both at the content creation level and at the intermediation level.

As a result, their conclusions about the efficiency of existing institutions, and especially about the efficiency of those aggregators, have no foundation since those factors that are ignored are those that would make it possible to say something about economic efficiency and social welfare.

As observed previously, by treating the processes of content creation and production on one hand and of intermediation on the other, as all being inside a single black box, the scope of economic analysis has been reduced, and its ability to address key policy issues eliminated. More seriously, such studies sidestep fundamental economic issues such as the treatment of fair use in a Peer-to-Peer world and the impact of the high concentration among aggregators on the economic efficiency of the sector, as well as on the ability to foster competition through technological change and innovation.

One of the proper social concerns with the industrial organization of the sector is its impact upon the creation of new content by artists. As we can see by the disaggregated analysis we have outlined above, where we consider the unique characteristics of the content creation activities, the failure to treat separately content creation and production on one hand and intermediation on the other means that those analyses cannot consider the impact of alternative institutions on the creative sector.

We have just reviewed some of the factors that contribute to the unique idiosyncrasy of copyrighted content, namely, individual works produced by entertainers and producers to expand an ever-changing film, music, and entertainment library. Individuals and small firms produce those works and bear most of the risk by putting on the hat of an entrepreneur and contributing to various functions that are required to ensure the success of their endeavor. Those functions include creators and producers of film, music, and other digitalized forms of content.

This characteristic of content, namely the alternative categorization of outputs, has limited meaning in terms of the individual consumer's willingness to pay. That willingness to pay will itself depend upon factors such as the way the individual is likely to learn about the specificity of the artist's work and the context within which this happens.

The consumer's willingness to pay is a direct function of the marketing and distribution system. Some artists may be inherently good at positioning their works in the mind of the public. After all, this has to have been the case with Salvador Dali as described by Riding (2004), or, earlier Caruso. Some such as Oprah Winfrey and Georges Lucas are also exceptionally good at managing their assets. However, this cannot be generalized. This heads towards a need for a range of intermediation services between artists, entertainers, and consumers. In an Internet era, such intermediation may take the form of services of firms such as Music Dish to help publicize the works of artists.

Historically, intermediation functions have become increasingly consolidated in today's major content aggregators such as the major labels in the music industry. The transfer of ownership has emerged as the dominant financial characteristic of today's intermediation, at least among the more successful artists.

The services those aggregators provide vary across media with various levels of integration across those media. For instance, while a substantial portion of the risk associated with new production is provided through separate channels, in the music industry the aggregators generally integrate most functions. Intermediation continues to evolve through time.

The two dimensions that are key in shaping the role of intermediation and the social, legal, and institutional context within which artists produce and consumers "consume" the entertainment commodities are the ability of aggregators to manage their market power and the constraints new technologies such as Peer-to-Peer may impose on their exercise of market power.

The Artist's Work as a Product and Intermediation

Technological innovations such as Peer-to-Peer impact the content sector in two ways. Firstly, they impact the value of accumulated copyrights assets that are largely in the hands of aggregators. Secondly, they impact the costs for and benefits of those who create new content. The large concentration of the control of copyrights assets in the hand of a small number of aggregators has reinforced their incentive to act as incumbents who concentrate their resources on creating an environment that is friendly to their market position. Trivially, this also means that this process is at the expense of innovation, flexibility, and adjustment to institutional constraints.

The concentration in the ownership of copyrights can only take place in the intermediation activities. Individual artists would not be able to manage their benefits with the kind of concentration we observe today unless they could cumulate the intermediation role. However, there is no clear benefit in such a step. As we suggested earlier, the benefit of concentration would appear to go completely to the intermediates.

Today's intermediation process creates ambiguities about the content market, about what the products that are commercialized to end-users might be, and about the ways the market can be expected to react in response to consumer and technological pressure. One of these ambiguities has its roots in the economic concepts of stocks and flows. Those concepts are typically neglected in today's economic analysis, if not altogether ignored.[53]

In the technology theory of the firm, one works on the basis of a technology that specifies the stock of capital and its organization as well as the flow of capital. Where the process is in equilibrium, i.e., where there are no external forces on the system's internal equilibrium, then the stock dimension of the model can be taken as a parameter. Such a hypothesis makes it possible for us to work solely with the flow of capital. Today's economic literature on copyrights is built upon that implicit hypothesis.[54]

The main source of ambiguity is the confusion today's intermediation creates between the stock of content that is controlled by the aggregators, and the flow of new content that may be – but need not necessarily be – intermediated. It may be appropriate to ignore the stock and focus exclusively on the flow in a static world where the economy produces widget. Whether or not this is the case in a static, stable world, it is hard to conceive how it could ever be optimal in the dynamic world of content. This is a world where each individual's new work has to compete through its unique entertainment characteristics, i.e., through product differentiation, with other new works.

As existing copyrighted material is largely in the hands of aggregators, it is also obvious that the flow, i.e., the stream of new works artists are producing, has also to compete with existing copyrighted material. If there is no change in technology or in the institutions, then there is no strong reason to be uncomfortable with the system. On the other hand, if there are changes, then the attractiveness of the current range of intermediation that aggregators are offering to artists may not have the attractiveness it had prior to the change.

It could be that the economic rationale artists have been using to trade intermediation services for their copyrighted material may not be desirable any more. It could just as well be that artists would be better off pursuing a different course. The idea that the Internet in general and Peer-to-Peer in particular justify essentially different strategies for artists and entertainers is in fact the position taken by new firms such as MusicDish.[55] Such firms are redefining intermediation and, as a result, changing the relative balance in the market power of the artists and the content owners.

There are several reasons why new technologies may directly affect the aggregators and the artists, and the artists' willingness to pay for the services aggregators provide is straightforward. For instance, as far as the creation of art and entertainment content are concerned, technology does not impact heavily the contribution of artists. However, it does strongly impact the contribution intermediation can make to promoting those works. It is obvious that the internet and, more recently, Peer-to-Peer, have a very significant impact on marketing, distribution, and retailing costs; hence it impacts the value of the services aggregators can offer.

There is another way in which a change in technology can impact aggregators in a different way from artists and content creators. Intermediation is the means through which aggregators have been able to gain control over the artists' copyrighted material and those assets are creating a unique source of market power. The implication is that, today, aggregators have become above all the managers of copyright assets; hence, they have been increasingly concerned about the way innovation might undermine the value of their assets. From that perspective, new content creation may contribute as a revenue source to their intermediation function. However, it could also dilute the value of their present assets and threaten their market power.

Conclusion

In this paper we study Peer-to-Peer from the perspective of the commons. Although the "commons" have been mostly associated with publicly-held properties, the notion applies to all exchange regimes. Likewise, a new market like online music creates a commons jointly owned by consumers, hosting firms, record companies, and musicians.

Good institutions and governance create incentives to achieve efficiency, while their neglect can result in a "tragedy of the commons." For example, music copyrights are a commons that have been disrupted by several subsequent innovations: the record, the radio, and, today, Peer-to-Peer.

The paper suggests that this outcome can be avoided. It is conceivable that many of the members of these new Peer-to-Peer commons may be willing to shift to commercial Peer-to-Peer networks, as the commercial success of new services such as iTunes shows. Furthermore, the willingness of individuals to participate in voluntary programs such as SETI also points towards the possibility of avoiding such an outcome.

Viewing exchanges as a commons can improve regulation and business strategy, and can guide entrepreneurs in promoting new markets. For co-ordination to succeed, the rules and norms of this commons must encourage cooperative behavior. Markets are based on the presumption that all players are opportunistic. This is not a generic requirement for a commons that recognizes diversity of attitudes among members of the society as a possibility. Interestingly, it is this diversity vis-à-vis opportunism that makes it possible to find governances that support efficient exchanges in the context of market failures.

Consumers play a key role in facilitating the emergence of credible Peer-to-Peer content commercial services. Peer-to-Peer is transforming the content into a good that is, in and of itself, more attractive to consumers. However, the actual economic impact is still very sensitive to the strategies suppliers have been pursuing. Our best guess is that the rigidity of their position has contributed to the emergence of today's Peer-to-Peer networks creating an even greater chasm between copyright owners and consumers.

The owners of copyright content may point to their property rights. First, they neglect the business dimension of those rights, namely that a narrow and rigid interpretation effectively destroys the value of those property rights. It is not good business to enforce copyrights too narrowly. A property right is not to be imposed by sheer power or ruthless fiat but rather if it is to be a factor within a democratic society, it cannot be arbitrarily imposed on that society. Rather, it must reflect the society's acceptance of the granting of power that the society's recognition of owner-ship de facto implies. This means that the society must find it reasonable in the long-run. It is this social and political dimension of property rights that is so often neglected and overlooked in discussions.

Looking at the extent to which Peer-to-Peer platforms have evolved technologically in response to institutional factors, the paper concludes that the RIAA's victory over Napster and other networks such as Aimster, and its unwillingness to negotiate intermediate solutions, created strong incentives for entrepreneurs to favor the new generation of Peer-to-Peer networks. This new generation was conceived to eliminate the technological elements, such as the centralized catalog, that had led to the demise of the first generation of Peer-to-Peer networks in courts. In that respect, it is not unreasonable to conclude that the copyright owners' strategy may have largely backfired making it that much harder to develop a Peer-to-Peer network that could meet reasonable industry demands while responding to customer demands that became apparent through Napster and other such networks. In addition, such policies by copyright aggregators have led Peer-to-Peer network operators to take a layered approach with respect to file transfer in order to build business models that are also immune to challenges by copyright owners.

The need for additional research to design incentives to encourage a stronger cooperative behavior among the different players is highly recommended.[56]

Notes

We thank Loretta Anania and Fabrizio Balassone for their helpful comments. The views here expressed do not represent the positions of the organizations the authors belong to, but only the authors' personal standpoints.

1. Bourdeau de Fontenay and Bourdeau de Fontenay (2002).
2. Peer-to-Peer networks are essentially software designed, and their parts are largely provided by those who use the network (Bourdeau de Fontenay and Liebenau 2004).
3. The analogy here is to the "common lands" in the Middle Ages in England, where anyone could let their sheep graze. Not all such environments are subject to the infamous "tragedy of the commons." If there is enough open space and a good enough legal or customary rules managing individual action, a commons can survive without rapid exhaustion.
4. Ostrom (2000).
5. Liebowitz (2004).
6. The Economist, "Profit from Peer to Peer."
7. An excellent discussion of the role of intermediation in the music and movie industries in the USA is available in Fisher (2004), "Promises to keep," Stanford University Press, Chap. II.
8. Baumol (1965,1971).
9. OECD INFORMATON TECHNOLOGY OUTLOOK (2006).
10. "File sharing activity doubles." The Seattle Times, July 13, 2004.
11. "Films Fuel Online File-Sharing," World Entertainment News Network, July 15, 2004.
12. "The Effect of File Sharing on Record Sales – An empirical Analysis" March 2004 – working paper.
13. "Peer-to-Peer networks: Creative Destruction or Just Plain Destruction," July 2006, working paper. In particular he claims that: "The effect of sampling (more music-listening services at constant CD prices) is to lower the price of music-listening services. The net effect should be to lower the revenues generated by music-listening services. With a price per CD that is independent of the sampling effect, this implies that the quantity of CDs will fall due to sampling," p. 9.
14. To date, there are overall five empirical papers that tackle this issue: Martin Peitz and Patrick Waelbroeck (January 2004), "The Effect of Internet Piracy on CD Sales: Cross Section Evidence," CESIFO Working Paper No. 1122; Alejandro Zentner (April 2006), "Measuring the Effect of Online Music Piracy on Music Purchases," Ph.D. Dissertation in progress, Princeton University; Eric S. Boorstin (April 2004), "Music Sales in the Age of File Sharing," Senior Thesis, Princeton University. But those by Liebowitz (2004) and Oberholzer and Strumpf (2004) can be considered to be the leading ones. The former for comprehensiveness and the latter for the specific data sets used for the analysis.

15. At the Cato Conference on The Economics of Peer-to-Peer in Washington of June 2004, Strumpf, while commenting on the results from Liebowitz's paper, argued that correlation does not imply causality and that Liebowitz's indirect approach based on time series does not help in this case. Indeed, he asked "how do we explain that in the last 9 months, while file-sharing was slightly increasing, the sale of CDs were up to between 7 and 10%?"

16. The other studies previously mentioned used proxies to estimate the number of downloads such as the share of internet users and different units of analysis such as sales of sound recording in different countries (Peitz and Waelbroeck; Zenter) or different cities in the USA (Boorstin). According to Liebowitz's paper, the ones that use the countries run into heterogeneity problems while Boorstin runs into specification problems.

17. According to Liebowitz (2004), there are two potential problems with Oberholzer and Strumpf's paper. First, we are not sure whether using records as the units of observation can enable us to infer the impacts on the entire industry as opposed to the impacts on individual records (i.e., if it can be shown that a given set of albums was not affected by file-sharing, it may be difficult to say that the entire music industry will not be affected by file-sharing). Second, the model runs in specification problems in the use of instrumental variables necessary to take into account the serious simultaneity problem due to the fact that popular songs are, at the same time, the ones purchased and downloaded the most.

18. "Peer-to-Peer booming as users swap large files," ZDnet UK, July 14, 2004.

19. "Movies in the digital age," MIT Communications Forum, April 8, 2004.

20. See "Peer-to-Peer Gaming: Guerrilla gameplay," New Media Age, September 23, 2003.

21. See: "Atzio Technology Announces Arrival of Legitimate Peer-to-Peer Television," Tech-News, August 31, 2004.

22. Commons have typically been defined in the literature in a much narrower sense. Faulhaber and Farber (2003) define it as "an asset available for the use of all, with common restrictions governing use restrictions for all," using the FCC Part 15 spectrum rule as an example. In general, the "common restrictions" they refer to could be any form of restriction, including price restrictions as in the case of toll highways or the tolls charged historically for lighthouses (Coase 1974). Further on, they differentiate "a property right regime from a commons… [in terms of] (i) scarcity and (ii) transaction costs" (208). They do not elaborate upon those points even though, excluding some of the commons Hardin (1998) called "unmanaged," commons have associated property rights even though they can be private at the level of an individual or at the level of a community, or still, public as with the FCC Part 15 spectrum. They point out correctly that property rights will make it easier to deal with transaction costs, but this has nothing to do with ownership characteristics. For Frischmann (2001), the Internet is a commons. Frischmann (2004) summarizes the current literature by concluding that "'commons' … means that the resource is openly accessible to all within a community regardless of their identity or intended use… the antithesis of private property and

an alternative to government ownership or control...." In his analysis, he uses "'open access' and 'commons' interchangeably to mean that the resource is openly accessible to users regardless of their identity or intended use." We have not generalized the terminology gratuitously. Rather, it is our observation that one of the main characteristics of a commons is to provide sustainable and viable solutions to market failures. That perspective highlights the benefits of looking at a commons as the broad context within which to study economic exchanges, i.e., the benefit of looking at markets as a subset of a commons (Bourdeau de Fontenay and Liebenau 2004).

23. Smith (1776) and Yang (2001).
24. Baumol (1971).
25. We use here the terminology of license rather than of property right that is used in economics to avoid to have to detail every time the actual property rights that are sold by the copyright owner to the individual. The license is used as a generic term to describe those very circumscribed property rights; hence it is used to avoid ambiguities in the discussion.
26. Krishnan. The lack of governance is illustrated by the inability of such communities to protect themselves from actions such as the RIAA's spoofing.
27. Hardin (1968).
28. Asvanund et al. (2003a,b), Li et al. (2003), Chu et al. (2004), Dewan and Dasgupta (undated), Garcia-Martinez and Feldman (undated), Krishnan et al. (2004), Kung and Wu (undated), and Ionescu et al. (2004).
29. Demsetz (1967).
30. Currently, the lack of participation of a substantial fraction of the population of a Peer-to-Peer network community does not seem to threaten the viability of the community itself. This may not be true anymore in the near future as video Peer-to-Peer becomes increasingly important. This is an unknown factor that will have to be addressed at the time.
31. The commons appear to take forms other than markets primarily where there are market failures as in the problem Hardin (1968) studied. In particular, historically many of the commons were designed to provide for economic exchange where there was both a lack of excludability and also rivalry. In addition, the commons were typically organized in a way so as to lower transaction costs, including where, as in Sengupta (2001), transaction costs overburdened the system to the extent that they were not only inefficient but also resulted in a market failure.
32. Coase (1974).
33. Ostrom (2000).
34. Bourdeau de Fontenay and Liebenau (2004). Transaction costs would seem to be the primary factor that differentiates the subset of markets from the more general commons. Markets are used where the size of transactions is sufficiently large in relation to transaction costs. Where market-based transactions – as with local telephone calls – are very small and can easily be swamped by transaction costs, and/or where people show a clear preference for simpler pricing schemes, then pricing strategies evolve away from "marginal pricing"-based criteria to more generic, commons-like criteria as with flat-rate

telephone pricing. The same can easily happen where the product's characteristics invite moral hazard as with Coase's (1974) lighthouses. The reason is simple. It reflects an attempt to bypass the market failure of neoclassical pricing through a broader contractual strategy. Those broader pricing strategies can resolve the neoclassical market failures.

35. Bourdeau de Fontenay and Liebenau (2004).
36. Barzel (1997).
37. We need to underline that we are not considering here the efficiency of the process. This is because our analysis does not permit us to consider the efficiency of the search and the convergence characteristics of the existing process.
38. Ionescu et al. (2004).
39. One of the arguments used in Canada to deregulate small satellite antennae was that the enforcement of a consumer level of those antennae was effectively impossible.
40. Ostrom (2000).
41. Ostrom (2000).
42. Krim (2004).
43. Technology is assumed to be endogenous in a number of other fields in economics, e.g., in economic growth. There are even segments of the industrial organization literature, such as the study of patent strategies, where such endogeneity is natural and fundamental. In addition, it was central to the classics such as Adam Smith (Stigler 1951). We have also demonstrated in Bourdeau de Fontenay et al. (2004) how its neglect in regulatory economics results in a causality reversal, a basic flaw in today's analysis.
44. Demsetz (1966).
45. Brel, Jacques. "Les bourgeois," words and music by J. Brel and J. Corti (1962). (accessed November 2004, http://www.paroles.net/nix/poster/11798).
46. Van Cayseele (undated).
47. Coase's (1937) conditions under which it is unambiguously efficient for a Coasian firm to be vertically integrated are particularly difficult to meet. When a Coasian firm chooses to carry out simultaneously both an intermediate activity and the activity that produces the final commodity, the action of that firm must not impact on the efficient functioning of the intermediate market. In other words, other firms' decisions to maintain their disintegration must not be affected, and the relative merits of vertical integration and vertical disintegration must remain unchanged.
48. Einhorn and Rosenblat (2004).
49. Bowles (2004).
50. Thierer (1994).
51. http://www.aufdermauer.com
52. It is evident that we use the terminology of transaction costs in a very heuristic manner. Such a heuristic approach is, for good or for bad, the characteristic of today's institutional economics. It is a heuristic approach that appears, at least, on the surface, to clash with much of today's literature. With roots in Coase (1937) and the Chicago School, it dominates much of today's

new institutional economics, and survives in Williamson's work. An empirical economic analysis of Peer-to-Peer requires more solid foundations. For instance, it would have to push much further the tally of the sector's vision, the key factors that we have aggregated under the label of transaction costs (Spulber 1999). In a setting as the one we are considering here, we do not believe that more precise definitions would seriously impact our conclusions.
53. Georgescu-Roegen (1967).
54. Einhorn and Rosenblat (2004).
55. http://www.musicdish.com
56. Alain Bourdeau de Fontenay is a visiting scholar and Senior Affiliated Researcher with the Columbia Institute for Tele-Information (CITI), Columbia University. Email: ad2239@columbia.edu. Eric Bourdeau de Fontenay is founder and President of MusicDish LLC, magazine publisher and artist development/management. Email: ecfont@pipeline.com. Dr. Lorenzo Maria Pupillo is an Executive Director in the Public Affairs Unit of Telecom Italia and Affiliated Researcher at Columbia Institute for Tele-Information. Email: lorenzo.pupillo@telecomitalia.it.

References

Asvanund, Atip; Clay, Karen; Krishnan, Ramayya and Smith, Michael D. "An Empirical Analysis of Network Externalities in Peer-to-Peer Music Sharing Networks." *Information Systems Research*, 2004, 150(2), pp. 155–174.

Asvanund, Atip; Krishnan, Ramayya; Smith, Michael D. and Telang, Rahul. "Intelligent Club Management in Peer-to-Peer Networks," H. John Heinz III School of Public Policy and Management Working Paper. Pittsburgh: Carnegie Mellon University, 2003.

Barzel, Y. *Economic Analysis of Property Rights*, 2nd Edition. Cambridge, UK: Cambridge University Press, 1997.

Baumol, W.J. "On the Performing Arts: The Anatomy of their Economic Problems," *The American Economic Review*, 55(1/2), 1965, 495–502.

Baumol, William J. and Bowen, W.G. "On the Performing Arts: The Anatomy of their Economic Problems," *American Economic Review*, 1965, 55(1/2), pp. 495–502.

Bollow, N. "Market Economies of Peer-to-Peer Networks and of the Software Industry." 28 January 2004.

Bourdeau de Fontenay, A. and Bourdeau de Fontenay, E. "Peer-to-Peer, Digital Commodities, and the Governance of Commerce." *Cyber Policy and Economics in an Internet Age*. Lehr, W. and Pupillo, L. (eds.). New York, NY: Kluwer Academic Press, 2002, pp. 169–196.

Bourdeau de Fontenay, A., Liebenau, J., and Savin, B. "A New View of Scale and Scope in the Telecommunications Industry: Implications for Competition and Innovation." 2004.

Bourdeau de Fontenay, A. and Liebenau, J. "Investment in Broadband: Theory and Policy from the Perspective of the 'Commons'." Presentation to the FCC, Washington, DC, October 2004.

Bourdeau de Fontenay, Alain and Liebenau, Jonathan M. and Savin, A. Brian. "A New View of Scale and Scope in the Telecommunications Industry: Implications for Competition and Innovation." *Communications and Strategies*, 2005, 60(4), pp. 85–103.

Bourdeau de Fontenay, Alain and Liebenau, Jonathan M. "Modeling Scale and Scope in Telecommunications Industry." *Communications and Strategies*, 2006, 61, pp. 139–156.

Carruthers, B.G. and Ariovich, L. "The Sociology of Property Rights." *Annual Review of Sociology*, 30, 2004, 23–46.

Cheung, Stephen N.S. "The Fable of the Bees: An Economic Investigation." *Journal of Law and Economics*, 1973, 16(1), pp. 11–33.

Christensen, C.M. *The Innovator's Dilemma*. New York, NY: HarperBusiness, 2000.

Chu, Y.-H., Chuang, J., and Zhang, H. "A Case of Taxation in Peer-to-Peer Streaming Broadcast," SIGCOM Workshops, Portland, OR, 30 August–3 September 2004.

Coase, Ronald H. "The Problem of Social Cost." *Journal of Law and Economics*, 1960, 3, pp. 1–44.

Coase, Ronald H. "The Nature of the Firm." R.H. Coase, *The Firm, the Market and the Law*. Chicago: Chicago University Press, 1937, 33–55.

Coase, Ronald H. "The Lighthouse in Economics." *The Journal of Law and Economics*. 17(2), 1974, 357–376.

Cuenca-Acuna, Francisco Matias and Nguyen, Thu D. "Text-Based Content Search and Retrieval in Ad Hoc P2p Communities," *The International Workshop on Peer-to-Peer Computing*. Springer-Verlag, 2002.

Demsetz, H. "Some Aspects of Property Rights," *Journal of Law and Economics*, 9, October 1966, 61–70.

Demsetz, H. "Toward a Theory of Property Rights," *American Economic Review*, 57(2), May 1967, 347–359.

Dewan, Prasun and Dasgupta, Partha. "Securing Reputation Data in Peer-to-Peer Data." *16th IASTED International Conference on Parallel and Distributed Computing and Systems (PDCS 2004)*. Cambridge, MA, 2004, 1–10.

Economist, The."Profit from Peer-to-Peer," *Economist.com*. 2001.

Einhorn, M.A. and Rosenblatt, B. "Peer-to-Peer Networking and Digital Rights Management: How Market Tools can Solve Copyright Problems." Washington, DC: Cato Institute, 2004.

Faulhaber, Gerald R. and Farber, David J. "Spectrum Management: Property Rights, Markets, and the Commons," L.F. Cranor and S. Wildman, *Rethinking Rights and Regulations; Institutional Responses to New Communications Technologies*. Cambridge, MA: MIT Press, 2003.

Fisher, W.W. "Promises to keep." Chicago, IL: Stanford University Press, 2004.

Frischmann, B.M. "An Economic Theory of Infrastructure and Sustainable Infrastructure Commons" (Accessed November 2004:http://papers.ssrn.com/sol3/papers.cfm?abstract_id=588424).

Frischmann, B.M. *Privatization and Commercialization of the Internet Infra-structure: Rethinking Market Intervention into Government and Government Intervention into the Market*, 2 COLUM. SCI. & TECH. L. REV. 1 (June 8, 2001) <http://www.stlr.org/cite.cgi?volume=2&article=1>.

Garcia-Martinez, Antonio and Feldman, Michal. "Gnushare: Enforcing Sharing in Gnutella-Style Peer-to-Peer Networks." Berkeley: University of California at Berkeley, 2002.

Garcia-Murillo, Martha A. and MacInnes, Ian. "The Impact of Incentives in the Telecommunications Act of 1996 on Corporate Strategies," *29th TPRC Conference*. 2001.

Georgescu-Roegen, N. *Analytical Economics, Issues and Problems*. Cambridge, MA: Harvard University Press, 1967.

Hagel, John III and Armstrong, Arthur G. *Net Gain: Expanding Markets through Virtual Communities*. New York: McKinsey, 1997.

Hardin, G. "The Tragedy of the Commons." *Science*, 162, 1968, 1243–1248.

Hardin, G. "Extensions of 'The Tragedy of the Commons'." *Science*, 280, 1998, 682–683.

Ionescu, Mihail; Minsky, Naftaly and Nguyen, Thu D. "Enforcement of Communal Policies for P2p Systems." *Coordination Models and Languages: 6th International Conference*. Pisa, Italy: Springer, 2004.

Krim, T. "Les Nouveaux Modèles de Distribution de Musique: Concurrence et Complémentarité." Paris: L8Rmedia, 1er Mars 2004.

Krishnan, Ramayya; Smith, Michael D. and Telang, Rahul. "The Economics of Peer-to-Peer Networks." *Journal of Information Technology Theory and Applications*, 2003, 5(3), pp. 31–44.

Krishnan, R., Smith, M.D., Tang, Z., and Telang, R. "The Impact of Free-riding on Peer-to-Peer Networks." Proceedings of the 37th Hawaii International Conference on System Sciences, IEEE and School of Public Policy and Management. Pittsburgh, PA: Carnegie Mellon University, 2004.

Kung, H.T. and Wu, Chun-hsin. "Differentiated Admission for Peer-to-Peer Systems: Incentivizing Peers to Contribute Their Resources," 2003.

Li, Cuihong; Yu, Bin and Sycara, Katia. "An Incentive Mechanism for Message Relaying in Peer-to-Peer Discovery." *Second Workshop on the Economics of Peer-to-Peer Systems*. Cambridge, MA: Harvard University, 2004.

Liebowitz, Stan J. "File-Sharing Creative Destruction or Just Plain Destruction." *Journal of Law and Economics*, 2006, 49(1), pp. 1–28.

Oberholzer-Gee, Felix and Strumpf, Koleman. "The Effect of File Sharing on Record Sales: An Empirical Analysis." *Journal of Political Economy*, 2007, 115(1).

OECD. "OECD Information Technology Outlook 2006," T. a. I. Directorate for Science, OECD, 2006.

Ostrom, E. "Collective Action and the Evolution of Social Norms." *The Journal of Economic Perspectives*, 14(3), Summer 2000, 137–158.

Peitz, Martin and Waelbroeck, Patrick." An Economist's Guide to Digital Music," *CESifo Working Paper*. CESifo, 2004.

Riding, A. "Unmasking a Surreal Egotist: Two Blockbuster Reassess Dali's Legacy at the Centenary of his Birth." The New York Times, Tuesday 28 September 2004, p. E1.

Sengupta, N. *A New Institutional Theory of Production: An Application.* New Delhi: Sage Publications, 2001.

Smith, Adam. *An Inquiry into the Nature and Causes of the Wealth of Nations.* London: Methuen, 1776.

Spulber, D. *Market Microstructure: Intermediaries and the Theory of the Firm.* Cambridge, UK: Cambridge University Press, 1999.

Stigler, George J. "The Division of Labor is Limited by the Extent of the Market." *The Journal of Political Economy*, 1951, 59(3), pp. 185–193.

Thierer, Adam D. "Unnatural Monopoly: Critical Moments in the Development of the Bell System Monopoly." *Cato Journal*, 1994, 14(2).

Van Cayseele, Patrick and Van den Bergh, Roger. "Antitrust Law." B. Bouckaert and G. De Geest, *Encyclopedia of Law and Economics*. Cheltenham, U.K.: Edward Elgar, 1999.

Williamson, Oliver E. *The Economic Institution of Capitalism.* New York: Free Press, 1985.

Yang, X. *Economics: New Classical Versus Neoclassical Frameworks.* Malden, MA: Blackwell Publishers, 2001.

Zentner, Alejandro. "Measuring the Effect of File Sharing on Music Purchases." *Journal of Law and Economics*, 2006, 49(1), pp. 63–90.

PART II – Peer-to-Peer: Market and Technology

4

The Implications of Video Peer-to-Peer on Network Usage

Kevin Werbach

University of Pennsylvania

Rewritten by machine and new technology,
and now I understand the problems you can see.
Oh-a oh
I met your children
Oh-a oh
What did you tell them?
Video killed the radio star.[1]

Introduction

The tsunami is upon us. A rising tide of video Peer-to-Peer[2] activity is already beginning to affect data networks. And video Peer-to-Peer traffic will inexorably grow in the years ahead. Video Peer-to-Peer will expand beyond unauthorized sharing of commercial pre-recorded content, becoming a significant driver of broadband usage and potentially creating new revenue streams. Meanwhile, because of its sheer bulk and technical characteristics, video Peer-to-Peer traffic will place significant strains on broadband networks. Thus, video Peer-to-Peer will influence both the outputs and the inputs of the Internet of the future.

The network usage implications of video Peer-to-Peer are not widely appreciated. To date, most of the attention devoted to Peer-to-Peer has focused on the content of the files being transferred.[3] The unauthorized dissemination of copyrighted material through Peer-to-Peer systems has considerable implications for users, artists, network operators, technology developers, device manufacturers, investors, and content distributors. Yet

E.M. Noam and L.M. Pupillo (eds.), *Peer-to-Peer Video*, doi: 10.1007/978-0-387-76450-4_4,
© Springer Science + Business Media, LLC 2008

Peer-to-Peer, and especially video Peer-to-Peer, would have significant impacts even if none of the files involved were subject to intellectual property protection. And, though it is quite early in the development of the market, there are indications that video Peer-to-Peer will be used more actively than audio Peer-to-Peer for sharing content not subject to copyright limitations.

Focusing on commercial content provides only a partial view of the economics of video Peer-to-Peer. In the eyes of lawyers and entertainment industry executives, there is a vast difference between my home movies, which I freely make available to any prospective viewers, and the latest *Star Wars* prequel. One is a potential source of several hundred million dollars in revenue; the other is, at best, a reason to spend a few hundred dollars on a video camera. From a network engineering perspective, though, both are simply large amalgamations of data. And to me personally, both are valuable, though in different ways. Understanding likely usage patterns and network impacts is critical for any realistic assessment of the consequences of video Peer-to-Peer.

Bits and Bytes

All information transferred across digital networks such as the Internet is ultimately fungible. A bit is a bit. Thus, a large file requires more network capacity, typically expressed in terms of bandwidth, than a small file, regardless of what that file contains. However, data in motion is not equivalent to data at rest. In other words, there are differences in network impacts based on how files are used. A popular file consumes more network resources, because it is transferred more times, even though it takes up the same number of bytes on a hard drive as an unpopular file. This creates a rough parallel with the content-oriented perspective. It is quite likely that more viewers would download a pre-released print of the *Star Wars* movie than the Werbach family's summer vacation highlights.

On the other hand, what matters from a network perspective is the aggregate impact of all user activity. There are many more home movies shot each year than Hollywood feature films. And some non-commercial content achieves significant popularity – witness the spread of the Paris Hilton sex video, or the original installment of what became the animated show *South Park*, mailed out as a video Christmas card by a Hollywood executive. Before the Internet came along, distributing video content was beyond the means of individuals, and small commercial operations had limited reach. Now, when any content can become instantly available to a global audience of more, a bright-line distinction between commercial and non-commercial video is more difficult to draw. Each is likely to have significant economic and network capacity consequences as it becomes more feasible to distribute them across the Internet.

Technology adds another layer of complexity to the economic analysis. A television episode is subject to the same intellectual property law regardless of how it is delivered across the network. Yet content creates very different network loads depending on whether it is streamed, downloaded explicitly, or downloaded automatically in the background over a period of time. Video captured in real-time from a wireless device will create different choke demands than fixed video files such as recorded television programs. A video file pulled together from fragments stored on many different users' hard drives will have different network impacts than one delivered in a single piece from a central server on demand.

The network impacts of video Peer-to-Peer activity are significant for several reasons. Network capacity has a cost. If video Peer-to-Peer imposes costs on network operators, they will have incentives to limit it, especially if they do not receive a commensurate benefit from the activity. How the network infrastructure delivers Peer-to-Peer content also influences user behavior. To take one example, an individual may be inclined to use – or pay for – a Peer-to-Peer service that quickly and reliably delivers content, but not a service that is slow and prone to connection errors. Some applications, and some users, have more tolerance for poor quality than others.

Those tolerances are loosely connected to the type of content involved, though the relationship is synergistic. A Peer-to-Peer service used to swap Hollywood movies will have a different profile than one used to aggregate assorted content streams into a personalized television network, or one used to share running video diaries of life experiences with family and friends. What the network supports will influence which of these applications are more popular, and application popularity will influence network design. The legal and economic battles now being fought over Peer-to-Peer activity are exogenous factors which will have a significant bearing on this dynamic. Impediments to certain types of Peer-to-Peer activity will make some applications impractical or impossible, whether or not those applications are the actual target.

None of these issues is necessarily specific to video. However, because of video's unique characteristics, it will create different challenges than other media types. The rise of video Peer-to-Peer promises much greater network impacts than the largely music-dominated traffic heretofore. And video as a medium lends itself to certain applications and usage patterns that have heretofore not been widely adopted.

The remainder of this paper sketches the likely consequences of video Peer-to-Peer on networks and usage patterns. The sections focus on: reviewing of data on the level of video Peer-to-Peer activity, concluding that it already represents a substantial share of Internet traffic, and that share is likely to grow; Peer-to-Peer technology for transferring video, in particular the new class of swarming file-transfer software typified by BitTorrent; four major categories of video Peer-to-Peer applications that are likely to become significant in the coming years; evaluation of how the proliferation of these applications will affect different segments of the Internet; and consideration of how network operators and other service providers will respond to the capacity challenges and revenue opportunities of video Peer-to-Peer.

Rise of the Videonet

To a first approximation, video Peer-to-Peer file transfers *are* the Internet.

Comprehensive and reliable data on video Peer-to-Peer are just starting to become available. The distributed nature of Peer-to-Peer services, the short time that video has been an appreciable component of Peer-to-Peer activity, and the difficulty in segmenting among types of Peer-to-Peer traffic all make it hard to obtain accurate measurements.[4] Nonetheless, what we do know is striking: virtually everywhere measurements are done, Peer-to-Peer transfers of large files such as video are the single biggest component of network utilization.

Peer-to-Peer file-sharing in general represents a substantial proportion of Internet traffic. A study by network monitoring appliance vendor CacheLogic, released in July 2004, found that Peer-to-Peer is the largest consumer of data on Internet service provider (ISP) networks, and is still growing.[5] CacheLogic is one of a new breed of vendors whose equipment is capable of deep packet inspection at the application layer, allowing it to monitor and differentiate Peer-to-Peer applications more finely than previously possible.[6] In a single 30-day period, one CacheLogic appliance tracked Peer-to-Peer accesses from 3.5 million unique IP addresses. CacheLogic estimates the worldwide simultaneous Peer-to-Peer user base at 10 million – over 10% of all broadband accounts. And those users are sharing over 10,000,000,000 megabytes (10 petabytes) of data.[7]

Despite legal action by the record industry against individual users as well as distributors of Peer-to-Peer file-sharing software, Peer-to-Peer traffic continues to represent an increasing share of Internet traffic.[8] Peer-to-Peer file transfers represent an absolute majority of traffic on many networks, as high as 80% in some cases.[9] The numbers are especially high for broadband access networks.[10] Email and the World Wide Web, the "killer apps" of the Net, are small by comparison.

Video in particular is a significant and growing element of Peer-to-Peer traffic, especially since 2003. A study of BitTorrent, a Peer-to-Peer system popular for video, found between 237,500 and 576,500 daily BitTorrent transfers in progress between December 2003 and January 2004, of which roughly 100,000–150,000 per day were movies.[11] These numbers represent a small percentage of the Peer-to-Peer file-sharing user base, most of which is still engaged in trading music files.[12] However, video Peer-to-Peer transfers are rapidly eclipsing Peer-to-Peer distribution of music files in bandwidth usage. The CacheLogic study concluded that BitTorrent alone consumed more than one-third of all Internet bandwidth worldwide.[13]

The reason is simple: video files are enormous. As Table 4.1 shows, a feature motion picture, encoded using common compression mechanisms, may be a thousand times the size of a song, or even larger.[14]

Table 4.1 Relative sizes of different file types

File type	Approximate size (kilobytes)
Email message	5–100
Web page	25–500
Music audio file (MP3)	2,000–10,000
Music video	50,000–200,000
Feature film	500,000–4,000,000

Thus, video files have an impact on network usage that is grossly disproportionate to the number of users sending or receiving them. Ten thousand people viewing a 100-kilobyte (kB) Web page would move the same number of bits through the network as a single person downloading a 1-gigabyte (GB) movie. In fact, this comparison may actually understate the differences between the two traffic types, for reasons discussed below.[15]

The data bear out these predictions. One study of traffic on the popular KaZaA Peer-to-Peer file-sharing service found that while 91% of requests were for objects smaller than 10 megabytes (MB), a majority of the bytes transferred (65%) were from objects greater than 100 MB, primarily video files.[16] According to the Organization for Economic Cooperation and Development (OECD), video and other transfers made up a majority of Peer-to-Peer traffic in OECD countries in 2003, for the first time exceeding music.[17] Another study by economists Peter Lyman and Hal Varian concluded that video files represented 59% of total file-sharing traffic in 2003, compared to 33% for audio files.[18]

If these numbers sound shocking, it may be because the United States is something of a laggard in usage of video Peer-to-Peer. Video distribution on Peer-to-Peer networks is significantly more common in other parts of the world. One reason is that US Broadband penetration lags many other countries in Europe and Asia.[19] Countries such as Korea, where users have significantly more bandwidth available to them at significantly lower prices, unsurprisingly have higher rates of usage of Peer-to-Peer networks for video.[20]

Even today's relatively small level of video Peer-to-Peer activity is influencing overall network demand. In contrast to music, therefore, network operators may feel the economic impacts of video Peer-to-Peer distribution before commercial content owners do. Over the coming decade, video Peer-to-Peer usage will expand greatly, for two reasons: enhanced technology and new applications.

Video Peer-to-Peer Technology

Peer-to-Peer file sharing burst on the scene with the 1999 release of Napster, a software application written by college student Shawn Fanning. Fanning was an inexperienced programmer, and it showed. Though millions downloaded Napster and it quickly created an earthquake in the music industry, the application itself was unsophisticated. It wasn't even truly Peer-to-Peer. The files involved were transferred directly between users, but those transfers were coordinated through a central directory maintained by Napster.[21] That central coordination point was Napster's undoing on both a legal and practical level[22] when the company was sued by the record industry.

Peer-to-Peer technology has come a long way since Napster. The functions of today's Peer-to-Peer file-sharing applications may be similar, but the mechanisms differ in important ways. How Peer-to-Peer services operate has important consequences for their impacts on networks and economics, especially in the case of video.

Peer-to-Peer Techniques

There are two basic processes for acquiring rich media content[23] over the Internet: file transfer and streaming. File transfer involves delivering the entire file over the network to the user's computer. Once the transfer is completed, the file can be played, copied, or transferred elsewhere.[24] In streaming, the user receives a small initial segment of the file, which is stored locally in a buffer file. The file begins playing from the buffer, while the next segment is transferred over the network. In this manner, the user has the experience of hearing or viewing the entire file almost immediately. However, the file is only transferred as fast as it can be played back, and only the segment of the file being played is stored on the user's computer, making it impossible to copy or replay the file locally.[25]

From a pure network standpoint, file transfer is more efficient. Because the file is not actually being played across the unpredictable network link, there is more tolerance for delay and lost packets. Pieces of files can be transferred out of order, up to the speed of the network connection, rather than being limited to the playback speed of the file. These capabilities are particularly well-suited to a Peer-to-Peer architecture, in which information flows between heterogeneous and intermittently connected nodes at the edge of the network rather than centrally managed servers. The major Peer-to-Peer applications, including Napster, Gnutella, FastTrack, and BitTorrent, are all file-transfer systems.[26]

Beyond that, the Peer-to-Peer services differ in their technical architecture. None of the currently-popular systems employ Napster's central directory. Some use dynamically-created "supernodes," which turn users with high-quality connections into temporary directory nodes for other users. Other systems, such as Gnutella, relay requests from one node to another, until the request finds a directory including the desired file. BitTorrent, described in greater detail below, further distributes the directory function through the use of multiple "trackers," which keep track of pieces of files.

Every major Peer-to-Peer system has its strong and weak points. Some scale well to large numbers of simultaneous users (popularity); some compensate well for the inherent unreliability of Peer-to-Peer network nodes (availability); some offer higher file transfer speeds (download performance); some allow files to remain available for long periods of time (content lifetime); some offer content (such as movies) soon release (content injection time); and some are resistant to accidental or deliberate uploading of files with incorrect names or corrupted contents (pollution level). A recent study compared five leading Peer-to-Peer systems along these axes, showing that no single factor accounts for popularity.

The FastTrack platform, which is the basis of KaZaA and several other Peer-to-Peer software applications, has until recently been the most popular Peer-to-Peer service. eDonkey has enjoyed greater success in Europe and Asia than in the USA.[27] This is partially because eDonkey's queue-based scheduling and distributed downloading capabilities are useful for transferring video and other larger files. Such files are a larger proportion of the Peer-to-Peer mix outside the USA, where broadband speeds and penetration are greater.

As already noted, the distinguishing characteristic of video files is their immense size. Downloading performance is the biggest hurdle to obtaining such files across the network. Though video files have been available on Peer-to-Peer systems since the beginning, they typically represented a very small fraction of available files and network traffic. Performance simply wasn't reliable enough to make transferring large video files such as movies worthwhile (Table 4.2).

Table 4.2 Characteristics of the five most popular Peer-to-Peer systems

Peer-to-Peer system	Strong points	Weak points
FastTrack (KaZaA)	Popularity, availability, content lifetime	Pollution level
Overnet (eDonkey)	Popularity, content lifetime	Download performance
BitTorrent	Popularity, download performance, content injection time, pollution level	Availability, content lifetime
DirectConnect	Download performance, content lifetime	Availability
Gnutella	Download performance	popularity, pollution level

From J.A. Pouwelse, P. Garbacki, D.H.J. Epema, and H.J. Sips, "A Measurement Study of the BitTorrent Peer-to-Peer File-Sharing System," at 7, preprint available at http:// www.pds.ewi.tudelft.nl/reports/2004/PDS-2004-003/pdsreport.html

BitTorrent and Swarming

Even with a fast broadband link and a sophisticated Peer-to-Peer platform, downloading an entire movie or other long video clip in one fell swoop is difficult. Real-world transfer speeds on Peer-to-Peer services are significantly below the peak download speed of the broadband connection, generally in the range of 20–50 kilobytes per second. At those rates, a large video file may take many hours, even days, to transfer completely. The chances that the originating node will be online and reachable that entire time are small. And if a transfer is interrupted in the middle, it may be impossible to pick it up again.

The solution is what is sometimes called swarming technology.[28] Swarming breaks up large files into many small pieces.[29] When a user wishes to download the file, rather than pulling it all from a single source, the system locates and downloads the pieces from many different locations in parallel. When more than one user attempts to download a file at the same time, the downloaders simultaneously upload pieces of the file to each other.[30] Thus, instead of choking a node hosting a popular video file, a swarming system automatically distributes the file transfer load.

Swarming is a key element of BitTorrent, which was first released in mid-2002. This explains why it is used so heavily for video and large software files.[31] The BitTorrent architecture involves three components: .torrent files, trackers, and user nodes. The .torrent files, which are accessed through ordinary Web servers, provide basic information on the file to be obtained, but not the actual content itself. They also include pointers to trackers, which are a form of directory server. A tracker maintains information about who has what pieces of the relevant file. Using the tracker, the BitTorrent software begins downloading and uploading pieces of the file among other nodes. At least one node must function as a seed, which means it has a complete copy of the file, to verify integrity. The other nodes are in the process of downloading, and may only have a small portion at any given time.

Unlike other popular Peer-to-Peer services, BitTorrent does not directly provide search functionality. In order to obtain a BitTorrent file, a user must locate it through other means than the BitTorrent software itself. The most common way of doing so is through Suprnova.org, an independent website which maintains a moderated list of new BitTorrent files.

BitTorrent addresses a significant limitation of other Peer-to-Peer systems known as free riding. Free riding is a significant problem with some Peer-to-Peer systems, notably Gnutella; one study in 2000 found that 70% of users shared no files at all, and merely downloaded.[32] BitTorrent users do not have the option not to share files. The system also incorporates a bartering mechanism.[33] In other words, users who upload are rewarded with the ability to download more rapidly, while those who do not upload are punished with limited download capacity. Bram Cohen, the developer of BitTorrent, calls this "leech resistance."[34]

The BitTorrent software is open source. This allows developers to build their own client software based on the protocol, and several have. Developers are incorporating BitTorrent into different kinds of applications, including video syndication feeds. Commercial software developers are also evaluating BitTorrent as a technology platform for video distribution.

If widespread video Peer-to-Peer distribution does continue to take off, especially for applications other than unauthorized sharing of copyrighted material, BitTorrent or BitTorrent-like swarming technology will likely be part of any popular application. Faster broadband connections, especially in the upstream direction, will make it easier to transfer entire video files, but without a bartering system to limit traffic imbalances, any system will have difficulty scaling. The market appears to be moving in this direction. eDonkey, already one of the most popular Peer-to-Peer file-sharing platforms, especially outside the USA, has added BitTorrent-like swarming capability called Horde in recent versions.

It is important to recognize that BitTorrent and the Horde-enabled eDonkey are recent arrivals. Though released in 2002, BitTorrent was originally used primarily for software distribution. In essence, it has been less than a year since well-designed tools became available for effective video Peer-to-Peer transfers. And those tools are far from perfected. BitTorrent lacks a straightforward user interface and integrated search functionality, while eDonkey can't yet match the performance of BitTorrent's swarming implementation. As software to distribute Peer-to-Peer video reliably and simply becomes more widely available, video Peer-to-Peer traffic will grow. Any predictions at this stage of the market must necessarily be speculative. Given the growth of video Peer-to-Peer traffic in the past year, though the question is when, not if, today's usage level will expand.

Video Peer-to-Peer Usage Scenarios

The other half of the video Peer-to-Peer equation is the demand side. Good tools can only go so far without killer apps to drive usage. In the case of video Peer-to-Peer, there has been relatively little consideration of novel usage scenarios. Though the economic and legal discussion around video Peer-to-Peer centers on trading of commercial video content such as movies and television programs, this is not likely to be the only substantial form of video Peer-to-Peer activity.

As with the technology and network impacts, the precise timing and contours of popular usage scenarios is hard to predict. Video Peer-to-Peer is still in the early stages of development. Many entrepreneurs and even established companies have failed miserably in predicting usage patterns for new forms of media, which video Peer-to-Peer represents. So any predictions should be taken with a grain of sale. Nonetheless, it is possible to sketch out some likely developments, given the capabilities that will soon be available and known user demand.

Video as a medium is different from audio. The richness and emotional impact of video lends itself to different experiences. Just compare the number of people who shoot home movies or otherwise use video recorders to the number who make personal audio tapes. A song can be played in the background, while engaged in other activities, while most video content requires full attention. And, although movies as a form of pre-recorded commercial content are somewhat analogous to record albums, a great deal of commercial video content, such as television news and sporting events, is live. All these examples suggest that, as video becomes a more prominent part of the Peer-to-Peer world, different applications may predominate than the song-sharing that dominates audio Peer-to-Peer usage.

Four primary classes of application are likely to drive utilization of video Peer-to-Peer: sharing of pre-recorded video files; distribution of personal video among families and friends; dissemination of "do it yourself" entertainment and news content; and monitoring and sensor applications. The first, which dominates video Peer-to-Peer today, is a fixture of the broadband wired Internet. The second and fourth will, to a great extent, grow out of the wireless Internet, including both local-area WiFi wireless "hotspots" and wide-area cellular data networks.

Video File Sharing

Peer-to-Peer platforms are used to distribute copyrighted commercial video files such as movies, music videos, and television episodes. The pattern here is similar to the sharing of music files, though so far the level of activity has been smaller. Because video files are much larger than songs, they take much longer to download. Thus, in the same amount of time, a user can obtain fewer video than audio files. Moreover, large video files such as movies are still difficult to download reliably, though with faster broadband pipes and systems such as BitTorrent, downloading movies is becoming more feasible.[35]

Still, there is evidence to suggest that a reasonable amount video file-sharing is taking place. A Jupiter Research survey found that 15% of European Peer-to-Peer users download at least one movie per month.[36] A study by the Motion Picture Association of America found that one in four American Internet users interviewed said they had downloaded movies via the Internet, and 60% of Korean users said they had.[37] These numbers may sound frightening for the movie industry, but keep in mind that one movie download per month is likely to be small relative to both the equivalent music-sharing activity and the number of films the user views legitimately during that period. Moreover, evidence from music sharing has been inconsistent on the critical question of whether Peer-to-Peer file sharing leads to reduced record sales.[38]

If the music experience is any guide, video Peer-to-Peer file sharing is likely to become increasingly popular as time goes on. Efforts by the record industry to limit Peer-to-Peer file sharing through legal actions, including suits against end-user uploaders and software developers, have not significantly curtailed Peer-to-Peer activity.[39] The limiting factors on video Peer-to-Peer trading – principally, the size of the files – will diminish over time. Broadband access providers will offer faster transmission speeds, and software based on video-friendly technology such as BitTorrent will becoming increasingly widely distributed and easy to use. On the other hand, the appeal of downloading commercial video content will be limited until that content can more easily be viewed on a television screen, as opposed to a computer monitor.

Because it so closely tracks the audio Peer-to-Peer experience, file sharing is the least interesting application of video Peer-to-Peer. Whether content owners are successfully able to thwart unauthorized video file trading through lawsuits or licensed downloading services is an important economic and social question, but one being actively considered in relation to audio file sharing. The novel question is whether video Peer-to-Peer will produce something new and different. Even within the realm of file sharing, there are reasons to believe it will.

First off, not all video file sharing involves copyright violations. BitTorrent is widely used for sharing of high-quality audio concert recordings.[40] Many bands have given permission for fans to record and swap concert bootlegs. A network known as etree.org is dedicated to using BitTorrent to share such legal concert recordings, using lossless compression mechanisms that provide higher-quality audio than MP3 or similar formats.

In addition, some content owners are exploring the possibility of using Peer-to-Peer systems to distribute their content, subject to digital rights management restrictions to prevent unauthorized distribution. The BBC has openly discussed the possibility of using Peer-to-Peer platforms for distributing rich-media program guides.[41] Independent film developers may want to release their movies onto Peer-to-Peer networks to build demand, much as some independent bands have with their songs.[42] Peer-to-Peer distribution makes even more sense for small content producers of video than for music, because the content creators can distribute trailers or segments of their works rather than the whole film.

The same platforms will be used for large non-video files, principally software. BitTorrent is used for unauthorized distribution of games and other software. However, as with video, not all the activity involves copyright violations. Some distributors of the Linux operating system now use BitTorrent as a regular method for making new software versions available. Linux distributions can be several hundred megabytes in size, and when new versions are released, high download requests can clog originating servers. By using Peer-to-Peer services, the distributors save on hosting and bandwidth costs to get the software out to users.

Life Sharing

Video is a window on personal experiences. Sharing with someone what you *see* is so much richer than sharing what you hear that it forms a qualitatively different experience. A video clip of you or what you see around you, whether live or transferred asynchronously is a piece of your life. As such, it is likely to be of some interest to your friends and family, but less so to the general public. Personal video communications are not the same as phone calls, as four decades of failed videophone efforts show. Nonetheless, there may well be markets for video Peer-to-Peer life sharing. Content that is of interest to a small audience becomes significant in the aggregate when there are enough originators.

For the first time, many million people now have digital video camcorders, with unit sales exceeding 10 million in 2004.[43] This eliminates one of the hurdles to Peer-to-Peer life-sharing: the capability of encoding video. Because video life sharing is largely a personal experience, it does not require professional quality production values, which are expected for most of the music files shared on Peer-to-Peer networks. All that is necessary is a reasonable-quality recording, which is now widely affordable.

The second element is to get those recordings onto the Internet. Digital video editing software is now inexpensive and easy to use, but that still requires an additional step to transfer the content from a camera to a storage device such as a hard drive or rewriteable DVD drive. Two developments are likely to change the equation: networked video recorders and video cameraphones. A variety of short-range unlicensed wireless technologies, including WiFi and WiMedia, could be employed to transfer data directly from a video camera to a home network server, from which it could be uploaded over the Internet. Or, with a webcam or other built-in video capture device, an existing PC, media, or gaming device becomes a networked video origination point.

The bigger impact may come from the continued proliferation of camera-enabled mobile phones. The mobile phone is the world's most popular personal computing platform, with over 1.5 billion users worldwide. Annual handset sales worldwide exceed 500 million units annually. Handset vendors are now adding applications, data networking, and cameras to phones, turning single function mobile phones into digital smartphones. An estimated 200 million cameraphones will be sold in 2004, compared to roughly 50 million digital cameras and 60 million film cameras (excluding single-use models).[44] That number is expected to grow to over 600 million a year by 2008.[45] Thus, in less than a decade, there will be over one billion users carrying networked digital cameras around with them at all times.

Since video is, in essence, simply a series of still photographs, the basic hardware for a still cameraphone can also handle video. Many existing cameraphones offer video modes, and as resolutions, storage, and wireless network capacity increase, a greater share of cameraphones are likely to offer this capability. The resolution and other capabilities of cameraphones are a function of hardware performance and miniaturization. The information technology industry has developed fabulous expertise in applying standardized processes to improve performance and reduce costs steadily over time. Higher unit sales mean lower per-unit costs. Whatever the price-performance of a video cameraphone today, it is therefore a safe bet that the standard device a year from now will be better, cheaper, or both. High-resolution video cameraphones selling for less than $200, or much less when tied to service plans, are inevitable by the end of the decade.

For the first time, therefore, a substantial and growing audience exists with all the fundamental capabilities necessary for wireless life sharing: video encoding capability, direct network connectivity from the device, and a broadband data pipe. Exactly when and how quickly personal video sharing takes off will depend on other factors, including the pricing and ease-of-use that service providers offer.

What is clear is that people love to share their personal experiences, either with social networks of family and friends, or with anyone who cares to view them. The proliferation of personal World Wide Web pages is testimony to this fact. So are the sales of still and video cameras. As Andrew Odlyzko has shown, "communications" applications involving user-generated content have consistently outpaced services delivering professionally-created content to a passive audience.[46] From giving grandparents who live far away a glimpse of their grandchildren to keeping a running diary of your European trip to showing your doctor what that bump on your arm looks like to immortalizing the time you ran into a celebrity, there are countless situations in which people will want to share their experiences.

Much of this content will only be of interest to a small circle of recipients. That makes it ideal for a distributed Peer-to-Peer environment, with the video files flowing directly between individuals. Making this experience seamless will require new software tools that build on social networking services such as Friendster, Orkut, and LinkedIn. Already, a startup called Ludicorp has developed a social networking service, Flickr, designed around digital photo sharing, and sold it to yahoo! Similar services for video, tied together with other networking features, will be the glue for video Peer-to-Peer life sharing.

Some life-sharing is not, strictly speaking, Peer-to-Peer. Video streamed live from a camera or cameraphone to a server, and then viewed, involves a client-server broadcast model. Apple's iChat DV integrates a webcam and software for real-time video conferencing. Services such as SightSpeed, Viditel, and Convoq support reasonable-quality videoconferencing for both consumer and business applications over ordinary broadband connections. Instant messaging services, such as AOL's AIM and ICQ, Yahoo! Messenger, and Microsoft's Windows Messenger, are adding video chat functionality.[47] As gaming consoles such as the Microsoft Xbox and Sony PlayStation morph into multi-function digital hubs with integrated broadband and media capabilities, they are also likely to serve as real-time video communications endpoints.

Distributed Media

Where life-sharing is episodic and usually directed to a narrow social circle, distributed media involves aggregation of content for and by a wider audience. Until now, media has been centralized. The high fixed costs of producing and distributing content gave an advantage to large entities, such as television broadcasters and cable system operators, who packaged the programming for viewers. Though the media has become more fragmented and somewhat more interactive in recent years, it still follows the same basic template.

Now, thanks to the proliferation of devices and networks described in the preceding section, the ability to create high-quality content is within the reach of a far greater number of people. Drazen Pantic, who created the Internet department of pioneering Radio B92 in Serbia, explained the potential for distributed media in a recent manifesto:

"Today, everyone has access to the latest high quality consumer electronic devices. Every cell phone has the ability to capture images, even movies. Once people begin to use these devices to record the significant events of their lives, there is no way to prevent them from slipping cameras into any location. When sensitive material is captured in digital form, it takes on a life of its own. Circulating across the Internet, it becomes a fact in itself."[48]

Imagine, then, the opening ceremonies of the 2008 Olympic Games in Beijing.[49] Tens of thousands of spectators will crowd into the Olympic stadium, and it is a safe bet that many of them will have video-enabled mobile phones.[50] What they see and hear will be available instantly to many millions of potential viewers, who are no longer limited to the official broadcasts of the games. And this will be the case for unexpected events as well. For any major breaking news story, there will be dozens if not hundreds of potential journalists on the ground, if they care to take on that role.

Another nascent form of video-based distributed media is video-blogging. Blogs, or weblogs, are online personal commentary or diary sites, organized in a series of date-stamped "posts." The vast majority of blogs today are text-based Web pages. However, there is a small but growing community of bloggers whose posts take the form of video. Videoblogs are not Peer-to-Peer today, in that the content is uploaded to a Web server and downloaded from that central location. However, as with all video content, it is possible that in the future the files will be transferred directly between end-user nodes.

The key element in the chain is syndication. Blogs have been the primary driver for the growth of syndication protocols such as RSS and Atom.[51] Using the simple syndication protocols, blog software automatically tags each post with standardized metadata: information such the subject matter, author, and time of posting. Software packages called aggregators can read that information and automatically pull in the latest posts from dozens or hundreds of blogs their users subscribe to. Experiments are underway to integrate syndication and video. Some involve linking RSS with BitTorrent, so that an aggregator would automatically download video content using BitTorrent's efficient Peer-to-Peer technology.

Syndication and its corollary aggregation are the glue that can turn a cornucopia of content around the network into something approaching a unified media experience. Users can subscribe to feeds, either representing content creators they find interesting or new information automatically retrieved that meets certain criteria. Once the aggregator pulls in that latest material, it can be viewed or organized in many different ways, because it is already marked with standard metadata. The full value chain for this new media form hasn't been formed, but companies are working on many of the piece-parts.

The end-product will be a sort of personal TV on steroids. Users will have the ability to select from a vast array of programming that meets their needs, which they can view whenever they choose. Companies such as Tivo[52] and Akimbo are taking baby steps in this direction with their digital video recorders. Akimbo's service, which just launched, allows users to select from a huge library of programming on the Internet and download it directly to a hard drive on the Akimbo box, from which it can be played on a television.

Wireless video Peer-to-Peer distribution may also converge to some degree with interactive and on-demand television. Many vendors and service providers are working on TV-over-broadband offerings that would include far more program choices and flexibility than existing cable and satellite systems. However, these are still centrally managed networks. The content is delivered to the user from a remote server, rather than Peer-to-Peer.

In the interim, video is making its way from traditional broadcast and cable networks to other kinds of devices. Services such as MovieLink offer downloadable movies directly to personal computers. Sprint's MobiTV streams broadcast video directly to mobile phones. And a small startup called Slingbox is building a device that bridges the gap between TV and Peer-to-Peer.[53] The $199 device, scheduled to go on sale before the end of 2004, plugs into a set-top box or digital video recorder. It converts the program signal to digital form, resizes it for delivery to a wireless device, compresses it, and sends it out over the Internet. The user can then watch the program on a mobile phone or handheld computer with a suitably fast wireless connection.

Sling Media is a tiny startup, and it may well face legal obstacles from television and movie industry as it launches its product. Conceptually, though, the Slingbox shows the potential for a new mode of media distribution, one in which content is reflected Peer-to-Peer even if originally delivered through centralized systems. Just as Tivo and other digital video recorders are challenging the advertising-driven economics of television despite still relatively limited sales, the Slingbox model could have significant disruptive impact whether or not the company succeeds in building a business.

Monitoring and Sensors

The final category of video Peer-to-Peer usage may ultimately be the largest in terms of bits, even though much of the content will never actually be viewed. With networked video cameras becoming increasingly cheap and widely available, many opportunities for monitoring will become apparent. Sprint PCS now offers a service called EarthCam mobile, which allows users of certain handset models to view streaming video from any Internet-connected webcam.[54] Security and traffic monitoring are two obvious applications, but there will be many more. Thanks to the WiFi unlicensed wireless protocol, it is now easy to deploy networked video cameras even where wired Internet connections are unavailable.

Some video monitoring scenarios overlap with the life sharing. Networked video-capture devices, such as webcams, can be used for real-time monitoring of family-related activity. The classic example is the so-called "nanny cam," which lets a parent look in on a babysitter or day care center watching his or her children. Unlike the life-sharing applications described above, most of the video delivered in these scenarios will never be viewed. It need not be. With inexpensive networked video cameras widely deployed, the mere possibility than what they record will be of interest will be enough.

In time, more intelligent software will be developed for automatically categorizing, filtering, aggregating, and searching this mountain of video. Excerpts from real-time streams could then be transferred automatically over Peer-to-Peer connections, avoiding the wasted bandwidth of sending the entire stream across the network. Imagine an oil company that wishes to monitor the condition of its equipment deployed in remote locations around the globe. Or a medical service that monitors older people who wish to continue living at home.

As with the life-sharing applications, most content generated through monitoring devices will be of immediate interest to a small audience.[55] However, because the content is generated with little or no human effort, there will be a tremendous amount of it flowing through the network. A Peer-to-Peer architecture, which avoids central repositories on services within the network, would seem to be the only logical approach to take for such information.

Peer-to-Peer Impacts on Networks

What will all this video Peer-to-Peer activity mean for networks? To answer this question, it is useful to divide the network into three segments: private corporate or campus networks (intranets), access networks, and transport networks.

Intranets are feeling strain from Peer-to-Peer traffic because of their relatively limited capacity, especially through the edge gateways connecting it to the public Internet. University networks have been especially hard-hit, because students are heavy users of Peer-to-Peer file-sharing. Many university network administrators have implemented bandwidth caps, terms-of-service restrictions, or other limits to corral Peer-to-Peer file-sharing, because of the network capacity costs rather than objections to potential copyright violations. Video Peer-to-Peer activity will likely increase the strains on these networks. Campuses and businesses that build intranets do so to support the demands of their users; they are not primarily in the network access business.

Access networks also face significant issues from Peer-to-Peer traffic. Capacity on these networks is at a premium. Most broadband operators engineer their networks with significant contention rates, frequently ten to one or more. In other words, the capacity coming into their network is many times smaller than the total theoretical download speed they offer their users. This approach saves on unnecessary capacity investment. It is feasible because not all users access the network at the same time, much of the time they are online they are not actually requesting data, and the access providers consumer terms of service do not guarantee throughput rates.

Wireless Internet connections are particularly ill-suited to handle large volumes of video Peer-to-Peer traffic. Cellular data networks offer substantially lower speeds and reliability than wired broadband access networks, due to the difficulty of sharing capacity over the air. Even newer wide-area wireless data services only offer top speeds of about 200 kbps, and operators frequently enforce monthly caps on data transfers. Thus, although a video-enabled cameraphone is an ideal device for capturing and uploading personal video for Peer-to-Peer distribution, such an application is unlikely to spread widely in the current environment.

This may change as performance of wireless data networks improves, though a more likely path is through alternate distribution mechanisms that do not tax the wide-area wireless networks. Automatic synchronization of media files between the phone and server is one option.[56] Another is to offload the video content from the wide-area network onto a local-area wireless link such as a WiFi hotspot. Dual-mode WiFi/cellular handsets are now coming on the market, and major wireless operators such as Verizon Wireless and T-Mobile operate significant hotspot networks. With wide-area network capacity at a premium, the operators would have incentives, either through service restrictions or pricing, to encourage Peer-to-Peer over WiFi delivery for the video content created through their phones.

Another alternative is to transfer information directly from one phone to another, Peer-to-Peer. With mobile phones increasing in technical sophistication, they could incorporate mesh networking technology to route traffic from device to device, avoiding the central network. Such a configuration would be particularly useful for applications involving video transfers within a limited geographic area.

The problem of video Peer-to-Peer usage is less acute on backbone transport networks. Peer-to-Peer traffic represents about 20% of traffic on Internet backbones, still large but substantially less than its share of access traffic.[57] Transport networks generally are over-provisioned, in contrast to access networks, because the cost of adding additional capacity to fiber-optic backbones is relatively low.[58] The greatest capacity constraint in the backbone is over international links, especially those involving undersea cables or satellite connections. Despite vast capacity increases during the telecom bubble, the data capacity available across the oceans is still far less than in-country for the developed world.

Fortunately, Peer-to-Peer traffic is relatively local. This is so for technical reasons, encouraged by the Peer-to-Peer software itself, but also because of the nature of the content. Popularity of media content often differs from country to country, for language and other cultural reasons. As noted, popularity of Peer-to-Peer file-sharing software also tends to be regional, with eDonkey more popular in Asia and Europe, and FastTrack in the USA. Such regional fragmentation means the Peer-to-Peer traffic itself is more highly concentrated on national or regional backbones, rather than spanning limited international connections.

Symmetry

Beyond the sheer volume of bits, Peer-to-Peer traffic stresses networks by confounding established traffic patterns. Network architects engineer systems based on assumptions about how and when traffic flows. A system used for one-way video broadcasting of a limited set of content, for example, may employ caching servers or a technique called multicasting to eliminate redundant flows of the same traffic. An electronic data interchange (EDI) network for business trading partners, by contrast, will be optimized for relatively symmetric, relatively unique traffic.

Video Peer-to-Peer traffic is inherently more symmetric than the Web and rich media broadcast content that most broadband networks have been optimized for, and its usage patterns differ from the baseline in other significant respects.

Some network traffic flows roughly equally in both directions. The telephone network as a whole, for example, has this characteristic. On average, people make and receive about the same number of calls. In local cases, though, this symmetry does not hold. Ticket agencies, for example, receive many more calls than they make, while outbound telemarketing call centers have the reverse pattern.

When networks designed for one type of traffic encounter a new distribution, they can experience economic and technical problems. Thus, when local phone companies first experienced high levels of dial-up Internet access in the mid-1990s, they complained that the increased number of long, outbound calls to ISPs forced them to make unplanned investments to add ports to their local switches.[59]

Though dial-up Internet connections are exclusively upstream from the perspective of the phone network – people call their ISP, not the reverse – Internet access traffic itself has historically been primarily downstream. Users of the Web request content from Websites. They rarely operate servers which send content out to others.[60] The asymmetry of Internet traffic traditionally tended to *increase* as file sizes grew. Text-based emails are largely symmetric, static graphics are largely sent downstream from Websites, and rich media content is almost always received in one-way broadcast mode.

Broadband access providers have architected their networks to take advantage of this asymmetry. Asymmetric access networks allow providers to save on capacity, improving downstream performance at a lower cost. One of the fundamental properties of information theory is Shannon's Law, which postulates a maximum information carrying capacity for a given communications link. Introducing asymmetry allows communication in one direction to exceed the apparent Shannon's Law limit. Moreover, asymmetric networks simply do not require the same investment in upstream capacity. This distinction is particularly important for cable modem systems. Cable networks were built for television, which is almost exclusively a downstream application.[61] Cable operators have had to spend money upgrading their networks for upstream capacity, which still comes at a premium.

Asymmetric broadband networks offer other benefits to access providers. They may be able to charge premium rates for specialized video, audio, and gaming content that flows down from their servers to their users. Even if they cannot, they have much more control for traffic engineering purposes over traffic that originates in their network or flows in through a limited number of peering points, compared to that originating at a large number of individual users' edge machines.

With Peer-to-Peer traffic, every user is potentially an originator as well as a recipient of content. This is true even when the content is something, such as an episode of *The Sopranos* that end users only intend to view. Most Peer-to-Peer file-trading applications either encourage or require users to upload as well as download. BitTorrent, for example, has a built-in mechanism to incentivize symmetric utilization. This addresses performance issues that hobbled other Peer-to-Peer systems, including early versions of Gnutella.

Moreover, some Peer-to-Peer traffic *is* user-created. This is an important distinction between video and other forms of Peer-to-Peer traffic. Very few ordinary people record and distribute their own music. Quite a few, however, take photographs and shoot home movies. With the plummeting cost of digital video cameras, video-enabled mobile phones, personal computers capable or running powerful video editing software, and storage devices such as rewriteable DVDs, more and more end-users have the ability to be content creators as well as consumers. Thus, video Peer-to-Peer traffic is likely to involve even more upstream activity than music. This poses a dilemma for broadband access providers in the USA, who have uniformly deployed asymmetric access networks.[62]

The symmetry of video Peer-to-Peer traffic will primarily be an economic issue for access networks. Backbone transport networks have always been largely symmetrical, because they aggregate traffic among different kinds of access networks. For every downstream-heavy broadband access service there is an upstream-heavy server farm. And, as noted above, Peer-to-Peer traffic represents a significantly smaller share of traffic on the backbone than on access networks.

Usage Patterns

As discussed above, video Peer-to-Peer file transfers can take many hours to complete. This extended period of activity contrasts with most Web and email sessions, which are relatively short-lived and require active participation by the user. Peer-to-Peer software, especially when used for video, is often left online for extended periods when the user himself or herself is not present. Consequently, the time of day in which the Peer-to-Peer activity takes place does not necessarily track the daylight or work hours the way other Internet traffic does. This confounds traffic engineering metrics that network operators use to allocate capacity.

In addition, users of Peer-to-Peer file-sharing systems typically only download a particular file one time. Once they have the file on their computer, assuming it is complete and functional, there is no reason to download another copy. A movie today will be the same movie next week. The Web is different. The home page of CNN.com six hours from now may be very different than the same page right now. Users download the "same" web page many times, either because it has in fact changed, or to determine whether it has done so. Therefore, traffic patterns on the Web are driven largely by the speed of changes to content. On Peer-to-Peer file-sharing networks, they are driven by addition of new items.[63]

Because of these various differences, Peer-to-Peer usage does not follow the "power law" distribution that marks Web traffic and many other network phenomena.[64] The most popular objects on KaZaA are significantly *less* popular than a power law would predict.[65]

Again, these variations from standard Internet traffic impose costs on network operators by throwing off their models for allocating capacity. Service providers also engineer peering points with other networks in the most efficient configuration, based on traffic flows. As more and more traffic reflects video Peer-to-Peer content rather than traditional Web content, these peering point allocations will also become less accurate.

Likely Consequences and Responses

Video Peer-to-Peer will impact network usage in two ways: by changing what users do, and by changing traffic loads. Both will create incentives for service providers to respond.

Historical network-stressing applications

The rise of video Peer-to-Peer represents the fourth instance that a shift in online usage patterns has created significant new stresses for network operators. In every previous case, the Internet has been up to the challenge. The response to the prior strains did, however, lead to changes in Internet architecture and to Internet economics.

The first situation was the rise of the dial-up Internet in the mid-1990s. The Net was not the first online service, but its scope exceeded anything before. The Internet prior to the emergence of commercial services providers and the World Wide Web was primary designed for non-commercial academic and research users. The growth of dial-up ISPs and the Web created two primary stresses on the extant Internet architecture: telephone switch congestion and peering congestion.

Dial-up users call ISPs through the public switched telephone network, which was engineered for analog voice traffic. The average voice call is 3–5 min, but the average Internet connection is far longer. Phone companies complained to the FCC that dial-up traffic was imposing significant costs on them and threatening to degrade service for other telephone users.[66] In the core of the network, the bottleneck was the limited number of locations, known as Network Access Points (NAPs), where major ISPs exchanged traffic. These open, multi-lateral peering points suffered increase-ing performance problems, leading the largest backbone ISPs to move to bilateral private peering and utilize traffic engineering techniques to route traffic more efficiently. There was also a major effort to construct exchange points outside the USA, limiting the traffic that had to traverse slow and expensive international links.

The second time when Internet infrastructure was inadequate to handle growing demand came in the late 1990s. Internet usage, especially World Wide Web and e-commerce activity, was ramping up explosively and globally. Early broadband deployments added to the load. Even with the sophisticated traffic engineering strategies of the backbone carriers, performance began to slow.

The problem was that any traffic forced to traverse the network to a remote Web serve faces delays, either en route or because the originated Web server was overloaded. The more popular the site, the more serious the problem. The response was the development of content delivery networks (CDNs), the most prominent of which was Akamai. CDNs function as network-wide distributed caches. Popular files are served from caching servers close to the user, rather than from the origin server. CDNs shifted revenue flows among Internet service providers and equipment vendors. They also created a new, albeit distributed, Internet point of failure. If Akamai's network goes down, as parts of it did in early 2004, it is as if the Internet failed.[67]

The growth of Peer-to-Peer networks for music file sharing, beginning with Napster, was the third major stress on the network. Though Peer-to-Peer networks generated a vast amount of traffic, there have been few reports of significant network performance impacts across the public Internet. This is likely due to the fact that Peer-to-Peer arrived on the scene in the midst of a frenzied overexpansion of long-haul network capacity, fueled by the Internet and telecommunications bubble. As fast as Peer-to-Peer file sharing ate up bandwidth, new bandwidth was going into the ground. The one area where Peer-to-Peer is having an impact is on last-mile broadband networks. Phone and cable companies have used terms of service and technically-enforced speed limits to prevent users from extensively sharing files. Nonetheless, many broadband ISPs complain that a small number of users are responsible for a significant percentage of their bandwidth utilization.

And now video Peer-to-Peer seems poised to eclipse all of them, at least in terms of absolute traffic loads. The good news from this historical survey is that the Internet has withstood all the prior deluges. As eminent a figure as Bob Metcalfe, the inventor of the ubiquitous Ethernet networking protocol and founder of network equipment vendor 3Com, predicted that the Internet would collapse under the load of the first growth spurt. He was forced to literally eat his words. In each case, the solution has been a combination of new technology and "throwing bandwidth at the problem."

Responses to Video Peer-to-Peer Traffic

Network operators facing the growing flood of video Peer-to-Peer traffic can and do take several steps to respond. Some of these involve network engineering. For example, the symmetric nature of Peer-to-Peer traffic is likely to cause broadband access providers to peer directly, rather than feeding traffic to peered transport providers.[68] So far, though, the most common responses involve restrictions on user behavior. For example, some broadband providers today limit users' ability to operate servers. These provisions have been used against heavy users of Peer-to-Peer file trading software. Service providers also can enforce caps on upstream traffic to kick heavy video Peer-to-Peer users off their networks.

Deep Packet Inspection and Blocking/Filtering

A new class of "deep packet inspection" hardware promises to identify Peer-to-Peer traffic directly, allowing service providers to exclude it entirely or throttle down capacity available to these applications relative to others. The difficulty up to now has been that Peer-to-Peer traffic does not use standard port numbers, which would allow it to be distinguished from Web or email traffic. The only way to identify Peer-to-Peer traffic is to analyze packets at the application layer, rather than the lower network layers where switches and routers typically operate. Doing so requires hardware able to read packets at extremely high rates of speed, which has only recently become feasible.

Service providers have other reasons to deploy deep packet inspection. The FCC has tentatively concluded that managed voice over IP (VoIP) and broadband access services are subject to the wiretapping obligations of the Communications Assistance to Law Enforcement Act (CALEA). If formally adopted, as seems likely, this requirement will obligate service providers to make their networks amenable to wiretapping of VoIP calls. To do so, however, requires knowledge about which traffic is VoIP – information available at the application layer.

Moreover, broadband access providers may voluntarily deploy deep packet inspection gear for other reasons. Classifying services at the application level potentially allows broadband providers to offer differentiated value-added services and enhance security. It also could be used to identify and either block or degrade third-party VoIP traffic. Though major broadband providers have so far disclaimed any intention of doing so, they may have economic incentives to tilt the scales in favor of their own voice offerings, absent regulation to the contrary.[69] An article in mid-2004 quoted a deep packet inspection vendor who stated that his company was in trials with major cable broadband operators, and that third party VoIP services "raped" the access providers networks.[70] Cisco's acquisition of P-Cube suggests the leading data networking hardware vendors are not ignorant of the potential demand for packet inspection technology.[71]

Service Provider Opportunities

Instead of seeing video Peer-to-Peer as purely a negative development, service providers could exploit it to develop new revenue streams. The "if you can't beat 'em, join 'em" strategy has already been employed on university campuses with regard to music sharing. In a 1-year period beginning in mid-2003, more than 20 universities struck licensing arrangements to grant their students access to Peer-to-Peer music downloads, subject to a monthly fee.[72] In these cases, however, there is proven demand for the application, and the universities are simply looking to manage their networks in a way that avoids both legal complications and excessive costs.

There are, however, reasons to believe that broadband service providers will look for ways to offer video Peer-to-Peer services. As more user activity by broadband subscribers reflects video Peer-to-Peer and related applications, service providers will have incentives to capture more of the revenues from those activities. Broadband services generally involve flat monthly rates with upstream and downstream bandwidth caps. Service providers do not benefit directly when users send more traffic; in fact, they may see such usage as a net loss, because it requires them to provision more capacity. If service providers could realize incremental revenue from video Peer-to-Peer transfers, they would have incentives to invest in the necessary network capacity to support them.

As noted above, there are reasons to believe that a smaller share of video Peer-to-Peer activity will involve unauthorized distribution of copyrighted material than is the case for music. The video Peer-to-Peer content that represents personal "life sharing" activities, distributed media, and monitoring, doesn't raise the intellectual property concerns that dominate audio file sharing. Yet these applications face the same network constraints.

Service providers can offer their customers enhanced service quality, ease-of-use, and additional features such as archiving that would enhance any of these usage scenarios. To the extent users have the opportunity to choose between access providers whose terms of service and affirmative offerings constrain their ability to engage in video Peer-to-Peer activity and those provide premium services tailored to video Peer-to-Peer, market incentives may help create a situation favorable to video Peer-to-Peer expansion. For distributed media, there is an opportunity for aggregation, filtering, and billing service providers who package content and make it available to users for a fee.

Service providers could deploy caches or "superpeers" within their networks to make video Peer-to-Peer file transfers more efficient, while offering their users software packages to take advantage of them. By keeping video

Peer-to-Peer transfers more local, such a strategy would also reduce capacity demands in the service providers' networks, thus reducing costs.

Conclusions

The enduring popularity of Peer-to-Peer file-trading for music, despite intensive legal efforts and licensed music distribution alternatives such as Apple's iTunes, shows that once Peer-to-Peer platforms achieve critical mass, they are virtually impossible to stamp out. In the case of video, the rising sales of video cameras and broadband connectivity seem destined to create the conditions for substantial new applications. Video Peer-to-Peer will place dramatic new demands on data networks regardless of what type of content it carries. And the opportunity to transfer non-commercial content will create new business opportunities and usage shifts.

Given the early stage of video Peer-to-Peer activity, especially in the USA, precise economic predictions are difficult to make. Many factors will influence future developments, including the pace of broadband rollouts for truly high-capacity connections (at least 10 Mbps, and ideally at least 100 Mbps, in both directions); the influence of disruptive actions by non-traditional participants in the networking world, including Apple, Sony, Nokia, and Microsoft; and progress on standardization of short-range high-speed wireless links between media-capable devices. Still, the question is *when*, not *if*. Video Peer-to-Peer is here to stay.[73]

Notes

1. THE BUGGLES, VIDEO KILLED THE RADIO STAR (Polygram 1980). This song was the first music video played on the MTV cable network when it launched in 1981.
2. Peer-to-Peer is a technical architecture in which individual nodes such as end-user personal computers connect with one another directly, rather than to a central switch or server. Peer-to-Peer systems can be used for many functions other than transferring files. For example, Peer-to-Peer architectures are being employed for distributed computing, storage, electronic commerce, search, and business collaboration.
3. Questions about the legal propriety and responses to Video Peer-to-Peer distribution, including matters of intellectual property enforcement, are outside the scope of this paper. However, it is worth noting that the legal standard for contributory infringement by a piece of hardware or software that can be used for copyright violations is whether it has "substantial non-infringing uses." *Sony Corp v. Universal City Studios*, 464 U.S. 417 (1984). If a higher percentage of video Peer-to-Peer traffic is in fact a non-infringing activity, then that may affect the outcome of future legal challenges.
4. Peer-to-Peer systems are also difficult to track because they do not use standard port numbers in communicating over the Internet. Port numbers are supposed to represent different applications; for example, the World Wide Web employs port 80. Not only do different Peer-to-Peer systems not use the same port number, but each client may employ a range of different numbers. This variation is partly for technical reasons of penetrating firewalls and ensuring reliable connectivity, and sometimes for purposes of obscuring activity from network operators or content owners.
5. *See* Andrew Packer, The True Picture of Peer-to-Peer Filesharing, *available at* http://www.cachelogic.com/press/CacheLogic_Press_and_Analyst_Presentati on_July2004.pdf, at 12 (CacheLogic Presentation).
6. *See infra* text at note 67.
7. CacheLogic Announces New Internet Data Analysis Platform, Provides Exclusive Data on Worldwide Peer-to-Peer Usage, press release, July 15, 2004, *available at* http://www.cachelogic.com/news/pr040715.php.
8. *See* T. Karagiannis, A. Broido, N. Brownlee, K. Claffy, and M. Faloutsos, "File Sharing in the Internet: A Characterization of Peer-to-Peer Traffic in the Backbone," UC Riverside Technical Report, 2003, at 11–12.
9. *See* CacheLogic Presentation, *supra* note 5, at 9.
10. Approximately 70% of bandwidth at one cable broadband access provider measured by equipment vendor P-Cube was attributable to Peer-to-Peer. *See* Approaches to Controlling Peer-to-Peer Traffic: A Technical Analysis, P-Cube Technical White Paper, *available at* http://www.p-cube.com/doc_root/ products/Engage/WP_Approaches_Controlling_Peer-to-Peer_Traffic_31403.pdf, (P-Cube White Paper) at 4.

11. J.A. Pouwelse, P. Garbacki, D.H.J. Epema, and H.J. Sips, A Measurement Study of the BitTorrent Peer-to-Peer File-Sharing System, *preprint available at* http://www.isa.its.tudelft.nl/~pouwelse/bittorrent_measurements.pdf, at 13–14.
12. CacheLogic Presentation, *supra* note 5, at 12.
13. Adam Pasick, File-Sharing Network Thrives Beneath Radar, Reuters, November 3, 2004, *available at* http://uk.news.yahoo.com/041103/80/f5x2i.html
14. Exact sizes vary, even for the same original file, based on the compression scheme used and, for video, the resolution of the original. For example, DVDs start at higher resolution than analog formats such as VHS (videotapes) or NTSC (over-the-air television).
15. *See infra* Part V. On the other hand, since a user may view several dozen Web pages in a day, but only download one movie. As bandwidth increases, though, the amount of video content it is reasonable to obtain will increase.
16. Krishna Gummadi, Richard Dunn, Stefan Saroiu, Steven Gribble, Henry Levy, and John Zahorjan, "Measurement, Modeling, and Analysis of a P2P File-Sharing Workload," http://www.cs.washington.edu/homes/gribble/papers/p118-gummadi.pdf, at 2.3.1. KaZaA is a Peer-to-Peer application based on the FastTrack platform. In the USA and much of the world, FastTrack was the most popular Peer-to-Peer file-sharing platform in the years between the shutdown of Napster and 2004, when video-oriented services surpassed it.
17. Organization for Economic Cooperation and Development, "P2P Networks in OECD Countries," pre-release of a section from the OECD Information Technology Outlook 2004, http://www.oecd.org/dataoecd/55/57/32927686.pdf.
18. Peter Lyman and Hal Varian, "How Much Information: 2003," *available at* http://www.sims.berkeley.edu/research/projects/how-much-info-2003/internet.htm.
19. As of January 2004, the USA ranked 11th in per-capita broadband penetration. *See* Jim Hopkins, "Other Nations Zip by USA in High-Speed Net Race," USA Today, January 18, 2004.
20. Regional Characteristics of Peer-to-Peer, Sandvine White Paper, *available at* http://www.sandvine.com/solutions/pdfs/Euro_Filesharing_DiffUnique.pdf, at 5. ("In short, there is more demand amongst European Peer-to-Peer users for video content.")
21. Ramayya Krishnan, Michael Smith, and Rahul Telang, The Economics of Peer-To-Peer Networks, September 2003 draft, at 2.
22. The court's rationale was that Napster provided the "site and facilities" for infringement. *A&M Records v. Napster*, 239 F.3d 1004, 1019 (9th Cir. 2001). A subsequent case involving Peer-to-Peer services without that central directory initially came out the other way. *MGM Studios v. Grokster*, 259 F.Supp.2d 1029 (C.D. Cal. 2003), *affd.*, 380 F.3d 1154 (9th Cir. 2004), but was later reversed by the Supreme Court. *MGM Studios v. Grokster*, 125 S. Ct. 2764; 162 L. Ed. 2d 781 (2005). Moreover, Napster's reliance on a central database meant that once Napster the company was shut down, Napster the service disappeared as well. This is not the case with the newer, more distributed Peer-to-Peer networks.

23. Rich media refers to content that is not static, in other words, sound and video recordings. These objects are inherently sequential and subdividable, which is what allows them to be delivered through streaming. Peer-to-Peer networks are also used to distribute non-rich media, such as photos and software applications, which are outside of the scope of this paper.
24. Digital rights management may be used to limit access to the file or prevent it from being transferred to other users.
25. There are hybrid approaches which provide some of the benefits of file transfer with the immediacy of streaming. For example, a file can be streamed but stored for later playing locally once the entire file has been streamed.
26. The major category of Peer-to-Peer streaming applications are instant messaging applications such as Yahoo! Messenger and Apple's iChat AV, which offer video chat capabilities.
27. Karagiannis et al., *supra* note 8, at 6–7.
28. Variations of swarming technology are used in several research projects. Some commercial ventures, such as OpenCOLA and Onion Networks incorporated swarming. However, BitTorrent is the first implementation of swarming to become popular as a means of distributing files across the Internet.
29. *See* Pouwelse et al., *supra* note 11 (describing BitTorrent architecture and performance).
30. Bram Cohen, Incentives to Build Robustness in BitTorrent, May 22, 2003, *available at* http://bittorrent.com/bittorrentecon.pdf. The standard size is one quarter of a megabyte. *Id.* at 2.
31. Recent versions of eDonkey include a swarm download system called Horde. At this stage, BitTorrent's implementation appears to be more effective, based on anecdotal user reviews and takeup rate. BitTorrent is growing more quickly than eDonkey, and it is used almost exclusively for video and other large files. However, it is possible that eDonkey (or some other platform) will surpass BitTorrent in the future.
32. Eytan Adar & Bernardo Huberman, Free Riding on Gnutella, First Monday, October 2000, *available at* http://www.firstmonday.dk/issues/issue5_10/adar/.
33. The algorithm is based on the well-known "tit for tat" strategy from game theory.
34. Interview Responses From BitTorrent's Bram Cohen, Slashdot.org, June 2, 2003, http://interviews.slashdot.org/interviews/03/06/02/1216202.shtml?tid=126&tid=185&tid=95.
35. The social experience of the two media types is also different. People often listen to music in the background, and they listen to the same song or album many times. Movies, by contrast, require full attention, and are often only viewed once. Irrespective of the technical differences, people typically own more songs than they do movies.
36. BBC News, Films "Fuel Online File-Sharing," July 15, 2004, *available at* http://news.bbc.co.uk/1/hi/technology/3890527.stm. The highest level was in Spain, where 38% of users admitted to downloading movies at least once a month. The rate in the USA was 12%; half the rate claimed in the MPAA study, but still significant.

37. Movie and Software File Sharing Overtakes Music, New Scientist, July 12, 2004.
38. *See* Felix Oberholzer and Koleman Strumph, The Effect of File Sharing on Record Sales: An Empirical Analysis, *available at* http://www.unc.edu/~cigar/papers/FileSharing_March2004.pdf.
39. *See* Thomas Karagiannis et al., Is Peer-to-Peer Dying or Just Hiding, *available at* http://www.caida.org/outreach/papers/2004/Peer-to-Peer-dying/Peer-to-Peer-dying.pdf, at 1. ("In general we observe that Peer-to-Peer activity has not diminished. On the contrary, Peer-to-Peer traffic represents a significant amount of Internet traffic and is likely to continue to grow in the future, RIAA behavior notwithstanding.")
40. For example, ETree (http://bt.etree.org/index.php) is a site specifically for high-quality recordings of concerts by artists who expressly permit their fans to record and share their performances.
41. Lucy Sheriff, BBC Ponders Peer-to-Peer Distribution, The Register, February 17, 2004, http://www.theregister.co.uk/2004/02/17/bbc_ponders_Peer-to-Peer_distribution/.
42. The appeals court in the Grokster case pointed to one prominent example, the band Wilco, in justifying its conclusion that the Peer-to-Peer software had substantial non-infringing uses. *Metro-Goldwyn-Mayer Studios, Inc. v. Grokster Ltd.*, 380 F.3d 1154, 1161 (9th Cir. 2004).
43. Reuters, Canon to Pull Out of Analog Camcorders, May 12, 2004, http://reuters.com/newsArticle.jhtml?type=technologyNews&storyID=5115158 (stating that Canon expects sales of 2.6 million digital camcorders in 2004, representing 20% of the global market).
44. Nokia's Ollila Says Global Mobile-Phone Users Reach 1.7 Billion, Bloomberg News, November 3, 2004 (estimating sales of 200 million cameraphones in 2004). Camera Phone Sales to Outstrip Film, Digital, PhoneContent.com, August 14, 2003, http://www.phonecontent.com/bm/news/gnews/camera.shtml (comparing cameraphone sales to film and digital cameras).
45. Dinesh C. Sharma, Study: Pretty Picture for Camera Phone Sales, CNet News.com, March 11, 2004 *available at* http://news.com.com/2100-1041_3-5172377.html.
46. Andrew Odlyko, Content is Not King, *First Monday*, February 2001, *available at* http://www.firstmonday.dk/issues/issue6_2/odlyzko/.
47. A study by the Pew Foundation, based on data from February 2004, found that 42% of American Internet users, representing 53 million adults, used instant messaging. *See* Pew Internet & American Life Project, How Americans Use Instant Messaging, September 1, 2004. Five percent of those users, or nearly three million people, claim to use instant messaging to send music or video files. Even higher percentages, including 21% of respondents of age 18–27, and 12% of those of age 28–39 said they used streaming audio or video to see or hear people they instant messaged.
48. Drazen Pantic, Anybody Can Be TV: How P2P Home Video Will Challenge the Network News, http://journal.planetwork.net/article.php?lab=pantic0704.

49. I first heard this scenario from Jonathan Schwartz, President of Sun Microsystems, at the Supernova conference which I organized in June 2004.

50. China is the largest mobile phone market in the world, and with its vast population, it lead seems certain to grow in the years ahead.

51. RSS stands for either "really simple syndication" or "rich site summary." There are several variations of RSS, and the competing Atom protocol is similar in its basic approach. Both are built on the extensible markup language (XML).

52. Tivo purchased a startup called Strangeberry that was developing technology to integrate Internet content with television. Kim Gerard, Saving TiVo, Business 2.0, September 2004.

53. Elizabeth Corcoran, Shifting Places, *Forbes*, August 2004.

54. Sprint Launches New Live Webcam Application for Mobile Handsets, http://144.226.116.29/PR/CDA/PR_CDA_Press_Releases_Detail/1,3681,111 2170,00.html

55. The exception is information such as live traffic pictures. Such content is a perfect fit for the syndication/aggregation model of distributed media.

56. Mike Masnick, Taking The Upload Out Of The Camera Phone Process, The Feature, http://www.thefeature.com/article?articleid=100917&ref=2725973, July 24 2004 (describing a startup called Cognima that offers mobile synchronization software for cameraphones).

57. Karagiannis et al., *supra* note 8, at 12.

58. Moreover, the locality of much Peer-to-Peer traffic means that a relatively small share traverses long-haul network backbones. Gummadi et al., at 5.

59. Kevin Werbach, Digital Tornado: The Internet and Telecommunications Policy, FCC Office of Plans and Policy Working Paper No. 29, March 1997. It is not clear that this argument was justified. The FCC declined invitation to impose per-minute access charges on the ISPs, which the phone companies argued would compensate them for their increased costs. In time, complaints about switch congestion died down.

60. The commercial Website operators typically use specialized Web hosting providers who offer high-capacity outbound links under a significantly different pricing framework than that available to individual end-users.

61. Cable TV networks have a limited upstream channel for telemetry and basic interactive functions, but this alone is insufficient for any Internet usage.

62. Karagiannis et al. at, *supra* note 8, 11 ("Technologies such as DSL and cable modem were quite sufficient when downstream throughput was the main concern. Their attractiveness will fade and their market share dwindle if alternative broadband technologies are deployed that offer comparable upstream and downstream performance.").

63. Gummadi et al.

64. Albert-Lazlo Barabasi and Reka Albert, Emergence of Scaling in Random Networks, Science, October 15, 1999, at 509.

65. Gummadi et al., at 2.3.3.

66. *See* Digital Tornado, *supra*.

67. Paul Roberts, Akamai outage hobbles Google, Microsoft, others, Infoworld, June 15 2004, http://www.infoworld.com/article/04/06/15/HNakamaioutage_ 1.html.
68. Karagiannis et al., *supra* note 8, at 11.
69. *See* Tim Wu and Lawrence Lessig, Ex Parte Submission in CS Docket No. 02-52, *available at http://faculty.virginia.edu/timwu/wu_lessig_fcc.pdf*
70. Eric J. Savitz, "Talk Gets Cheap: Internet telephony is bad news for the Bells, but maybe great news for the cable guys," Barron's, May 24, 2004.
71. *See* Reuters, Cisco to Buy P-Cube for About $200 Million, August 23, 2004.
72. John Borland, College Peer-to-Peer use on the decline? ZDNet, August 24, 2004, *available at* http://zdnet.com.com/2100-1104_2-5322329.html
73. Kevin Werbach is an Assistant Professor of Legal Studies and Business Ethics at The Wharton School, University of Pennsylvania. Email: kevin@werbach.com.

5

Peer-to-Peer Video File Sharing: What Can We Learn From Consumer Behavior?

John Carey

Fordham Business School

It is difficult to assess the adoption path for media technologies and services that are very new, as is the case with Peer-to-Peer video file sharing applications. Many critical elements will affect how the services grow. These elements include technology development, regulations, business investment, competition, advertising revenue, content models, and consumer appetite for the new services. Other chapters in this volume address many of these issues. Here, the emphasis will be on content models and consumer behavior.

A starting point in this assessment is current media behavior by consumers. What types of video files are consumers currently downloading and sharing? Are there overt needs that video file sharing meets? Are there latent demands that could grow into video file sharing or current behaviors that might be transferred to this new activity? For example, will large numbers of people who like to take cell phone photos and send them to friends, use the latest generation of cell phones to capture short video clips and share these files with friends? How many of those who have digital still cameras with video capability are using this new feature? Will the instant messaging craze among teenagers expand into video instant messaging? Are people who once recommended TV programs to co-workers at the water cooler ("Water Cooler TV") now passing along clips of favorite shows in email? In general, how much of video file sharing is new, disruptive behavior and how much a transfer of existing behaviors into the video file sharing realm?

E.M. Noam and L.M. Pupillo (eds.), *Peer-to-Peer Video*, doi: 10.1007/978-0-387-76450-4_5,
© Springer Science + Business Media, LLC 2008

Beyond the questions associated with consumer behavior, what types of content do people want to share with others – clips from a child's Little League game, frivolous behavior of teenagers at a party, movies and TV programs, pornography, video blogs (Vlogs), webcams of a beach, or other content? Who is creating the content – amateurs, large media production groups, government, or education groups? There may be many surprises, for example, a summer camp that takes videos of campers and posts them on the Web for parents to share.[1] Why do ordinary consumers and other non-professionals create videos? Is it a lark, a component of social networking, a desire to become a professional video producer, or to gain status on a video-posting site by having enough viewers to achieve a level of prominence within the site? New technologies enable new forms of video file sharing, e.g., monitoring household security cameras from a cell phone while traveling or creating web-based television programs from amateur videos that consumers share with a producer, and these are being tested in the marketplace.

History also provides clues. For example, there has been much discussion about a new generation of videophones that allows the sharing of live video or video e-mails between people or groups.[2] The videophone has been introduced a number of times over the past four decades and has failed each time. A group-to-group version of the videophone, often called video teleconferencing, has achieved moderate usage.[3] However, those who have promoted each new generation of videophone have claimed that the problem in the past was poor video quality, the new technology has improved video resolution, and this will lead to broad acceptance. Research about videophones indicates that there are many other obstacles to wide acceptance such as a feeling of embarrassment in being seen.[4] Perhaps all of these obstacles will be overcome and a generation that grew up with instant messaging will embrace video messaging, but it would be foolhardy to ignore the lessons from the past.

In order for Peer-to-Peer video filing sharing to grow into a mass medium, consumers must have the tools and bandwidth to support it. How many households have broadband access to the Web (A majority of US households at the end of 2007, or, two-thirds of households with Web access, and projected to grow to more than 70 million by 2010)? Video file sharing is not limited to the PC, but also includes devices such as advanced cell phones, video MP3 players, and personal video recorders (PVRs). These devices are growing in penetration, for example, the PVR was in an estimated 22% of US households at the end of 2007 and is projected to grow to 33% by the end of 2010.

The core concept of Peer-to-Peer video file sharing is not clearly defined and many academics as well as industry groups disagree about the scope of activities it includes. Video file sharing overlaps with the more general category of Web video viewing. People can access video by downloading or streaming from a content producer's site such as CNN.com; download or stream from a content aggregator such as YouTube.com or social networking sites such as MySpace; receive videos attached to emails or instant messages; and use Peer-to-Peer networks such as BitTorrent to access videos. While the definition of Peer-to-Peer video should not be so wide as to include any form of video sent over the Web or other digital network,[5] it may be appropriate at this point to define it loosely. For example, there is likely to be much interaction, both positive and contentious, between the sharing of video files among people and the publishing or transmission of video content by traditional sources such as broadcasters and movie distributors. Similarly, institutions such as universities and government agencies are likely to be sources for video files that are shared among consumers. In this sense, video file sharing goes beyond consumer-to-consumer and includes business-to-consumer, business-to-business, entertainment companies-to-consumer, government-to-consumer, and institutions (e.g., universities)-to-consumer.

The Technology Context and Behavior Indicators

Peer-to-Peer video file sharing must grow in a context of transmission networks that support video (e.g., broadband Web access and advanced digital cell phone networks), access/storage devices that can accommodate video (e.g., PCs, DVDs, advanced cell phones, PVRs, and portable media devices), players or software that can download and display video (e.g., RealPlayer, iTunes and Windows Media Player), and, for some applications, technology that can capture or create video (e.g., digital camcorders, Webcams, digital cameras with video-capture capabilities, and PCs with video editing software).

In many ways, the context of equipment and networks to support video file sharing is strong. By the mid 2000s, a majority of US Web usage at home was from households with broadband Web access, and the penetration of broadband has continued to grow. There are also high penetration rates for digital camcorders, digital cameras, and DVD players. These technologies tend to cluster in the same set of households, i.e., broadband households have more digital camcorders, DVD players, and digital cameras than dial-up households.[6] Further, broadband households do much more video downloads than dial-up households. Video player software is also ubiquitous on computers. DVD burners, PVRs, and cell phones with video capture or playing capabilities are in fewer households, but they too are growing in penetration. Similarly, cell phone networks in the USA are being upgraded and a number of companies have begun to offer video services for cell phones.

If much of the enabling technology and transmission networks for video file sharing is in place, what about consumer behavior? Are people using these technologies to access and watch video? Video streaming has grown sharply over the past few years, rising more than tenfold between 2000 and 2006. Many of these sites receive very high volume of usage – some download hundreds of millions of videos per month.[7] The types of video content consumers are accessing through video streaming include short clips (the average viewing time is 2 min per clip): music videos, sports highlights, and news stories. Some longer form video streams have increased in usage, e.g., downloading of TV shows. There is little evidence so far that many consumers are directly sharing large video files that they created (e.g., emailing them to family members), such as highlights from a vacation. The capability to share very brief video files taken with advanced cell phones has increased. However, most sharing of amateur-produced video is passed along through postings on file sharing sites such as YouTube or social networking sites such as MySpace and then telling friends where they can access the videos. There is also much sharing of "hot" video clips and uploading of video clips to news sites when there is a disaster. The former included a *Saturday Night Live* clip of Ashley Simpson caught lip synching and a clip of Jon Stewart clashing with the host of CNN's *Crossfire* on *The Daily Show*.[8] These were transmitted as attachments to email or links within email by millions of people. Examples of the latter included thousands of postings to news sites by people who shot video clips of the tsunami in the Indian Ocean and the London underground bombings. All forms of postings and retrievals help increase the number of people with the skill set to create, transmit, find, and view Peer-to-Peer video.

There are indicators of a potential latent demand for video file sharing based on some current activities. For example, many consumers share music files, send photos to others, refer friends to Web sites with cartoons or photos, and lend tapes or DVDs of movies and TV programs to friends. Does this indicate a latent demand to share camcorder tapes of family events, cell phone videos of a party, music videos, television programs, and movies? Probably yes, but the scope and size of these forms of video file sharing are difficult to estimate. It is important to examine some of this behavior more closely. For many consumers, it is relatively easy to take some digital photos, select a few of the best shots, and send them to someone else. It requires much more work to edit a videotape and send a video file of the edited version to a friend or family member. Downloading songs, compiling a song list, and sharing the file with others requires a modest amount of work. However, music listening is highly repetitive, justifying the work involved. Will the same work-to-reward ratio hold for music videos that may not be viewed as repetitively? In the case of television programs and movies, there is a high value in being able to share the video files with others. What is unclear, however, is the work, cost, and risk (in the case of pirating copyrighted work) involved. In some cases, such as using Tivo to capture, store, and share a television program, it appears that the work, cost, and risk is low.[9] In other cases, such as burning a DVD of a television program on the first generation of DVD burners then transmitting it over the Web, the work, cost, and risk were high. As the cost of DVD burners decreased and the user interface improved, the attractiveness increased.

Early Adopters: A Younger Generation

It is typical for the first group of users for a new technology or service to be different from later groups when adoption of the technology has spread widely.[10] In the past, early adopters of new electronic technologies have typically been males in their late 30s to early 50s, with high income. However, with broadband Web services, early adopters of many applications have been younger, more diverse in terms of gender and with a greater range of household income.[11] This has been the case for Peer-to-Peer video file sharing as well. The author conducted a study of the media habits of a core component of these early adopters – those between 18 and 34.[12] What are their media usage habits and how does Peer-to-Peer video file sharing fit into their existing habits?

In trying to understand the media usage patterns of this group and their interest in video file sharing, the place to start is not technology but lifestyle – where and how they live, and the ways lifestyle affects media usage. First, they have very hectic and irregular schedules. Much of their media use moves later into the evening and their apartments are crammed with media options: multiple TVs, PCs, cell phones, videogame consoles, and MP3 players. In order to reach them, media have to fit flexibly into their irregular schedules because they may not be available when regularly scheduled media are playing. Peer-to-Peer video file sharing is an effective way to do this since it is predominantly unscheduled – a user can access a file at any time.

Second, the settings where most 18- to 34-year-olds live, work, or attend school are different from the images we have of average American households, offices, or colleges. By virtue of their age, most are just starting out in life, so they typically have smaller office and household spaces. Yet, they are generally well equipped with media. Further, many 18- to 34-year-olds use media in public locations such as a gym, sports bar, or coffee shop. A number of these locations are well equipped with media and young people often bring their own media to these locations. In addition, it is very common for people in this demographic group to carry media such as a cell phone or an MP3 player with them wherever they go. This generation has come to expect pervasive access to media and demand portability. So, access to video files is not an obstacle for this group. These experiences in turn shape attitudes about media and have led to some important changes. For example, many young people in the author's research indicated that they have easier access to the Web than to a newspaper, reversing earlier notions that newspapers are portable while computers are a burden to lug around.

The college environment has changed significantly compared to a decade ago. Access to the Web, through wired and wireless broadband networks is pervasive – by one measure, more than 80% of college students have broadband access to the Web.[13] Students can access the Web in drop-in labs scattered around campuses, library carrels, hallways outside of classes that are equipped with rows of computers, lounge areas near dining halls, and ubiquitously throughout dorms. In addition, some campuses have wireless wide area networks so students can access the Web virtually anywhere on campus via a laptop computer. A more subtle change is the use of better speakers on most computers compared to a few years ago. This relates to the growing use of computers for entertainment and video is a significant part of their entertainment experience on the Web.

Equally startling to an observer who attended college 10 or more years ago, cell phones are everywhere. As students exit a class, it is common for half of them to go on their cell phone; some professors schedule cell phone breaks during long class sessions to keep students happy. The cell phone as well as MP3 players/iPods further strengthen the core expectation of this young generation for portable access to media. In addition, this group replaces their cell phones frequently and wants the latest generation of the technology, which now includes access to video.

At the same time, the core functions of Web video are not very different from the core functions of television: escape, entertainment, and information. They watch Web video to escape from everyday tedium and enter a fantasy world that is fun and offbeat, or for simple entertainment such as music videos and TV programs. In addition, Web videos keep them informed about the world around them through news, weather, and sports.

The Web is perceived by this group as convenient, customizable to personal interests, and giving people control over content. One young woman said, "It gives me what I want, when I want it." MP3 players are characterized by their portability, depth, and control. Cell phones are characterized by their portability, instant communications, and lifeline to a person's network of family and friends. In addition, many are using added features of cell phones and perceive it as a multi-application device. All of these attitudes influence their expectations for Peer-to-Peer video file sharing.

What matters a great deal in the current media environment for 18- to 34-year-olds are their schedules and place in life, and the ways these interact with the media that are available to them. Media that are relatively schedule-free fit more easily into the irregular schedules of many 18- to 34-year-olds and the narrow slices of time available to others. Downloaded and streamed video files fit flexibly into the lifestyles of 18- to 34-year-olds – they can access desired content at any time.

College students in particular have been among the earliest adopters of video file sharing. Gali Einav conducted a study of the file sharing habits and attitudes among college students.[14] She found that nearly all of the students did some form of file sharing. Further, video file sharing was very common in dorm settings. Students did file sharing for reasons of convenience, control, and immediacy. They also used file sharing to check out new content before buying it – a form of sampling. Very few were concerned about copyright issues.

Who are the early producers of Peer-to-Peer video files? Reviewing the current scene of Web videos that are created by people outside established media companies shows that they include video bloggers, underground filmmakers, political activists, and amateur videographers. Much of this content is satirical or self indulgent, for example, political satire, funny pet videos, and karaoke-style musical performances. These appeal to the tastes and sensibilities of a younger audience.

There are two others groups who create and share video files over the Web with consumers. One group is businesses that create and share promotional content as well as many forms of consumer information as video files, e.g., a video tour of a hotel resort or a video about how to build a patio. Businesses also create video training materials for employees and share these across the Web to sites in multiple locations. The second group is institutions such as universities that create and share video courseware, distance learning materials, and video newsletters, e.g., a video of a college lecture or a video of the groundbreaking ceremony for a new building on campus. Much of this content falls below the radar of media analysts because it lacks the star power or broad appeal of entertainment content.

Clues from the International Scene

The USA does not lead in many areas that are crucial to the development of Peer-to-Peer video file sharing. Finland, Norway, and Japan have higher ratios of broadband to narrowband Web users; Korea leads the USA in penetration of advanced cell phones[15]; and the UK is more advanced in the development of interactive television applications that could be adapted for broadband Web file sharing.[16]

Are there lessons to be learned from these countries about applications that are likely to take hold in the USA? Certainly, some applications have migrated from foreign shores to the USA in the past. Text messaging migrated from Europe and Asia to the USA. Cell phone photos migrated from Japan to the USA. It is important to monitor video file sharing activities outside the USA. However, this analysis requires at least two filters. The first is cultural. Different cultures may adopt or reject a technology, or differ in how they use it, based on how they perceive privacy, personal space, individual expression, and other values. For example, in Japan it is common for teenagers to decorate their cell phones with tassels, stickers, and other symbolic objects, treating them as an icon of personal expression and displaying them prominently for others to see.[17] There is no equivalent in the USA, although specialized ringer tones add some degree of personalization to cell phones and have been very popular.

In the case of shared video files, the question is how they might serve as an expression of values for different groups within each country? Do people place a value on the number of files they have accumulated (as in the case of music files), securing taboo content such as pornography, or sharing pirated content because it is illegal? A second filter is the existing infrastructure in each country. There are many differences between the USA and Europe in attitudes about new media based on the history of earlier technology deployments, e.g., interactive television services have developed more quickly in the UK than in the USA in part because they had a lower installed base of PCs and broadband Web, making the television a natural host for interactive video services. In the USA, these services are spread across a wider range of technologies. In the case of Peer-to-Peer video file sharing, there are many technologies that can act as a host for the video files, but the deployment of these technologies varies widely, e.g., in the USA there is very high penetration of PCs but a relatively low penetration of PVRs.

It is also likely that video file sharing will cross national boundaries. The USA is a major exporter of television programs and movies. These transactions are controlled by contract and regulations, although piracy is a significant problem, e.g., pirated DVDs of movies. Video file sharing via the Web adds new opportunities, complexity, uncertainties, and greater risk of piracy. On the one hand, countries with higher penetration of broadband such as Japan and Korea provide millions of potential consumers of US video content. On the other hand, copyright laws differ from country to country. The Web crosses national boundaries with impunity and makes copyright law difficult to enforce. Much Peer-to-Peer video file sharing is pirated content from international sources such as China.[18] Attitudes about piracy also differ internationally. Jonathan Marks' research indicates that in some countries where people pay a license fee for television, many young people feel they have a right to download any content from file sharing sites since they have already "paid" for it.[19]

The Importance of Mobile Access to Media

One important value that is affecting the development of Peer-to-Peer video file sharing is mobile access to media. Over the past decade, we have become accustomed to accessing a number of media in mobile settings. These include cell phones, laptop computers, TVs in airports, building lobbies, and sports stadiums, WiFi hotspots and cybercafes, portable DVD players (including rental units at airports), MP3 players, and two-way pagers. More recently, the list of mobile media has expanded to include satellite radio and entertainment centers for cars, and a new generation of portable media players. Further, many new services have emerged to serve these mobile media technologies, e.g., TV programs, video blogs, and even pornographic movies for cell phones.[20] It is unclear which of these new services for cell phones will succeed. Early research suggests slow growth and a number of obstacles such as a need for longer-lasting batteries that do not drain quickly when used for video.[21]

It is important to ask how this reliance on portable media and expectation for media access just about anywhere will condition demand for Peer-to-Peer video file sharing? One piece of the equation is the presence of so many mobile technologies that could be used to access, store, or display video files. Another piece is how these technologies have conditioned the habits and appetites of those who are saturated with mobile media content and services, for example, an appetite for using a laptop computer as an entertainment device and expecting access to entertainment just about anywhere. The context of media access may, in turn, affect what types of content are consumed in these settings just as the television content consumed by one person in a kitchen setting often differs from the type of content consumed by a family group in a living room setting.

There are many issues associated with style of use. First, what is the role of these video sessions in everyday life? In general terms, they are for entertainment and information. However, a closer examination of usage suggests that many sessions are to kill time, take a break from work, check out the latest sporting news or music video, or simply a habit that has started to develop. It is also a conversation starter, as in the case of students who show sports clips from a video cell phone to buddies at school as a way to start a conversation about sports.

Some people use mobile video device as an alternative to Tivo or a DVR. That is, they use it to time shift their viewing of a favorite program because they were not available to watch it at its scheduled time. Just as ease of recording is very important to Tivo use, convenience and ease of downloading is very important to those who use a mobile video device for time-shift viewing. Perceived control is another important attribute of mobile video. In the author's research, people have indicated that they feel more in control of what they are watching on their mobile video device compared to regular TV. Part of this perception is freedom from the TV schedule. Another element is the perception that video files from the Web are uncensored and there is a wide variety of content.

The overall design and screen size for mobile media devices have a strong impact on content that users will download. In the case of video cell phones, the small screen size limits the length of time people are willing to watch content – it leads to eye strain. For this reason, most content is short clips, including some original TV series with 60-second episodes. The screen size also makes it difficult for users to find content. Often, they must navigate through many layers of menus to find specific choices.

The Role of Interactivity and Mashups

In trying to assess the value of interactivity in Peer-to-Peer video file sharing, it is useful to begin by examining the ways in which people currently interact with media and interact with each other through media. There is much more interactivity in our media environment than appears at first glance. The Web is inherently an interactive medium. This includes person to person interactivity in the form of e-mail and instant messaging (IM) and the interactivity that takes place in navigating across and within Web sites. Cell phone conversations, text messaging, and videogames are also highly interactive. Sharing music files involves some interactivity through the process of sending and receiving the files, but the music content is not generally interactive.

Most video file sharing has the same low level of interactivity as music file sharing. However, this could change, depending on the actions of content producers and consumers. In the UK, the BBC set up a "Creative Archive" that gives Web users access to video files and encourages them to re-mix or otherwise interact with the content to enhance and customize it.[22] The term "mashup" has been coined to describe this type of content editing. In Europe, interactivity has been built into a number of programs and these could serve as models for interactive Peer-to-Peer video, e.g., *9Live*, a German call-in quiz show that generates millions of calls at 49 Euro cents per call.[23] This form of interaction has migrated to the USA in shows such as *Deal or No Deal*.[24] There has been some experimentation in bringing interactivity into American television, e.g., by MTV and Fox Sports,[25] but overall interest in European style interactivity has been modest. Many American distributors of programming perceive video-on-demand as a form of interactive television. This has been a common model for video distribution on the Web and advanced cell phones. However, this may change over time as a generation that is comfortable with file sharing and interacting with technology begins to control more of household spending.

Content Models

Starting from the perspective of current and past consumer behavior, it is possible to create models for Peer-to-Peer video content sharing. Notice in the examples below that most do not involve direct consumer to consumer file sharing. Often, there is a media organization that enables the file sharing, whether for a consumer-created video or content created by professionals.

Live Video Interactions

Videophone calls between people, as a form of video file sharing, appear to face long odds given the past history of videophones. However, there may be new versions of videophone calls that will be adopted. For example, instant messaging (IM) that has become so popular with younger audiences could evolve into video IMs. Similarly, some e-mails may evolve into video-mail. This form of video file exchange in non-real time may help to overcome the concerns of people in the past that they might get a videophone call while they were not dressed or otherwise didn't want to be seen.[26] Further, the Web can provide a cheaper alternative to business videoconferencing that is currently used by many companies.

Home Videos

Sharing home videos with friends and relatives faces a few hurdles. Digital camcorders have been widely adopted. However, it is not clear how many people edit their home videos. Photos are inherently easy to edit: a person selects from the photos he shot and sends them to a friend or relative. However, editing video footage is time consuming and requires special software. Sending an hour of unedited footage of a vacation or Little League game requires a lot of bandwidth and may lack appeal. This could change if new software emerges that makes it very easy to edit video footage or pull out a clip from a longer tape and send it as an email attachment. The current generation of cell phones and digital still cameras includes many models with a capability to shoot brief video clips and email them to friends. These models, typically with no editing capability, are popular with teens who readily adopted still photo emailing. Many of the postings to sites such as YouTube are short videos from these sources.

Niche Services to Build Awareness and Appetite

There are many services that have demonstrated modest (or, in some cases, wide) appeal but which collectively can build awareness and interest in video file sharing. These include short underground films, video blogs, and video promotions/press releases. Since these applications are promotional for the producer, it is less likely that there will be restrictions placed on the sharing of content among consumers. Some of these applications have become fads and generate "buzz" among peer groups. This could lead to broader interests in video file sharing. For example, in 2006 movie trailers and clips for *Snakes on a Plane* were released well before the movie. Fans did mashups of scenes, mixing actual footage from the movie with their own videos and distributed these widely on video blogs and file sharing sites. One person created a mashup that caught the attention of the producers and they shot a new scene for the movie based on it. This generated further publicity. This type of fad helped the movie in this case, but it can be hard to replicate.

Institution or Business-to-Consumer

There are many applications of video file sharing that have received relatively little attention but which build on existing services and needs. Many of these involve institutions such as universities or business services. These include distance learning, tapes of classroom lectures, video newsletters, guest speakers at universities, and business training tapes. These can be downloaded from an institution, then shared among people with no, few, or strong restrictions. In addition, security companies can distribute tapes of homes or businesses to appropriate parties who wish to monitor them. These can be powerful forces that introduce the concept of video file sharing to broad audiences who may then adopt other applications in the home. In the past, many technologies such as computers and cell phones were first adopted in business or education, and then moved into households.

Pornography

Adult content has been a part of the launch for many new technologies and services, from videocassettes to paid Web content, and it is a significant component in Peer-to-Peer video file sharing. It is often a greater share of content overall during the initial stages of a new technology introduction. Over time, the share of adult material diminishes as more mainstream entertainment applications grow. In the early stages of Peer-to-Peer video file sharing, x-rated movies, amateur adult content, and pornography for cell phones are readily available.[27]

Mass Entertainment

A conservative perspective on the demand for Peer-to-Peer shared content suggests that over time people will want to share the same content they currently watch at great length – movies and television programs – and those amateur videos will have a relatively small role in file sharing. Some will disagree with this. With mass entertainment, there is uncertainty about the principal way in which the content will be distributed over time. Will it be part of a store-and-forward service such as Tivo, video downloads from traditional distributors, or through (legal or illegal) video file sharing services? Other chapters in this volume address the many technical and copyright issues associated with file sharing of mass entertainment content.

In the first few years of video file sharing, much of the mass entertainment video that was offered consisted of movie trailers and promotions for TV shows. Many branded video producers such as TV networks and movie studios actively encouraged viewers of a clip to email a friend and include a link to the clip. More recently, some full length movies and many TV programs became available. Traditional video producers also serve as a re-distributor of some amateur video content, much as they have packaged some amateur content in programs about silly pet tricks or funny home videos. News programs re-distribute amateur videos by inviting people to email videos shot at the scenes of disasters and other breaking news events.

Generally, the mass entertainment industry for video content has accepted the Web as a distribution and file sharing medium in ways that the music industry resisted for years. However, the business plans for video content, for example, free with advertising or paid content as well as digital rights management models, are still evolving.

Creative Surprises

Whenever new services are launched, the opportunity emerges for new forms of content to be created. One interesting and highly creative form of video on the Web is long form commercials-on-demand such as those created by American Express and BMW. Peer-to-Peer video file sharing may encourage the creation of other new content forms that cannot be predicted but which emerge as creative people get their hands on the technology. One example is "machinima," a mixture of video gaming and cinema. Many video games such as Quake allow users to capture and edit a section of game play, then share the file with friends. They are a form of underground film and have developed a modest, cult-like following. There is an annual film festival for machinima and a Web site (Machinima.com) that serves as a portal to game-based films.[28]

Short form advertising is another wild card. As video commercials evolve on the Web, will they be the same type and length as appearing on television or will new, more entertaining commercials emerge to keep the Web user engaged? Will viewers who now tell friends about funny or interesting television commercials they have seen, send a file of the commercial to friends in Web environment? Some Web advertising has encouraged this practice.

As video files have proliferated on the Web, video search engines have followed. These include major search engines such as Google and Yahoo, which have developed a separate search engine for videos as well as smaller, independent groups, and search capabilities on video file sharing sites such as YouTube. As video files proliferate, search engines will be challenged to sort through millions of videos to return what users are seeking.

Obstacles

There are several potential obstacles to the mass adoption of Peer-to-Peer video file sharing. The first is price: what price are consumers willing to pay for content that they can share with others; and, what price will video distributors charge? A combination of "Web think" (i.e., "we don't pay for content on the Web") and unrealistic pricing by video distributors could slow adoption. At a practical level, will pay-per-view or a subscription model or free with advertising be more attractive to consumers? A second issue is complexity – will consumers be able to download and share video files without taking a 10-week course about how to do it. The devices for sharing files vary enormously in ease of use. Some, e.g., Tivo, iTunes and the current generation of video players for PCs, have received reasonably high marks for usability while others, e.g., the first generation of DVD burners, were panned by reviewers. Related to this is interoperability – will files move across devices transparently or will proprietary hardware and software restrict where video files can be stored and how they can be accessed? Many portable video players have followed the model of music players and made it difficult to download files from many sources. Legitimate concerns about piracy by copyright holders could also lead to draconian protection mechanisms that discourage people from using services at all. In this sense, will the Motion Picture Association of America (MPAA) follow in the footsteps of its counterpoint in the music industry, the Recording Industry Association of America (RIAA), which has sued thousands of individuals who engaged in music file sharing? There is some reason for optimism that video piracy will not be as harmful to copyright owners as music piracy. First, it is more complicated and time consuming to download long-form video compared to audio. Second, in the author's research with 18- to 34-year-olds, many indicated a fear that Peer-to-Peer file sharing sites with pirated content were often a source of viruses and were avoided for this reason.

The quality of video over broadband networks is also an issue. While video quality over the Web has improved significantly over the past couple of years, there is a great deal of variability in the quality of video experienced by consumers. This relates to a few factors including the speed of connection, the method of accessing video (e.g., streaming versus downloading), and the technical configurations of host servers. None of this is obvious to an average consumer who simply wants good video, just like TV. The quality of the user experience will also be affected by the length of time to download a file. This can vary enormously, depending on the size of the file and how the file is sent, from a few seconds to many hours. Badly produced videos are common on the Web, especially those produced by amateurs. The occasional gems that attract enormous publicity and usage are buried in a sea of boring and inane video content. Users need ways to sort the wheat from the chaff.

In the mobile video arena, obstacles include batteries that drain quickly when used for video, small screen size, poorly designed menus, and glare in some outdoor settings. Laptop computers are the most robust for storing and watching videos but they are heavy compared to other players. MP3 players with video capability and portable media players are a reasonable compromise. Cell phones are the most challenging in terms of screen size and menus. Further, if a cell phone battery drains, a person loses his connection to the world, not just music playback as with MP3 players.

Discussion

The development of Peer-to-Peer video file sharing will continue to evolve over time. It is important to distinguish applications and service features that have been adopted early in the process from applications and feature that will take time to develop. In the near term, it is likely that most shared video files (for PCs) will be shorter and work effectively in media player windows that are less than full screen. So, movie trailers and promotions for TV programs are easier to implement than full-length movies and TV programs. Many video applications for cell phones are rough approximations of where the technology is likely to be in a few years. Tivo-based shared networks support high quality video files. Over time, each of these video file sharing networks will support better quality and longer form video. In addition, there are currently many different content providers, from video bloggers and underground filmmakers to major entertainment groups. If history is a guide, a number of these early groups will fade away over time and mass entertainment will dominate in the longer time frame.

A core issue is whether the early users, applications, and devices will build towards a critical mass in which a large group of consumers develop an appetite for video file sharing that can spread with its own momentum and lead to a greater range of users and applications. Rogers has demonstrated that this pattern has occurred frequently with other innovations that were subsequently adopted by the mass market.[29]

The concept of Peer-to-Peer video file sharing also raises the question: which groups are targets for these services? There are many natural groupings based upon particular services, e.g., sports fans, movie buffs, alumni of a college, and business colleagues. These are likely to be younger people in the near term. The use of the Web as a network for file sharing suggests that the reach of Peer-to-Peer file sharing will span great distances. However, we should not ignore Peer-to-Peer file sharing within households or a neighborhood. Currently, much videotaping of television shows is by one household member for another person in the same household or friends at school.

There are many other uncertainties surrounding Peer-to-Peer video file sharing. One is whether many Web services will add video over time and if a mass audience of consumers will embrace video on the Web? Personal computer applications evolved from spreadsheets to word processing to email to entertainment. Will people who collect and share music files want to do the same thing with music video; will the millions of people who share photos over the Web share home videos? The actions of major video copyright owners are also uncertain. Will they embrace or fight video file sharing? Will major networks adopt the BBC model (i.e., the Creative Archive) and put some content into the public sphere, encouraging people to edit or alter it? Further, will they re-edit existing content (or create new content) and create video files of different lengths and with new forms of advertising, as American Express and BMW have? Will more media organizations encourage the public to send them video files and use them to create programming, either in the tradition of funniest home videos, news, or interactive programming?

In order for a mass audience of consumers to have a positive experience with Peer-to-Peer video file sharing, a number of pieces have to come together: continued expansion of broadband into homes; improved compression techniques to enhance video quality; interoperability among devices to access, store, and display video files; broadly accepted, safe, and secure intermediaries (i.e., player software and re-distributors) for video files; the availability of high quality content and special interest video; acceptable pricing; and well-designed user interfaces for hardware and software. Bringing video files into mobile environments is also likely to boost consumer appeal.

Video file sharing has been enhanced by the same types of support services that have made Web text browsing more appealing, i.e., video portals, search engines, and video content aggregators. A number of these have already been created, e.g., MSN and AOL have created video portals and a number of video content aggregators serve as an intermediary between consumers of various types of videos such as sports, news, independent films, and amateur videos. Some of these have evolved from photo post-and-share sites to video post-and-share. Further, a number of video search engines have emerged, including major search organizations such as Google and Yahoo, along with smaller, niche video search sites.

Does video Peer-to-Peer video file sharing pose a threat to major brands of video such as TV networks or movie studios? Putting aside the issue of pirating branded content, it does not appear that file sharing poses a threat to major brands. On the contrary, much of the content that is downloaded is from branded sites and viewing files from branded content providers appears to boost interest in the movies and TV shows from which they were excerpted.[30] Branded content providers also serve as enablers in the sharing of amateur content and search engines for video files.

Peer-to-Peer video file sharing is a fast moving target. A few years ago, it was barely on the radar and consumer experience of video, e.g., with dial-up networks, was poor. Today, it is in the marketplace and many consumers are actively sharing video files. If the pieces come together and no major obstacles slow it down, the novelty of video file sharing will likely become a core habit and Peer-to-Peer video will become a mass medium.[31]

Notes

1. Bonnie Morris, "For Fretful Parents, Online Postcards From Camp," The New York Times, July 29, 2004, p. G-5.
2. William Bukeley, "Better Virtual Meetings," The Wall Street Journal, September 28, 2006, p. B-1; Almar Latour, "Videophones: The New Generation," The Wall Street Journal, July 26, 2004, p. R10.
3. Robert Johansen, Teleconferencing and Beyond: Communications in the Office of the Future. New York: McGraw-Hill Publications, 1984.
4. A. Michael Noll and James Woods, "The Use of Picturephone in a Hospital," Telecommunications Policy, March, 1979, pp. 29–36.
5. See A. Michael Noll, "Internet Television: Definition and Prospects," in Eli Noam, Jo Groebel and Darcy Gerbarg (eds.) Internet Television. Mahwah, NJ: Lawrence Erlbaum Associates, 2004, pp. 1–8.
6. Ian Austen, "More Speed, More Stuff," The New York Times, September 6, 2004, p. C-5.
7. Kevin Allison and Richard Water, "MySpace Videos Most Watched," The Financial Times, September 23, 2006, p. 23.
8. Antonio Regalado and Jessica Mintz, "Video Blogs Break Out With Tsunami Scenes," The Wall Street Journal, January 3, 2005, p. B-1.
9. Based on the recent Ninth Circuit Court of Appeals ruling in San Francisco. See Nick Wingfield and Sarah McBride, "Green Light For Grokster – Federal Appeals Court Rules File-Sharing Program Makers Aren't Violating Copyright," The Wall Street Journal, August 20, 2004, p. B1.
10. See Everett Rogers, Diffusion of Innovations (Fourth Edition). New York: The Free Press, 1995.
11. For a treatment of the Web habits of 18- to 34-year-olds, see John Carey, "What I Want, When I Want It: Understanding The Media Usage Patterns of 18 to 34 Year Olds." New York: The Museum of Television and Radio, 2004.
12. Drivers and Barriers To Online Video Viewing. New York: Online Publishers Association, 2005.
13. Stephen Baker, "Channeling The Future," Business Week, July 12, 2004, pp. 70–72.
14. Gali Einav, "College Students: The Rationale For Peer-to-Peer Video File Sharing," presentation at Columbia University, September 10, 2004.
15. Seah Park, "Expanding Cells," The Wall Street Journal, July 26, 2004, p. R-10.
16. Gali Einav, Content, Demand and Social Implications of Interactive Television. New York: Columbia University Ph.D. Dissertation, 2004, Chapters 5–6.
17. Laura Forlano, "Wireless, Time, Space, Freedom: Japanese Youth and Mobile Mania." New York: Columbia University Department of Communication, 2003.
18. Geoffrey Fowler and Sarah McBride, "Newest Export From China: Pirated Content," The Wall Street Journal, September 2, 2005, p. B-1.
19. Jonathan Marks, Critical Distance, Volume 2, Number 6, July, 2005, p. 3.

20. See Walter Mossberg, "Watching TV on Your Cellphone," The Wall Street Journal, September 1, 2004, p. D-7 and Richard Wray, "Video Blogs Go Mobile in 3G Trial," The Guardian, February 23, 2004.

21. Knowledge Networks/SRI research cited in Media Daily News, July 11, 2006, p. 1.

22. "BBC Creative Archive pioneers new approach to public access rights in digital age," BBC Press Release, September 3, 2004.

23. Kevin O'Brien, "German Quiz Shows Thrive As Contestants Stay Home," The New York Times, August 9, 2004, p. C-8.

24. Anne Becker, "Text Messages 2 good 2 b tru," Broadcasting and Cable, September 25, 2006, p. 1.

25. Karen Brown, "Fans Show Their Best Game Face," Cablevision, April 24, 2000, p. 60.

26. Michel Marriott, "Waving Hello, From a Distance," The New York Times, November 25, 2004, p. G-1.

27. Jennifer Schenker, "In Europe, Cell phone Profits Go Up As Clothes Come Off," The New York Times, May 4, 2004, p. G-5.

28. "Deus ex Machinima," The Economist, September 18, 2004, p. 3.

29. Everett Rogers, op. cit., pp. 313–328.

30. Knowledge Networks, op. cit., p. 1.

31. John Carey is Professor of Communications and Media Industries at Fordham Business School. Email: johncarey@fordham.edu.

6

College Students: The Rationale for Peer-to-Peer Video File Sharing

Gali Einav

NBC Universal

"In this generation it's just something that people do" (John, 19, English Major)

Peer-to-Peer networking is not a new concept within the academic world. Universities have been utilizing the Peer-to-Peer architecture for decades. Before the advent of the world-wide-web in the 1990s, the original ARPANET connected UCLA, Stanford Research Institute, UC Santa Barbara, and the University of Utah and allowed direct information sharing between researchers.[1] Programs such as Bitnet allowed electronic communications between academics worldwide much earlier than e-mail and Instant Messenger.

College campuses have also provided a robust breeding ground for content file sharing. Napster, one of the most popular Peer-to-Peer programs used to share music files was developed by Shawn Fanning while a freshman at Northeastern University and was introduced in May 1999. By end of that year, Napster's membership had risen to millions – thanks to word of mouth advertisement at colleges and universities worldwide.

Peer-to-Peer file sharing is a growing phenomenon. By the end of 2004, it represented 60% of internet traffic,[2] with approximately one in four internet users who have downloaded movies and nearly two out of ten current "non-downloaders" likely to start downloading in the future.[3] The amount of television show piracy increased to 150% from 2003 to 2004, from 6–14%.[4] The number of downloaders can be expected to rise with the increase in Broadband subscribers and more internet users experiment with the technology.

E.M. Noam and L.M. Pupillo (eds.), *Peer-to-Peer Video*, doi: 10.1007/978-0-387-76450-4_6,
© Springer Science + Business Media, LLC 2008

File sharing is not necessarily seen as illegal copyright infringement. A MPAA worldwide internet piracy found that almost half of respondents believed it is acceptable to download movies after theatrical release and before DVD release. As for television, 50–80% feel it is legal to copy and share television programs they recorded.[5]

Peer-to-Peer usage is seen to be influenced by age. Internet studies show that the vast majority of file sharers on the internet are among the 18–29 age group.[6] Within internet households, those who house 18- to 24-year-olds are twice as likely to file share and download videos.[7] Examining the behavior of this age group can provide interesting insights into the current and future file sharing trends. Therefore college campuses, which allow students both access to the technology and a social breeding ground for Peer-to-Peer usage habits, provide an interesting case study for the examination of file sharing.

College students are a huge community, reaching approximately 14 million undergraduates in the USA.[8] A United States General Accounting Office report to congressional requesters from May 2004, states that 90% of students file share. Pew internet research shows that 80% of students don't care if the files they share are copyrighted.[9] College students are, in the most part, early adopters of technology, who have grown up with the internet. A constantly connected generation, many college students start their Freshman year as savvy file sharers, while for others, campus life provides their initial gateway into the Peer-to-Peer file sharing world.

Given this backdrop this research set out to examine the reasons for video file sharing among students, better understand how they share and shed light on their attitudes towards the technology and behavior. It also set out to inquire whether file sharing will be a habit students will continue beyond college years, thus potentially creating changes in future media consumption. This can have vast implications for content providers who are in a constant struggle with users on the other end of the computer screen.

The following are observations based on 15 in-depth interviews with students from six universities in the New York, Boston, and Washington, DC areas. The study was conducted in Aug–Sep 2004 and is an attempt to provide directional insights into behavior and attitudes of college students regarding Peer-to-Peer video (television and film) file sharing as well as their future expectations from this medium.

College Students: A Whole New World

"It's a great way to connect with friends." (Jay, 20, Computer Science Major)

"When I go to party and they hear that I don't download, it affects my social life. They look at me like I have three heads." (Michael, 19, Engineering Major)

Visiting a college campus today is a different experience than one might remember. A haven for the early adopter, it provides a gateway into a world of technology and connectivity over a myriad of devices such as laptops, cell-phones, and iPods. The social environment feeds and exposes students to new technologies and behaviors, file sharing being no exception.

Students interviewed for this study mentioned that file sharing is "something they just do" because other people around them do as well. This often creates awkward social situations in which those who do not engage in this kind of activity are seen as social outcasts. This doesn't necessarily deter the students who decide not to download due to a combination of moral qualms or just plain disinterest, but can make it difficult for others who just want to blend in. Those who don't engage in sharing do not try to convince the others to stop. They believe that although most students agree that it is wrong to file share, they will continue if they can get away with it, which they so often do. Attempts to change this behavior are seen as futile.

Video File Sharing – How?

"Give and ye shall receive." (Bram Cohen)[10]

"The University does a good job in protecting us. Outside we can get into trouble." (Eric, 20, Engineering Major)

Colleges and universities provide very easy access to file sharing. T-1 and T-3 internet connections provide fast, easy, and reliable internet connectivity. Students find it easier to hide behind a "university hub" that awards them the anonymity they crave on the web. Many of them feel protected by the university, enough to file share without thinking about the consequences.

Additionally, file sharing programs such as BitTorrent and DC++, which were mainly used by students interviewed in this study, operate without any involvement from central computers, making tracking individual users more difficult. Students download the programs on their laptops through their school hub and they are ready to go.

Since BitTorrent's architecture breaks the files into small "bits" and allows uploading of content while downloading, it ensures that the more files a user is willing to share, the faster any individual "torrent" will download to their computer thus preventing people from "leaching," i.e., downloading files and refusing to upload.[11] When asked about their download time, students said that by using BitTorrent or DC++ they can download a full length movie in less than half an hour. A half hour television show can download in minutes.

Many students said that they are connected to about 200 other university students simultaneously. They don't necessarily see it as a community tool for meeting people but a great way to connect with their friends, sharing their favorite videos among them. They believe that a file sharing community is possible, but anonymity is much more important. It is also very important to them to know that the file comes from a trusted source.

The scope of downloading is impressive. When asked how often they download video, students ranged between 1 program a week to 300 movies per semester. They create their own collections which they take wherever they go. As for storage, an important issue in crowded dorm rooms, students keep their content either on their computer drives or on CDs, depending on file size. Some only keep the rarities since content is easily accessible through Peer-to-Peer whenever they need it. Movies are not typically stored on a computer, since they take up a lot of storage space due to their file size. Many watch and delete them. Those who do decide to keep their favorite movies burn them on DVDs and create personal collections.

Main Reasons for File Sharing

"I never don't find what I'm looking for." (Katie, 19, Cultural Studies Major)

Convenience, Immediacy, and Instant Gratification

"I can't wait a week." (Michael, 21, Communications Major)

Contrary to what might be the first thought that comes to mind, the main reason students file share is not the cost, but the convenience. File sharing allows them to watch what they want and when they want to watch it.

Their viewing has to fit into their personal schedule. Immediacy and instant gratification are very important factors for them. They will download a TV show which hasn't been released on a DVD and they feel there is no other way to get it. They don't like to follow schedules and therefore will not wait for the summer for reruns of their favorite shows to air.

Many of the students don't have a TV set in their dorm room, and use their laptop/computer as their main viewing screen. They will download shows so they will have something to watch while in their rooms. Some reasons for downloading are more mundane. One student mentioned that he downloads movies because the video store would not allow him to rent since he didn't have a proper credit card. The student turned to file sharing to find the same movies, this time for free.

"Quality Control"

"I hope people stop paying for bad movies – it will make the movie business better." (Katie, 19, Cultural Studies Major)

Many students see file sharing as a form of "Quality Control." They want to sample the offerings and will not pay for them until they are sure they like them. Since most of them are on a tight budget they feel that it would be just a waste of money for them to go to a movie if it is not one hundred percent something they would like to see. This doesn't necessarily imply that students are watching fewer movies than they did before. Some students stated that through file sharing they are exposed to content they wouldn't previously consider watching, broadening their offerings. On the other hand, file sharing has been assisting in turning these students into more selective consumers, which expect a taste or preview of the content before they pay for it.

Promotional Value

"It's actually good for the studios." (Kristin, 19, Music Major)

Many students interviewed believe that file sharing is a very convenient way to introduce friends to new content, therefore, emphasizing the promotional value in their sharing activities. This also allows for rationalization of Peer-to-Peer sharing, since students believe they are promoting the content and not stealing it. In that sense, they see video file sharing as enhancing the entertainment business rather than disrupting it. Students feel that instead of fighting it, the best thing for the media companies to do is to make it flourish and utilize Peer-to-Peer networks to promote their offerings. Some mentioned that if networks would offer cancelled shows, for example, online, they would profit.

What content do college students share? Mostly, whatever interests them. They share episodes of favorite television shows previously viewed or missed. They are interested in re-runs, canceled shows, or any show which particularly appeals to them. In this study the most shared TV content mentioned was HBO's "Sex in the City," Fox's "Family Guy" and Bravo's "Queer Eye for the Straight Guy." One student mentioned that most recently he looked for, and found, a documentary on Noam Chomsky that he was interested in seeing.

When it comes to movies, the main content shared is new releases. The students interviewed were more likely to share to "check it out" for quality control to see if it's worth going to the theatre for. Interestingly, file sharing for "sampling content" did not replace going to the movie theatre or buying the DVD. Going to the movies was seen as a totally different experience that students aren't looking to replace. It also did not replace the purchase of a DVD. Students will buy a DVD of content they liked and wanted to keep but also to enjoy the additional features which provided an extra value that would justify the purchase. File sharing of movies did replace the trip to the DVD rental store, which was seen as an inconvenient and costly alternative.

Cost

"It's not so much the price, but the convenience." (Violet, 19, Music Major)

Avoiding paying for content is not a main reason that students file share. While some students did state directly that they would not pay for content over the internet, the majority of students interviewed clearly stated that they will pay for compelling content, good quality and no "annoying" limitations, specifically the ability to keep the content indefinitely. They will also pay to feel safe from computer viruses typically transmitted through file sharing programs.

Students did feel that they were not willing to pay much for content due to the financial constraints of student life. Some said that they would probably pay more when they have a job, but the basic idea of finding a way to access content for quality control and convenience would not change for them in the future.

In order to pay for content, price has to compare or be lower than a DVD rental, setting the bar to approximately 3–5 dollars per movie. As for television shows, most agreed that they would pay between 99 cents and 5 dollars per episode or series bundle.

Students also stated that they would pay more (between 5 and 10 dollars) for hard-to-get content such as cancelled TV shows or old classic movies or documentaries that are difficult to find through other venues.

Students welcomed innovative solutions. For example, they expressed interest in a service that will allow them to rent movies online and then stream them on their computers.[12] Most students liked the ideas of the iTunes music purchasing model describing it as a great example of a legal and cheap file sharing model.[13]

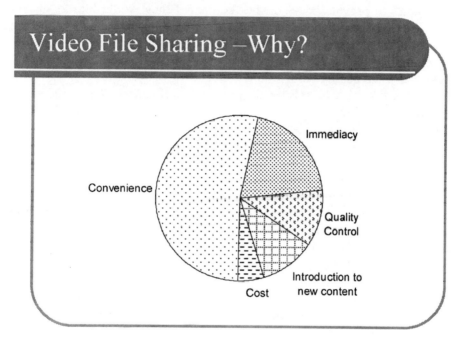

Fig. 6.1 Main reasons for file sharing

Moral Attitudes

"Someone has bought it and then decided to share it. You should be allowed to share it." (Nate, 20, Computer Science Major)

The majority of students interviewed do not have moral qualms about copyrights or revenue loss. On the contrary, they see big media companies as money making conglomerates, full of executives earning six figure salaries, who are making a hefty profit as is. They also believe that when they pay, their money doesn't channel directly to the artists but to the managers and offices that want to increase their profit.

As for television, the notion that TV is "free," despite the existence if subscription multi channel models still prevails. Therefore, they do not feel compelled to pay for it. Additionally, students could not think of many successful models for paying for content over the internet that they have ever previously used.

Many students admitted that they don't lose sleep over the fact that file sharing is illegal. They feel that they are supporting the artists that they do like by buying their CDs or DVDs, and feel that it is up to the media companies to provide better quality content if they would like to sustain the business. Some believe that music downloading has actually done the music industry a service and apply that example to video file sharing, believing that the movie industry can benefit as well since there are many "less than great quality" movies out there.

Qualms are closely related to personal preferences. One student, a classical music lover and violin player, said that she would never download "anything classical" because it is dear to her heart, but as for movies, if it's not a good movie, she wouldn't care, since she doesn't believe people would see it anyway.

Interestingly, many students mentioned that file sharing for them is a way to earn back their consumer rights which they feel have been taken away from them. They oppose the media companies' treatment of file sharers as "criminals," referring to some tactics used by content companies, explaining that it is unfair to consumers which are not given adequate alternative legal and cheap options to acquire content.

In their world of convenience and choice in media consumption, they feel they should not be forced into purchasing content they are not interested in, whether it is a full album for the one song they like, or a full price movie theatre ticket or DVD rental for a movie they are not sure they want to see.

Students believe that in the long run people will always find a way to access the content for free; therefore, it is up to these companies to develop methods to allow consumers to pay a reasonable amount of money for quality.

University Involvement

"It's really weird to be downloading SouthPark and have my parents pay for it." (Laura, 19, Physics Major)

Universities had attempted to develop collaborative solutions to address illegal file sharing on premises.[14] One suggested solution was for universities to negotiate deals with content companies to directly purchase content from them which will be offered to the students. Fees will be paid to the online service by the university; the service will pay royalties to copyright holders. The cost would then be factored into the tuition.

Students interviewed in this study were ambivalent towards these attempts. Some thought it was an excellent idea allowing the universities to point out the legal options that students have to keep using the file sharing programs, which they felt were the easiest to use to access content. Therefore, if the university could purchase the content and then give it to subscribers at subsidized rates they would endorse it.

Others either oppose having file sharing related to tuition or believe it just would not make a difference. Those students saw it as a waste of efforts, since there will always be those who will continue to file share and while it might partially prevent students from pirating content they will continue to do so if they could not find the content they are looking for. They also felt that these attempts are a bit patronizing since they would like to be the ones to decide what content they want to pay for. Some just didn't think it is appropriate for any form of file sharing to be affiliated with their education. They would only find it appropriate if the content downloaded would be a class requirement.

The Future

"As long as the software exists I don't think you can eliminate it completely." (Jay, 23, Engineering Major)

College years are seen as habit forming years by the students interviewed. Many students, both those who entered college with the Peer-to-Peer knowledge and those who were introduced to it for the first time during these years, believe that after 4 years, they will continue to file share, mainly for entertainment purposes.

The reasons for continuing to file share differ among students. Some out of habit, some would do it because it's available. There seemed to be a unanimous belief that there will always be those who will file share and that with increased technology the amount of sharing will increase as well.

Those who believe that they will discontinue file sharing, did not explain it for moral reasons, but also due to technological difficulties such as slower cable connections once they leave the campus. They also feel that at home the behavior is more likely to be detectable, which is a strong deterrent. They do feel that they will continue to use models such as iTunes, which allows legal and cheap content downloading.

Statements regarding future behavior are difficult to validate. Although it is probable that many will continue to file share after graduation, it will be interesting to track whether their media sharing habits will change with the time constraints that a demanding job and family life bring with them.

Discussion

File sharing is very common on college campuses. Students share content mostly for the convenience and immediacy and less due to the price.[15] Very few are concerned about the legality of sharing copyrighted material. Students view sharing, on the most part, as a form of sampling content to determine purchase intent. They lean towards the promotional value in file sharing, rationalizing their behavior in the belief that downloading and sharing video files will eventually enhance the entertainment business rather than disrupt it.

The study shows that while college students are still interested in television and movie content, the consumption and distribution models have changed. While video file sharing does not replace going to the movie theatre or purchasing a DVD, the study found that it does replace DVD rentals. However, most students interviewed admitted that they will pay same or less than rental for the convenience of accessing good quality content on their computers. As for television, in many cases the laptop replaces the television set within the dorms and students are looking for content to fill the screen, either catching up on existing shows without abiding to schedules, or enjoying content no longer available on air.

Looking into the future, students believe they will continue to file share after graduation. In many ways it is their way to oppose what they see as the dominance of media conglomerates by allowing them certain control over how much they contribute to the wealth of media companies.

Media companies are facing a challenge of providing this content to students while managing digital copyrights and revenue models.[16] Most students expressed interest in legal file sharing models that will allow them to access the content safely, and for a reasonable price. They expect media companies to treat them with respect rather than as thieves and provide models that will allow them legal and cheap access to video content. Apple's iTunes model was mentioned as a great example of a creative solution.

The overall agreement that file sharing will continue to grow as the technology develops and broadband penetration rises, creates a challenge for media companies. Not to say that they should not fight the phenomenon of piracy. There have been recommendations for creating educational Ad campaign to fight file sharing, but it would also be wise that media companies tap into these students online expertise and their willingness to pay to provide legal outlets for the students out there looking for content. This would allow college students to feel they are being treated with more of the respect they crave and in the long run, might yield better results in this battle.

The promotional value of Peer-to-Peer students mentioned should not be overlooked as well. Students can be introduced to new content which they will share with their friends, creating opportunities for reaching new or additional consumers. Entertainment companies should take notice of the appetite that exists for video content. Rather than fighting the phenomenon, new business models should be explored. Utilizing the Peer-to-Peer technology, especially second generation such as BitTorrent, in a legal way can be extremely helpful to utilize college students' expertise in a productive way. It is also helpful as a distribution system that will help, in this growing world of streaming content, to manage the interest in content without clogging the sites as in the case of providing multiple streams, thus allowing for a more robust online experience.

While revenue will always be lost to file sharing, there is an opportunity to capitalize on existing content. Providing good quality content for a reasonable price can prove very beneficial to media companies. They could capitalize on content which is currently not in use such as cancelled shows, and reruns, creating catalogues of content that students will be willing to pay small amounts for. Offering promotional segments from movies can help boost movie and DVD sales to a certain extent. It is important, however, that media companies assure that they own the digital distribution rights of their content.

Some networks are already trying to set up their own Peer-to-Peer networks to provide legal and hopefully profitable alternatives to video file sharing. The BBC, for example, is utilizing BitTorrent technology to provide free downloads of their programming.[17] Fox is looking at creating a youth skewed portal that will allow to download the company's film and television properties via Peer-to-Peer technology. In November 2005, NBC Universal and WurldMedia, the creator of the legitimate Peer-to-Peer service Peer Impact, announced an agreement that would make Universal movies and NBC Universal TV events available to Peer Impact customers on demand. Users would even be rewarded for sharing. By leaving their computers on they can be selected to receive "Peer Cash" that may be used towards future purchases.

In this world of file sharing many additional challenges arise. There is a need to better understand how students find the content they are looking for and how to promote content to that audience. Networks of the future might be morphed into content aggregators that distribute shows in Peer-to-Peer video torrents and sells ads or subscriptions to its portal.

Media companies would be wise to attempt to bridge the psychological gap that exists between them and file sharing students and try to change the way they are perceived by these students shake off their reputation of money making conglomerates.

There might be a long way to go to bridge the gap between media companies and the way the college students view them, as money making conglomerates. Earning the respect of the young consumer in this generation where power is transformed to consumer is a challenge for media companies. How to do that successfully is an interesting question for the future.[18]

Notes

1. See http://iml.jou.ufl.edu/projects/fall02/Moody/History.html
2. http://www.cachelogic.com/
3. See OTX/MPAA WorldWide Internet Piracy. Additionally, according to a Harris Interactive study, while Yahoo (33%) and Google (28%) are the top sites among those who only get free video downloads, 23% of respondents mentioned file sharing services as their main sources for free video downloads.
4. According to Envisional, sharing American Television content is a global phenomenon. Most Peer-to-Peer file sharing of television programs is done in the UK (16%) with 7% of traffic originating from the USA.
5. See OTX/MPAA WorldWide Internet Piracy Study and Gartner RSA Executive Briefing, 2004.
6. According to the Pew Internet and Life study, 2003, 82% of file sharers are 18- to 29-year-olds.
7. According to a Gartner Study, while a total of 19% of online households surveyed downloaded media from Peer-to-Peer networks, 41% of respondents, ages 18–24, said their household downloads media from Peer-to-Peer networks. 23% of the 18–24 age group downloaded video compared to 10% of the 25–34 age group, and 7% all. See "Free Downloads Depress U.S Online Purchases," Kydia Leong, Gartner Dataquest 7/8/04.
8. US Census Bureau; http://www.census.gov
9. Pew Internet and Life (July 2003).
10. See Clive Thompson, "The BitTorrent Effect," Wired, January 2005, p. 153.
11. See Wired, January 2005, p. 153.
12. Since the completion of this study, in September 2004, IP Video on demand models have been further explored by media companies.
13. As of Sep 2004, Video downloading via iTunes was not yet available.
14. In Aug 2004, a joint committee of the higher education and entertainment communities issued a report to congress on their latest efforts to curb illegal file sharing on college campuses.
15. Other studies have shown that another reason for illegal file sharing (movies mostly) is access to R rated movies. (UK TV addicts won't endure the lag time before episodes of new US hits air in Britain 9 like Desperate Housewives and 24) (Envisional, 2004, Television Piracy, Aug 2004).
16. Online advertising models were not discussed with students in this research.
17. The BBC made use of the Kontikis file sharing system in summer 2004 to send TV shows to 1000 households. See Jeff Howe, "The Shadow Internet," in Wired Jan 2005, p. 155.
18. Gali Einav is the Director of Digital Technology Research at NBC Universal. Email: gali.einav@nbcuni.com.

References

Envisional, "Television Piracy, An Envisional Briefing Note," Aug 2004, http://www.envisional.com

GAO, Report to Congressional Requesters, "File Sharing, Selected Universities Report, Taking action to Reduce Copyright Infringement," May 2004.

Gartner, RSA Executive Briefing, 2004, http://www.gartner.com

Harris Interactive, Entertainment On the Move: Video Downloading and Portable Entertainment, April 2006.

Jeff Howe, "The Shadow Internet," Wired, January 2005, pp. 155–159.

Madden Mary, Pew Internet & American life Project Memo: Music Downloading, File Sharing and Copyright, July 2003, http://www.pewinternet.org

Matt Moody, http://iml.jou.ufl.edu/projects/fall02/Moody/History .html

OTX, MPAA, Worldwide Internet Piracy Study, 2004.

Clive Thompson, "The BitTorrent Effect," Wired, January 2005, pp. 151–154, 178.

7

Peer-to-Peer and User Generated Content: Flash in the Pan or the Arrival of a New Storytelling Paradigm?

Steven Rosenbaum

Magnify.Net

User generated content (UGC) is driven by two factors – Technology and Community.

As we've reached the tipping point in the deployment of core technology that facilitates content creation and sharing, it's easy to theorize that technology is the key driver.

But I'd propose a different analysis. An analysis based on almost 15 years of experience developing environments that foster the creation of User-Generated Video.

So let's jump back in time, and I'll explain the evolution of UGV in its formative stages, and how what I learned in the early 1990s can help us understand the current explosion in UGV and the likely path it will take forward.

Back in the early 1990s, I was running a company that had broken new ground in local and then regional news magazine television. *BROADCAST: New York* was a weekly half hour television program syndicated throughout New York State. The program was seen by and large on NBC stations at 6:30 on Saturday evenings. It had a large following, had won two Emmy's, and had a staff of smart, hard working, young storytellers who were driven to explore ideas and issues in new ways. We'd defined a community (New Yorkers) and created a market for both content and advertising. The consumer Internet didn't exist. Neither did local cable news. These were early days. But magazine television programming was

E.M. Noam and L.M. Pupillo (eds.), *Peer-to-Peer Video*, doi: 10.1007/978-0-387-76450-4_7,
© Springer Science + Business Media, LLC 2008

"hot" and both network and local stations were adding programs. Increasingly, as the program's Executive Producer, I felt that the stories we were reporting weren't breaking new ground. Some months earlier we'd put in place a rather expensive 800 number so that viewers could call in and record a "letter to the editor" response to our weekly broadcast. We were getting 40 or 50 calls a week, and we'd choose the most interesting calls to broadcast on the following week's episode. We thought of this as a unique use of technology (the 800#) and interactivity (the audience could respond to us). But as pressure increased to develop more unique editorial, we were short of new ideas.

In May of 1991, I wrote a short promotional announcement for the program's host to deliver on the following week's episode. It read something like: "We've run out of ideas. We don't know what stories matter to you. And we need your help. Call our 800 number and tell us what we should be covering." Though I didn't know it then, it was a critical moment in my development as a journalist and storyteller. A number of events transpired that couldn't have been projected. First, of my 26 staff one quit on the spot. They saw the promo as irresponsible, an abdication of our job to figure out what mattered to our viewers. In their mind that was our job – knowing what mattered. And the 800 number logged almost a thousand calls.

Lesson #1. People are far more interested sharing their ideas with you than in "commenting" on the content created and distributed by mainstream media. That was instantly obvious.

From that moment on, *BROADCAST: New York* was a television program that listened. It was a transformative moment. The calls that came in where passionate, angry, crazy, charming, but above all authentic. We listened to them all, called many back, and within weeks were crediting audience members with their story ideas, tips, and editorial direction in each episode. The call volume never subsided. The audience never got tired of suggesting stories.

At some point thereafter, a local newspaper reporter doing a story about our company suggested we were doing something that was "technologically groundbreaking." I remember correcting him at the time – and suggesting that the only novel thing we were doing was answering the phone. Something any media outlet could do if they so chose.

Things proceeded for almost a year – until I found myself at a consumer electronics store holding one of the very first Sharp Viewcams. These hi8 cameras hand a large LCD screen and were the size of a large paperback book. They were no better than a VHS camcorder – save the fact that you could turn the lens around and photograph yourself. It was a "Max Headroom" moment. The next day I was on the phone to Sharp, who agreed to ship 5 loaner units to *BROADCAST: New York*. Once again, we gave our host the duty of inviting the audience to do our job – in this case replace the staff Videographer with first-person home-grown video.

The invitation took hold with instantly. And within two weeks we had a waiting list of viewers who wanted to do more than watch media, they wanted to make it. The segment, called "Viewers News" was an instant success. Our 5 loaner cameras were constantly in use. And while the quality of the material varied widely, we quickly learnt some key lessons that still serve us today. First, people knew what they wanted to say – they just weren't sure how to construct a coherent story with a beginning, middle, and end. After trying to get the show's producers to begin to mentor viewers, it became clear that anyone who thought of themselves as a professional storyteller wasn't going to be enthusiastic about handing those duties over to previously passive viewers. For a few weeks the stories that came in were authentic, but not dramatic. Then everything changed.

There was a call on the 800 number from a woman in Syracuse New York. She wanted to tell her story so that other women would be forewarned. She had had cosmetic surgery to increase her breast size. The surgeon used silicone implants. Both had ruptured, and she had been infected with a severe case of silicone blood poisoning.

A staff producer talked with her, and over the phone – there was no email – they outlined the story she would record. The camera was dispatched. And over the next 10 days she FedEx'd back tape so that the producer could give her feedback and constructive criticism. She had a checklist of scenes she was going to shoot, and she proceeded to record them all. She took the camera to work, where her disability left her unable to function on a full time basis. She recorded a trip to the grocery store, talking to the camera as it looked up at her from the shopping cart. And she interviewed her husband – an awkward and revealing conversation that had an extraordinary subtext.

Then she signed a footage release and returned the camera.

Once the camera and the last footage had been returned and was being reviewed, it was clear she'd done something beyond the original story proposal. The last day she had the camera she'd woken, as she did every morning, and made her way to the bathroom to get ready for her day. But this day, with her Sharp Viewcam in hand, she'd placed it on the bathroom mirror. Then, she'd unbuttoned her robe. The tape was unflinching. There she showed the camera, and us, two horrible scars where her breasts had been.

A much shaken Segment Producer summoned me to the edit room.

I remember the moment. It was shocking, disturbing, and honest. Could we show it on television? A few things were instantly clear. Had our crew recorded these images they would have represented such a staggering breach of etiquette that most likely the producer and the photographer would have lost their jobs. Had a producer from our company prompted the tape, or urged this kind of personal revelation, it would have crossed the line. But that hadn't happened. What happened was that a woman wanted to tell her story, and knew intuitively that the image of her marred chest was far more impactful and effective than any number of words she could record.

She wanted to tell her story in a way that would impact other woman profoundly. And that she had most certainly done.

We did two things next. We checked to make sure she wanted us to broadcast the images, and we alerted our affiliates that we were going to air video that some might find disturbing. They weren't sexual, but they were horribly graphic.

Then we held our breath. The woman said, yes she wanted those images on TV. And our stations didn't flinch. We aired it on 14 stations… and waited to see how the audience would react. The feedback was instantaneous – after all we had the 800 number. Woman cheered our Viewer/Storyteller, they supported us, and they talked at length about the issues of sexual identity, cosmetic surgery, and the impact of the media on women's body image.

Something had changed.

User Generated Video was born that day. Technology was enabled… but not the driver. The driver was far more human. A person whose pain and suffering had made her keenly aware of the dangers of silicone breast implants. A person who wanted to share her experience with others in her community.

Today

YouTube is reporting 70 thousand uploads and 100 million video views a day.

YouTube is notable in a number of ways. Its fast start is both remarkable and inevitable. From November of 2005 until June of 2006 it launched, grew with an adoption cure that is unlike any other software product, website, or piece of consumer electronics in history. And yet, if you return to the lessons learned at *BROADCAST: New York*, it's hardly surprising. Current projections for broadband content consumption peg growth from 13 million US homes today to 131 million by 2010.[1]

This tenfold increase in just 4 years suggests a consumer demand and adoption cure that will reach far beyond early adopters and teen consumers.

And looking back at the evolution of User-Generated Videos helps us understand this phenomenon.

1995. New York.

The evolution of content on *BROADCAST: New York* had allowed us to explore consumer content creation behavior for almost 2 years. And the results were surprising. The content makers came from a wide variety of backgrounds. There were certainly underprivileged crying out of justice, but within the middle class story ideas and extraordinary video tape continued to come in week after week. Demand didn't trail off. It was – from the moment we offered viewers a chance to create media – strong and consistent.

And so I went looking for a larger platform to test the concept of Viewers News on a national basis. In its original pitch, the concept was called "Viewers News Channel," a consumer reported 24-hour cable channel dedicated to first-person storytelling. I presented the idea with a great deal of enthusiasm to Frank Biondi, who was then the CEO of Viacom. Sitting in his office on the executive floor of 1515 Broadway we dialled into our 800# and played call after call of passionate personal storytellers. To his credit – Biondi immediately engaged the idea of new content sources and was supportive. Later in his role at Waterview Advisors, Biondi would be an early source of capital for a number of groundbreaking Internet start-ups including Atom Films. But he cautioned that the "channel" was too big a first step – why not start with a national television program to test the concept further.

With his encouragement and a tape full of "ViewersNEWS" segments from *BROADCAST: New York* programs to prove out the concept, I made a pretty elaborate presentation to MTV. Biondi had warned me that I should pitch it "cold" (not using his endorsement for fear that his notoriously independent exec would back away from anything that came from a "suit."). I presented to Joe Davola and Linda Corradina – and to their credit they were immediately enthusiastic about embracing consumer content. Yet they were wary. "Would people actually call in?" "Would the stories be interesting enough?" They wanted a test.

And so weeks later, we put on a 30 promo for a pilot series called "*MTV Interact*" and invited viewers to suggest stories they would report. The promo played just three times, and the calls were delivered to our 800# to be tallied and transcribed. Just 48 hours later – we had 5,000 calls. The series was given a green light to go into production. Interact became "*Unfiltered*," despite my protests. I argued that *Unfiltered* sounded too much like Unplugged (it did) and that my title was better – "Free Speech." But the push back at the time was that Free Speech sounded like a high school civics class, and that no one would ever care about the fact that *Unfiltered* was in fact *filtered*. On that point they were most certainly correct.

Unfiltered was an extraordinary experience. The core staff, the evolving editorial philosophies, and some of the hard fought internal battles all served to teach me about the opportunities and complexities that lay ahead as use-created-content moved toward the mainstream.

The process was formal and detailed. Each episode would invite viewers with a story to tell to call our 800# and pitch their story to *Unfiltered*. Alison Stewart, the show's first host had a remarkable way of exuding both trust and passion, and seemed to be able to reach through the set and coax audience members to dial the phone. The calls were transcribed and printouts of the day's calls were distributed to the show's Associate Producers, Producers, and Executive Producers. Early on we decided to let associate producers "adopt" stories that caught their eye. Certain AP's tended toward more visual pieces, adventure sports, and stunts, while others were drawn toward socials issues and injustice, and others toward personal stories and journeys. As the show's lead producer and Exec Producer (along with MTV's Dave Sirulnick), I would make sure that the stories all got "adopted" by someone. Everyone who called got a call back (read ClueTrain Manifesto if you want to know why). Having humans connect with humans was critical.

The calls were as broad as you might imagine. A girl from Penn State wanted to document and object to an annual male "streaking ritual" on her campus. Skateboarders felt they were harassed by the cops. A boy had painted his room black and painted over the windows, he was afraid to go outside. A teen father complained there were no baby changing tables in men's bathrooms. A cross dresser graduated from Florida State in drag. And then there was Shaun.

Shaun was 15. He seemed like an average teen. Then he committed suicide.

His best friend, a 14-year-old girl, had called the 800#, sobbing. She was angry. Angry with Shaun for the pain he'd caused. Angry that he'd left his friends to deal with the grief. She wanted to record her anger so that any teen thinking of suicide would know the pain it caused. She wanted us to send her a camera to tell her story.

At that point we had 30 cameras. They were sharp hi8 viewcams, and they were constantly on the move... shipped from one story to another. Each story was allocated just 10 days to shoot... but people often kept them longer. And as tape came in, we would often send a camera back for additional shots or new interviews, coaxing the story from the storytellers in little bites.

Each week we met, discussed stories, and Associate Producers lobbied for access to the few cameras that had freed up from the week before to start their stories. The Shaun story had been adopted by Dina Kaplan (who had left the Clinton White House to join Unfiltered). She wanted this story to be made.

Others weren't so sure. Suicide was a touchy subject. Was this really the right show to do such serious material? What images could actually be photographed? The story had happened. It seemed likely to be a waste of precious camera resources. Dina was adamant. She wanted a chance.

It was a pivotal moment for Unfiltered and for User-Generated Content as well. Dina won, and the camera was shipped. The result is a story that haunts me to this day. Heartbroken teens, home videos of Shaun both happy and deeply depressed. Interviews with the father, the mother, the sisters, the friends. My older son is 16 now, and on days when he's dealing with complex teenage things, I never forget Shaun, and always remember to hug him and tell him I love him. The naysayers in the room that day were right, suicide is a touchy subject. And that's why it deserved to be explored by people who'd earned the right to talk about how it feels to lose someone you love.

Not every *Unfiltered* story was that important or successful of course. Lots of viewers lost interest and didn't finish their pieces. Our associate producer walked a tricky line... in building bridges without crossing the line. Each camera that got sent out included a recorded introduction by the Associate Producer who would be working with the viewer. "We're going to see you, so you should be able to see what we look like" the tapes always began.

One storyteller who lived near our office in New York insisted on coming to pick up the camera ("don't fed ex it, I'll drop by"). Disaster. Once they'd met their associate producer, they wrangled him into "helping him shoot" and the result was an icky local news piece.

We learned something from that. We could provide assistance, help, tools, and a framework. But people needed to tell their own stories, in their own way. Technology was clearly part of what was driving the emergence of first-person storytelling. We'd be the first show at MTV to be cut on non-linear Avid editing equipment in large part because the stories came to gather in a non-linear way. And once the first crop of DV cameras came out, we shifted slowly from hi8 to DV improving picture and sound quality.

But Unfiltered's innovations weren't technical. They were philosophical. We thought what people had to say was more important than what we had to say. We thought our role was to create a framework, a support system, and a mentoring relationship. We trained our staff to this. If a viewer would say, "how should my story end?" we would say… "well, what do you think?"

We were more like shrinks than TV Producers.

By 1998 the Internet was clearly providing new opportunities for storytelling. And 3 years of producing Unfiltered at MTV had had only one drawback – the media had happily labeled User-Generated Content as "teen" or "Gen X" news. Despite my constant reminders of the early experiments with *BROADCAST: New York* and the large number of adult contributors, the power of the MTV brand (and the popularity of the show) had dwarfed the early days and the concept of Viewers News Channel.

This is worth a moment's consideration.

When consumers shift their function from consumption to creation, the impact is significant. And for content companies, the results will be earth-shaking – and potentially disastrous.

So when I approached MTV after 3 years on the air and suggested it was time for a change, I proposed a radical re-invention of the channel and its relationship with the audience.

In a meeting with Judy McGrath, then the President of MTV, I suggested that *Unfiltered* should end its run as a program and instead that the process of inviting content submission and content creation should be shifted to a wider network strategy. My proposal was to turn MTV into UGV. To invite viewers to submit stories about their world, their music, their fashion, and the trends in their town. Judy was willing to listen, since the early trend lines of the Internet were clearly being drawn. But months later, the decision was that it was "too early" and that MTV wasn't prepared to shift its focus from telling teens what was hip to having teens tell them. McGrath was right, in a way, because empowering the audience does have the potential to make MTV less central to the equation. Teach a man to fish, they go fishing. Feed a man a fish, they come back for dinner tomorrow night. MTV wanted to make sure it had return customers to its content buffet. And 8 years later, as MTV shifts to new delivery platforms –

there's no doubt that McGrath was right to continue to run the old model for as long as she did. The open question still remains, "can MTV morph into YouTube, or do those three magic letters not mean as much to today's teens?"

What drove *BROADCAST: New York* and *Unfiltered* and how does that connect to the emerging user-generated content trends we're seeing today?

Passion v. Profit

In August of 2005, I traveled to Oxford, England for a gathering of world changing thinkers called TED. TEDsters, as they're known, travel from around the world to hear talks from world-changing individuals and contemplate the nexus of technology, entertainment, and design.

The days are long. The topics are intense. And the pace somewhat blistering. By the end of the first day I'd been convinced that architecture, engineering, solar energy, and political photography all had world shaping potential. But it wasn't until 8 a.m. the next day that I knew why I'd come to TED.

Yoachi Benkler is a bearded bear of a man who teaches Law at Yale by day... and thinks deeply about consumer created content the rest of the time. In Oxford he had just 20 min – as do all TED presenters – to tell his story. It was Benkler who for the first time connected the Open Source Software moment to User-Generated Content. As Benkler sees it... its all consumer created content. And he makes a pretty compelling argument for the fact that something significant is changed. He points to server software like Apache, which is the work of an army of volunteers, and now has 66.9% of the server marketplace,[2] dwarfing Microsoft. Why do people participate in open source projects? Is there some hidden profit motive? Benkler says no. Instead, he says that people are creative, and people enjoy making things and people want to participate within communities of enthusiasts who have a passion for their craft. Stop and think about the explosive impact on Benkler's thesis. While software is a highly developed skill set, the impact on the content industry could be far more dramatic. Not everyone can write code. But *everyone* has a story, an idea, a project, or a skill that they can share in a video. Benkler's thesis promises a future of enthusiast content makers that latterly disassembles the current content creation/distribution/consumption eco-system. And talking to him, you can't help but get the sense that he thinks that can't happen soon enough.

After TED I contacted him, and we spent some time via email and then over coffee talking about the future of content, what's clear is that he is a passionate theorist. At one point I asked if his groundbreaking thesis on the web (coasespenguin.com) would be made any simpler when he published his book. His answer was a simple "no." And when you ask him to engage in an exploration of the slippery slope between "enthusiast" media and "pro-summer," he demurs. For Benkler, free is the single most interesting operating principal. And he may well be right. More and more I find that I'm relying on user-reviews, Google group comments, and Wikipedia for information and opinion. Sure, I consume some mainstream media, but it tends to be more "big" media that is as much a social phenomenon – the water cooler effect – and less for knowledge and information.

What is clear is that Unfiltered is very much driven by what Benkler calls Peer Production. And his thinking, combined with the motivation that drove Unfiltered and now YouTube, is creating an economy that increasingly leaves networks and distributors without a place to stand. No longer gatekeepers, no longer pipe owners, and no longer taste makers, the future of the current keepers of the media eco-system have much to be worried about.

In October of 2004, the Editor of Wired Magazine penned a thesis about how the connected word changed the content distribution equation. It was called The Long Tail. And much like Benkler, Chris Anderson's work clicked and fell into place. If Unfiltered had taught a generation that they could make content, and Benkler had developed a thesis that consumer content was likely to create a new model for content makers, then Anderson galvanized the future of micro distribution.

Simply put, The Long Tail re-imagines content distribution in a world where there is no cost of storage, no limits on shelf space, and highly evolved systems to discover and receive the media you want when you want it. It is both breathtakingly simple and wildly imaginative at the same time. It images a world without hits, without mass marketing, without mainstream distribution. Anderson might debate the scope of my summary (he does after all work for a company that prints and distributes a magazine), but it is my take on his analysis.

It is the future that Judy McGrath had hoped to postpone when she kept the Unfiltered phenomenon in its box, back in 1997.

And so, when the Wall Street Journal declares in a page one story in August of 2006 that "MTV can't seem to find kids online" they're actually chronicling a much more important underlying trend. The media wrongly presents MySpace traffic as a collective audience, when in fact the pageviews on MySpace are in fact thousands (more accurately hundreds of thousands) of niche channels made by and for young people. The Journal suggests that Viacom missed a critical moment when it didn't purchase MySpace, but that's hardly the point, because in the emerging world of Me Media, any attempt by a single company to capture and commoditize that audience will result in a defection to a new, less consolidated platform. Teens know what mass media smells like and they run the other way. And, they're not alone.

And so – we stand at a content crossroads. Not a moment driven by technology, but rather a moment powered by technology. Human beings tell stories. They gather and share knowledge. They entertain. They teach. There have always been gating factors that have separated community speakers from amplified speakers. The printing press, the radio license, the TV transmitter.

But those gates are gone.

And now the flood begins. Content made on the fly, content made by professionals. Content created by communities for communities. The impulses that drove people to call our 800 number back in 1994 are if anything more prevalent today than then. The world has become more complex, the news media more consolidated in its ownership and it's tenor. And the economics of cable and broadcast forces them to reach for broader and more disposable programming choices at the moment when media consumers are increasingly looking to highly specialized niche content sources including web sites and blogs.

In February of 2005, Chad Hurley and Steve Chen put online a web site to solve a problem they were having. Video sharing was difficult and they thought a public site was the solution. It was called YouTube, and it was neither slick nor complex. In fact, it was pretty bare bones. But in the aesthetics of web 2.0, it was extremely open and provided few barriers to upload and storage. It's pretty clear that the guys at YouTube didn't expect that they'd be lighting the fuse on the final explosion of conventional television as we know it. But it's pretty clear that's what is happening.

People formerly known as content "consumers" (or less kindly as "couch potatoes") began to turn their thoughts, hobbies, humor, and voices into a massive content creation engine. And the discussion of "exploding TV" became the hottest topic on blogs that debate the evolution of the net from text and pictures to full motion video.

Fred Wilson, who's influential blog AVC.Blogspot.com had been a bellwether for music technology and personal media, turned his attention to Television.

said Wilson: "I think the advent of the media-centric PC will cause this trend (bit torrent 'downloaded' TV) to accelerate. If my family room is driven by a PC with a DVR, set top box, and web browser built into it, connected to cable for both programming and high speed data, and then connected to a nice big flat panel display, the option to watch a show via live TV, VOD, DVR, or BitTorrent is just a click of the remote. And when it's that easy, why will my girls choose to watch One Tree Hill via DVR when they can just as easily get it via BitTorrent?"

And Jeff Jarvis, who blogs at buzzmachine.com and is the creator and founding editor of Entertainment Weekly, and TV critic for TV Guide and People magazines, has pretty strong feels about this as well.

Jarvis sees the "exploding" of TV in a number of critical ways. First, he proclaims "At some point, soon, content producers will get rid of all middlemen" and there's lots of reasons to believe this is true. But then Jarvis goes on to connect all this to Madison Avenue seeing a battle ensuing between old media companies moving online to complete and new media outlets.

Says Jarvis: "What excites me most is that reduced cost of production. That's really what drove weblogs: history's cheapest publishing tool reduced the barrier to entry to media and allowed anyone to produce and distribute text content. Now this will come to video. I've said it before (warning: I'll say it again) ... A half-hour of how-to TV that now costs X hundreds of thousands of dollars to produce can be done quite respectably – and probably with more life and immediacy – for a few thousand dollars. New content producers will pop up all over (just as they did in blogs) and now they can distribute their content freely (thanks to BitTorrent). That is where I want to play."

Jarvis sees a future in which citizen journalists and consumer content creators become central figures in the creation and consumption of editorial material. What makes his perspective so rare, and refreshing, is that he had a full-on membership in the ruling media elite. For him to set outside, and go from a TimeWarner/Conde Naste creator of MSM (mainstream media) to a blogger – a position of some less authority and power – is a sign of just how intoxicating the promise of personal publishing is.

Both Jarvis and Fred are on the money – the transformative changes that are roiling the media industry go deeper than technology or personal expression. At the core of the growth in first-person media is a passion that challenges the promises of the Democracy.

Big media, like Big Government, thrives by being able to monopolize the conversation. Media companies need to be able to control the conversation, set the agenda, and manage whatever role community members may want to have in the conversation. But consumer generated media isn't a parlor trick that's given credence by corporate media. It is in fact a Peer-to-Peer system that thrives on networks that fall below conventional radar.

That brings us full circle. *MTV Unfiltered* meets Tool replace networks, people replace search. We're standing on the eve of a new era in person-to-person storytelling. It is an era in which institutions that have for the past 50 years been at the center of mass media may find that they need to rapidly re-invent themselves or slip into obsolescence.

That brings me to Unfiltered 2.0, and one potential set of events that could unfold to create the new media landscape.

As I write this chapter the collective wisdom and mistakes of 12 years of work have been organized into code. Since my first day on the job at Unfiltered, I've been testing and evolving theories about UGC and the environments that foster the highest quality content. Over that time, content creators have proven time and time again that certain environment features stimulate the "network effect" in content creation. And turning those ideas into a set of web based tools and processes have the potential to nurture nascent content creation communities.

The code is a software platform called Magnify.net,[3] and it's available to any web based publisher or content entrepreneur. It – like all consumer driven products – will evolve as users teach us about how they interact with and modify the platform. But as of today, it is solid, growing, and increasing virally.

Can it be that software based rules and tools improve UGC? You decide. Here are the rules (more guidelines) that drive the Magnify Peer Production Platform.

Shared Spaces, Shared Stories

Communities used to be geographic. You were a part of a community where you lived, where you worked, or maybe where you found recreation or hobbies. But they were all driven by proximity. No longer. The web has changed that forever. I'm a member of a group of web-based entrepreneurs so secretive that I'm not allowed to even write the group's name down. They are some of the most well known leaders in web design, e-commerce, and technology. There are 68 of us. And I've only met one of them face to face. Yet I email all of them every day, read their blogs, and share private business concerns and questions with them. Why? Because we're a community. And as I catalog my interests and connections, it's clear that I can map my life as a series of concentric circles (communities of interest) that I subscribe to. These communities are shared spaces, and within them, much if not all of the value of these communities are the shared stories that reside within them. I drink from this well of knowledge often, and return to it knowledge that I think is useful and pertinent to others. Whether it is by commenting on other posts, or posting my own... these engagements are without a doubt editorial enterprises. The evolution from centralized knowledge creation and distribution networks (TV, Radio, and Print) to community based knowledge collectives is already underway. Whether you count on Wikipedia for research or Amazon reviews for consumer advice or Google Groups for tech support, chances are you're already dipping into knowledge networks for an increasingly large portion of what is your content diet. Video will be central to this change.

Peer Feedback Keeps the System Honest

There is no doubt that not all content is created equal. In fact, community-based peer review is critical to keeping both creators and critics honest. As we learned at MTV, no one-community member can assure that content submissions are accurate and honest. But dispersing the job to a wider group of community members assures that not one vote or voice will drive the process. Peer Filtering relies on anonymous distribution of contributed content to volunteer community reviewers. In the spirit of eBay, it's critical that both reviewers and submitters participate in reputation system that allows both comments and content that doesn't meet community standards to be identified and removed from the community.

Not all Community Members Have the Same Stature or Goals

There is currently a debate within the UGC world about the need to provided payments or revenue sharing with content makers. But not all communities are driven by the same motivators. And even within communities, not all creators have the same motivations. Compare the web sites Slashdot and Digg to the UGC created network "Current". Both of the tech-focused sites have extraordinary member involvement, both as submitters and as peer reviewers. Yet they don't pay anything for submission or participation. Current, on the other hand, pays submitters a flat $250.00 for each video submission that is used on the air. Yet as a ratio, members of Digg are far more engaged to contribute than Current. Why is that? Because members of both Digg and Slashdot are driven by their status in the community and reputation, and Current's decision making is centralized (and therefore not democratic). [Disclosure: Current's founder Al Gore was an early fan of MTV Unfiltered, and I was an early advisor to Current before its launch.]

Communities Organize Around Sparkplug Issues

In the old world of video content, programs were organized around channels. But in the emerging world of content communities, Sparkplug Topics drive contribution, collaboration, and community. The idea that small groups of people can be deeply passionate about narrow enthusiast niches is clear to anyone who has looked at Alexa.com to try and determine the key verticals emerging on the net. The quick answer is – they can't be deciphered based on conventional metrics. For example, www.rcuvideos.com has a very large base of users and more than 300,000 registered users. They are the best location for Radio Controlled model airplanes and helicopters. And, not surprisingly – they are also a terrific destination for the purchase of parts and supplies for that hobby,

The impact on these changes will be profound and unparallel. The coming changes will reshape marketing, sociology, journalism, and politics.

UGC will create powerful new voices from previously unheard minorities. As audiences organize around media made by their peers, the importance and value of commercially created content will be called into question. Already Wikipedia is roiling education as it's community curated editorial grows with breathtaking speed. Craig's list has gutted the cash-cow of local classified ads, and now Craig Newmark, the founder, says he's going to tackle local journalism. And YouTube has almost overnight snatched hundreds of thousands of video views away from Cable and Broadcast – forcing once mighty media companies to scramble to rethink how they can engage formerly passive media consumers in the content creation process.

It's a new media word. And "Bigness" may no longer be the gating factor. I'm not surprised.

Remember the first time you stopped by a farm stand and purchased big, fresh, red tomatoes right off the vine? Then remember the next time you tried to buy a tomato at the local super-market?

Well – UGC is fresh off the vine. And once consumers get a taste, the content grown in corporate-hot house environments just won't taste the same.

Back in 1992 it was entirely clear. Give people the tools and the platform and they'll make media that is personal, passionate, and compelling for others in their peer group. They'll do it for love rather than money. They'll put every ounce of their soul in the work creating media that has that indefinable "x" factor that connects with people on a gut level. It's the thing that a handful of Journalists, Filmmakers, Writers, and Poets can do. It's also the thing that corporations do poorly. Authenticity can't be produced by the pound. It just doesn't taste the same.[4]

Notes

1. http://www.instat.com/press.asp?ID=1758&sku=IN0602976CM
2. http://news.netcraft.com/archives/web_server_survey.html
3. Magnify turns web sites into community based video sites. The tools are simple to deploy and easy to modify and update. It's based on everything I learned with MTV, CBS Class of 2000, my project "Free Speech" at USA Networks, and more. It presumes that some communities will have the membership, sparkplug topics, and peer-driven feedback necessary to create new living, breathing, dynamic content communities. And others will simply be interested in searching and syndicating content from other like-minded communities to provide video for their sites. Unlike YouTube, Google, Yahoo, MSN or others – Magnify isn't a destination – and an enabling platform. And unlike sites that require submitters to play by a certain set of rules, Magnify can be configured to be highly vetted for established media brands, and provide a wide open publishing environment for sites interested in providing all comers with an unrestricted place to submit and engage in consumer created content.
4. Steven Rosenbaum is the CEO of Magnify Networks. Email: steve@magnify.net

8

A Survival Analysis of Albums on Ranking Charts

Sudip Bhattacharjee[1], Ram D. Gopal[2], James R. Marsden[3], Rahul Telang[4]

[1,2]*University of Connecticut*
[3,4]*Carnegie Mellon University*

Introduction

Maintaining security in the digital world continues to grow in complexity. Firms must protect operating hardware and sensitive data against increasingly innovative threats. With the emergence of digital goods comes a new security front where firms face the reproduction and rapid distribution of the digital goods themselves. Certainly, firms already have had to protect many of their goods from "knockoffs," but protecting digital goods represents a new level of challenge since the cost of copying and distributing such goods is virtually zero and can occur extensively within very short periods of time. The music industry has been the "poster industry" for facing such threats. The industry's goods are digital by nature. Further, the appearance of Peer-to-Peer networks offered the means to copy (download) the goods and distribute (share) them rapidly.

Through its industry association, the Recording Industry Association of America (RIAA), the music industry has continued to pursue mostly legal and technological strategies to eradicate the security threat of illegal copying and distribution. A recent study by Bhattacharjee et al. (2006a,b) provides evidence that, while individuals have tended to reduce their own sharing activity in response to RIAA's legal threats and actions, significant piracy opportunity remains. While individual firms may take steps to secure their digital goods, such constraints have two major drawbacks. First, such measures tend to impede the consumer's use of the digital good since they can restrict portability or require additional steps (e.g., security actions) that reduce consumer utility (Halderman 2002). Second, the measures have

E.M. Noam and L.M. Pupillo (eds.), *Peer-to-Peer Video*, doi: 10.1007/978-0-387-76450-4_8,
© Springer Science + Business Media, LLC 2008

proven less than "foolproof" and rather easily beaten (Reuters 2002, Felten 2003). Sony BMG's recent use of a rootkit with the XCP technology (Reuters 2005, Bergstein 2005) provides a prominent illustration of how an attempted technological security constraint can backfire (Bradley 2005):

Part of Sony's anti-pirating strategy is that some of its music will play only with media software included on the CD. When a user inserts the CD, he or she is asked to consent to an "end user licensing agreement" for a Digital Rights Management application. If the user agrees, the rootkit automatically installs and hides (or "cloaks") a suite of DRM software.

Unfortunately, the rootkit application created a possible secret backdoor for hackers which led Sony to "hastily" post a patch. However, the tool to remove the XCP application itself created new vulnerabilities (Russinovich 2005). The tale continues as California quickly filed suit under both unfair and deceptive trace acts and consumer protection acts, Texas filed suit for including "spyware" in its media player, and the Electronic Frontier Foundation filed suit seeking class-action status over its copy-protection software (Smith 2005). A posting (by concord (198387), 11/10/05, #13996982) in slashdot.org's bulletin board offers the following perspective on the Sony anti-piracy actions:

Now for the first time it is actually safer to download and listen to pirated music then [sic] it is to purchase and use compact disks and DVDs. Piracy will become a matter of self-preservation.

In addition, security professionals have consistently noted that all CD and DVD encryption techniques that have been tried by the entertainment industry have been broken by savvy consumers (Schneier 2000, Craver et al. 2001, Patrizio 1999, Clarke 2005, Associated Press 2003). Given wide dissemination of the encrypted music product among users (factors that make breaking encryption easier), it is not unusual to observe such copy protection technologies being defeated by smart users (Bergstein 2005, Felten 2005).

Thus a firm considering possible actions to protect its digital product may find little return in costly technological and legal anti-piracy measures. But can the firms identify and respond to the changing market they face? The post 1998–1999 period is characterized by consumers who increasingly search and consume music products in digital formats. Here we focus attention on what significant changes have occurred in the landscape of music products and their market life cycle since the introduction of significant new technology, including Peer-to-Peer networks, and other market forces (including online music stores, higher penetration of broadband into homes, digital rights management (SDMI initiative), and evolving copyright laws (DMCA 1998, Sonny Bono Copyright Term Extension Act 1998). We first develop an analytical model of music album life cycle to provide a robust foundation to develop effective decision making tools for a music company to better manage its music products in the market place. The model demonstrates how the pattern of album life cycle has undergone a shift in the years following the introduction of new technologies and other market forces. Following the analytic model, we examine how some of the album specific and artist specific variables affect the album survival. Thus, incorporating key exogenous factors helps a decision maker to better predict and respond to market success of a digital good in a dynamic environment. A firm's ability to act with these decision tools, which combine product life cycle analytics with analysis of consumer actions on online computer networks, would provide greater market value protection for the firm's digital products than would technological and legal anti-piracy measures alone.

The Landscape – Rankings and Survival Longevity

In a number of domains – including music, movies, books, university sports, and academics – rankings are the yardsticks to measure success. Appearance and longevity of survival on ranking charts are important for market success and job security. Rankings have limited slots (e.g., top 10, top 25, or top 100) and are reported on a periodic basis (ranging from weekly for music charts or in-season sports to annually for business school rankings).

High rankings and longevity on ranking charts would seem to have inherent links to the concept of "superstars," a phenomenon studied by Rosen (1981). Following Rosen's initial work, Adler (1985) suggested the existence of the superstar phenomenon in artistic industries where only a relatively small number of music artists and their products garner enormous success. Adler argued that consumers minimize the cost of search by simply choosing artists who are already popular among other consumers. Adler's "concentration of success" phenomenon has been empirically studied by several authors (Simon 1955, Yule 1924). Examples cover quite a range and include Albert's (1998) analysis of motion pictures, Cox and Chung's (1991) study of research output in academics, Simon's (1955) examination of the distribution of words in prose, and Levene et al.'s (2002) consideration of the growth of Internet websites. Approximately 30,000 albums are released annually by the major music labels alone (Goodley 2003). Given that a mere handful of successful albums can significantly affect the profitability of a music label, it is critically important for the labels to have an estimation of the potential life cycle of the albums released early in their release period. This would enable them to form informed decisions and channel limited marketing and promotional budgets towards potential winners.

But what happens if the landscape changes significantly and past business practices do not apply as well? What happens when advances occur in markets that make a consumer's search for information and product access far easier? Does ranking longevity, or life cycle on the chart, change dramatically? In fact, in the past few years, the music industry has seen such a technological and market revolution. Easier search for information and product sampling is an integral part of buying an experience product such as music. The advent of MP3 and online file-sharing technologies now allow consumers to access and exchange millions of digitized music files over Peer-to-Peer networks.[1,2]

We develop a stochastic model of the distribution of album longevity on the Billboard Top 100 Chart.[3] We estimate the model annually for periods before and after the major technological and market changes, that is, the introduction of MP3, broadband, and the Napster Peer-to-Peer online sharing technology that took place over the 1998–1999 period. What we find is that, despite declining numbers of new album releases after 1999 (Ziemann 2002), the probability of survival on the Billboard Chart had a major shift downward. We use this survival information and develop a regression model that incorporates consumer behavior on online file-sharing networks. This is used to estimate the continued success of albums on the Billboard Chart. We emphasize that the same stochastic model form yields similar useful fit results for the differing periods with, of course, different parametric estimation values. Continued refreshing of the model estimation can be utilized by firms as a benchmark to adjust their decision making on individual albums as the market continues to shift over time.

The Stochastic Model of Survival

Rankings and longevity on the charts is a key indicator of a music album's success, and is closely followed by music labels and music industry analysts each week. Since 1913, *Billboard* magazine has provided weekly summary chart information based on sales of music recordings (Bradlow and Fader 2001). The Billboard Top 200 Chart is based on "...a national sample of retail store sales reports collected, compiled, and provided by Nielsen Soundscan" (from Billboard website). We use the freely available list of the weekly top 100 albums in our analysis. Based on empirical observation, we assume that once an album drops off the Billboard Top 100, the album does not re-appear on the chart.[4] Thus each week, some albums drop off the ranking chart and an equal number of albums appear for the first time. At the end of a hypothetical "first" week of the chart, we would have 100 albums that have appeared on the chart for exactly one week.

Let p_i denote the probability that an album will remain on the chart for one more week after having been on the chart for exactly i weeks. In week 2, the expected number of albums that would remain on the chart is $100p_1$. The expected number of albums that drop out of the chart after the first week is $100(1-p_1)$ which is also the same number of albums expected to enter the chart for the second week since there must be a total of 100 active albums on the Billboard Top 100 chart in any given week. That is, we model a stochastic process with one absorptive state that might be termed "falling off the chart." Table 8.1 details the stochastic process for the first three periods.

More formally, let $C_{k,i}$ indicate the number of albums that appear on the kth week's Billboard Chart and have appeared for i weeks ($i = 1,...,k$). $C_{12,5}$ would be the number of albums on the 12th week's chart that had appeared for 5 weeks (charts 8 through 12). Let $D_{k-1,w}$ be the number of albums that appeared on week $k-1$'s chart, do not appear on week k's chart, and which were on the charts for w weeks. $D_{21,4}$ would be the number of albums that met the following criteria: appeared on chart 21, did not appear on chart 22, and appeared on the chart for 4 weeks (from weeks 18 to 21).

Table 8.1 Illustration of Stochastic Process

	Expected number of albums that have been and are currently on the chart for:				Expected number of albums that had dropped out of the chart after:			
	1 week	2 weeks	3 weeks	4 weeks	1 week	2 weeks	3 weeks	4 weeks
Week 1	100	0	0	0	0	0	0	0
Week 2	$100(1-p_1)$	$100p_1$	0	0	$100(1-p_1)$	0	0	0
Week 3	$100p_1(1-p_2) + 100(1-p_1)^2$	$(1-p_1)p_1$	$100p_1p_2$	0	$100(1-p_1) + 100p_1 100(1-p_1)^2$	$(1-p_2)$	0	0

The following summarize the stochastic process (for convenience, we ignore expected value signs and use a general "n" rather than the 100 total for our Billboard Chart):

$$\sum_{i=1}^{k} C_{k,i} = n$$

(In each week, k, there must be $n = 100$ albums on the chart so summing across various weeks on the chart, from 1 week to k weeks, must yield 100 albums.)

$$TD_{k-1,w} = \sum_{j=1}^{k-1} D_{j,w}$$

(At the end of the k-1 chart, this is the total number of albums that were on the chart exactly w weeks before falling off.)

$$\sum_{w=1}^{k-1} D_{k-1,w} = C_{k,1}$$

(The number of new albums coming onto the kth chart must be equal to the number of albums that fell off the charts after week k-1; we sum across those that were on for 1 week, 2 weeks, up to k-1 weeks to get the total number that dropped off after the k-1 chart.)

$$C_{k,i} = p_{i-1} C_{k-1,i-1}$$

(*Note expected value operators are not shown.) (Expected number of albums that appear on chart k and have then survived for i weeks. Value is obtained multiplying the eligible albums (those which have been on the chart i-1 weeks) and the probability of remaining on the chart for an ith week given album was on the chart i-1 weeks.)

$$D_{k-1,w} = (1 - p_w) C_{k-1,w}$$

(Expected number of albums that drop off after week k-1 having been on the charts for w weeks is obtained by multiplying the probability of dropping off given that the album has been on the charts w weeks times the number of eligible albums, those that have been on the charts w weeks in the k-1 chart.)

Let T_k be the total number of music albums that had appeared on the chart at the end of week k. The steady state ($TD_{k,w} / T_k$) for this stochastic model can be shown to be (see Appendix):

$$\lim_{k \to \infty} \frac{TD_{k,w}}{T_k} = (1 - p_w) \prod_{j=1}^{w-1} p_j$$

Note that when $p_i = p$ for all i, the steady state is that of the geometric distribution (see similar distributions, e.g., Chung and Cox (1994), going back to Simon (1955) and Yule (1924)).

For $k > i$, by expansion, we have $C_{k,i} = p_{i-1}, p_{i-2}, \ldots, p_2, p_1, C_{k-i,1}$. At one extreme, it is possible that all p_i's are equal, that is, that the probability of an album remaining on the Billboard Chart is independent of the number of weeks the album has already been on the chart. At the other extreme, all p_i values could be different. From empirical observations, we choose a step function for the p_i values as explained below. It is consistently the case (see below) that the largest "falling off the chart" occurs for albums that have been on the chart just one week. In addition, there appears to be at least one clear "shift" point. After albums have been on the chart for some number of weeks, the probability of remaining on the chart shifts upward. As an example, for three shift points (four "p"s), our model would utilize p_i values as follows:

$$p_1 < p_2 = p_3 = \ldots = p_a < p_{a+1} = p_{a+2} = \ldots = p_b < p_{b+1} = p_{b+2} = \ldots = p_{k-1}.$$

Data and Stochastic Model Estimation

Our Billboard Chart data includes all weekly data over the periods 1995–1997 and 2000–2002, the pre- and post-change periods in the markets. We investigate whether the market landscape has shifted and, if so, what the implications are for music firms. We note that the data observations are not a random sample and, in reality, are the entire populations for the two periods studied. We view them as all realizations from a stochastic process for the selected periods.

Preliminary evaluation of the data and discussions with individuals knowledgeable about the industry suggest that the album "chart drop-off process" is quite rapid. During the years studied, while one album did in fact remain on the chart for 151 weeks, the vast majority of albums had much shorter chart life spans. Table 8.2 summarizes the number and percentage of albums that debuted in a given year and the number of weeks they remained on the chart before departing.

Table 8.2 Album Dropoff Behavior on Charts

	Year of Debut					
	1995	1996	1997	2000	2001	2002
Number of albums debuting on the Billboard 100 during the year	323	339	361	341	366	383
Total number of albums dropping off after 1 week	43 (13.3%)	41 (12.1%)	55 (15.2%)	86 (25.2%)	91 (24.9%)	91 (23.8%)
Total number of albums dropping off after weeks 1 through 4	122 (37.8%)	119 (35.1%)	120 (33.2%)	190 (55.7%)	189 (51.6%)	197 (51.4%)
Total number of albums dropping off after weeks 1 through 8	162 (50.2%)	169 (49.9%)	189 (52.4%)	252 (73.9%)	262 (71.6%)	282 (73.6%)
Total number of albums dropping off after weeks 1 through 13 (3 months)	205 (63.5%)	222 (65.5%)	234 (64.8%)	284 (83.3%)	310 (84.7%)	331 (86.4%)
Total number of albums dropping off after weeks 1 through 20	247 (76.5%)	267 (78.7%)	282 (78.1%)	290 (85.0%)	324 (88.5%)	344 (89.8%)

Since the majority of albums dropped off the chart within the first three months, we decided to focus on modeling and estimating a stochastic process of that length.[5] As outlined in the previous section, the family of stochastic processes we are utilizing includes an array of shift points from 1 to 13. That is, one case would be where the probability of falling off the chart remains the same no matter the number of weeks the album has appeared on the chart. The other extreme would be 13 shift points where the probability is different for each of the 13 possible weeks an album could have remained on the chart.

We used a brute force solution process beginning with one p value. Table 8.3 summarizes the outcomes for the single p stochastic process.

Table 8.3 Single p Stochastic Process Estimates

	1995	1996	1997	2000	2001	2002
$\hat{p}$	0.83	0.85	0.84	0.76	0.79	0.80
Computed χ^2	23.47	16.62	29.29	13.89	28.14	32.93
α^*	0.0240	0.1646	0.0036	0.3077	0.0053	0.0010

Table 8.4 Multiple p Stochastic Process Estimates

	1995	1996	1997	2000	2001	2002
$\hat{p}_1$	0.86	0.89	0.86	0.72	0.74	0.76
$\hat{p}_2$	0.92	0.90	0.91	0.82	0.85	0.85
Weeks: $\hat{p}_1$	2	3	2	1	1	1
Computed χ^2	11.16	7.99	17.60	7.52	8.16	14.46
α^*	0.4301	0.7138	0.0913	0.7556	0.6993	0.2087

We used the χ^2 goodness of fit test for the null hypothesis that the stochastic model is appropriate for the observed process. The α^* values (normally indicated as p values, but we use α^* here to avoid any confusion) indicate that level of significance at which we would begin rejecting the null hypothesis. That is, we only reject the null hypothesis for a level of significance greater than α^*. Thus, at a 0.05 level of significance we would reject the proposed stochastic model for years 1995, 1997, 2001, and 2002. We would accept the null hypothesis (the proposed model) for years 1996 and 2000.

We then repeated the brute force solution process for a model with one shift point (two "p"s). The results are summarized in Table 8.4. This time, using the χ^2 goodness of fit test and a 0.05 level of significance, we would accept the null hypothesis of model appropriateness for all years. The α^* levels ranged were quite high: 0.4301 (1995), 0.7138 (1996), 0.0913 (1997), 0.7556 (2000), 0.6993 (2001), and 0.2087 (2002). Repeating the process for two shift points (three "p"s), we found little improvement and thus focus on p_1, p_2 stochastic model with parameter estimates as indicated in Table 8.4 and illustrated in Fig. 8.1.

Consider the model specification differences in the periods before (1995–1997) and after (2000–2002). We note the following:

1. the shift period occurs earlier (the $\hat{p}_1$ estimate has only a 1-week duration in each of the 2000–2002 years compared to 2- or 3-week duration in each of the 1995–1997 years); and

2. in every year during the 2000–2002 period, the $\hat{p}_1$ and $\hat{p}_2$ values are less than the corresponding $\hat{p}_1$ and $\hat{p}_2$ values for each year in the 1995–1997 period.

The 2000–2002 values of $\hat{p}_1$ are 0.72, 0.74, and 0.76, respectively, compared to $\hat{p}_1$ values for 1995–1997 of 0.86, 0.89, and 0.88. The 2000–2002 values of $\hat{p}_2$ are 0.82, 0.85, and 0.85, respectively, compared to $\hat{p}_2$ values for 1995–1997 of 0.92, 0.90, and 0.91. These outcomes suggest quite different parameters for our stochastic model before and after the 1998–1999 market shift. The probability of remaining on the chart after 1 week fell by an average of 0.1 (0.84 before and 0.74 after). Further, the probability of remaining on the chart (after the process shift) was, on average, 0.07 lower (0.91 before and 0.84 after). Table 8.5 provides the estimated probabilities of remaining on the chart for a set number of weeks for each of the years.

Table 8.5 Estimated Probability of Survival on Chart

Weeks	1995	1996	1997	2000	2001	2002
2	0.86	0.89	0.86	0.72	0.74	0.76
3	0.74	0.79	0.74	0.59	0.63	0.65
4	0.68	0.70	0.67	0.49	0.53	0.55
5	0.63	0.63	0.61	0.40	0.45	0.47
6	0.58	0.57	0.56	0.33	0.39	0.40
7	0.53	0.51	0.51	0.27	0.33	0.34
8	0.49	0.46	0.46	0.22	0.28	0.29
9	0.45	0.42	0.42	0.18	0.24	0.24
10	0.41	0.37	0.38	0.15	0.20	0.21
11	0.38	0.34	0.35	0.12	0.17	0.18
12	0.35	0.30	0.32	0.10	0.15	0.15
13	0.32	0.27	0.29	0.08	0.12	0.13

The results provided in Tables 8.2, 8.4, and 8.5 and Graph 8.1 indicate a shift in chart life cycles of music albums following the technological and market innovations of 1998–1999. In the 1995–1997 period, 50% of the albums that appeared on the chart would be expected to last at least 7 weeks and at least 40% would be expected to last 9 weeks. In the 2000–2002 period, less than 50% would be expected to last 5 weeks. Less than 40% would be expected to make it to the sixth week. It is important to note that although the probability of remaining on the chart has changed before and after the 1998–1999 period, the structural robustness of the model with one shift point (two "p"s) is maintained in both periods.

The nature of the estimated models indicates a shift after the technological innovations of MP3 and online file-sharing that occurred over
the 1998–1999 period. The 2000–2002 period is characterized by a much
shorter life cycle. In our stochastic life cycle analysis, we utilized the
entire set of outcomes (Billboard Top 100 rankings) for the comparison
periods: 1995–1997 and 2000–2002. We find that music as a digital good
has been significantly impacted by market changes brought about by easier
information dissemination and product access to potential consumers.
While overall album survival has decreased in the 2000–2002 period, the
chances of survival increase dramatically after an album has survived
beyond the first week during this period. This indicates a pattern that the
"good" albums survive more. This also suggests that the new environment
brought on by technological and other market innovations is not conducive
to lower quality music albums. Easier sampling and information dissemination hurts the lower quality albums. In general, the life cycle of lower
quality products will tend to diminish faster under this new environment.
The analysis also suggests that albums face a shorter life cycle overall.

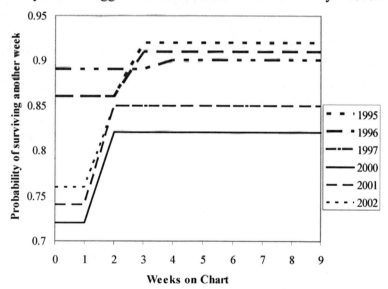

Graph 8.1 Multiple p Stochastic Process

Our analysis in this phase also emphasizes the robustness of our stochastic
life cycle model and consistency of results within each of the 3-year
periods, together with the differences between the two periods. Even with
significant "churn" in the music market and related environment between
the 1995–1997 and 2000–2002 periods, our simple yet robust model effectively captures the stochastic component of the chart life cycle process.

Duration Model of Album Survival

The stochastic model above does not easily yield to analyzing various exogenous factors that affect the survival probability of an album. For that, we turn to duration models in economics which allow for "regression"-like approach. The underlying process of survival is a weekly stochastic process that governs whether an album exits the charts (hazard of an album exiting the charts). Thus, in a hazard framework, one assesses the impact of an explanatory variable on the hazard of exiting the chart rather than on the length of survival time. A proportional hazard model (PHM) would allow for including various exogenous regressors and estimate the probability of an album exiting the chart given a certain number of weeks already on the chart. Thus PHM specification is of the form

$$h_1(t_i, X) = h_0(t_i) \exp(X_i \beta) \tag{1}$$

$h_0(t)$ is the baseline hazard function. A hazard function is simply $f(t)/(1-F(t))$ where $f(t)$ is the probability distribution and function and $F(t)$ is the cumulative distribution function. $(1-F(t))$ is also referred to as survival function. While a Cox PHM specification uses non-parametric form for baseline hazard function (Cox 1972), a Weibull PHM specification employs a parametric form to estimate this hazard. X is a set of covariates which shift the hazard function proportionally and β are the parameters to be estimated. A more "regression"-like framework is Accelerated Failure time (AFT) model. In AFT one can write the survival duration on Billboard chart as a regression model

$$\ln (T_i) = X_i \gamma + \varepsilon_i \tag{2}$$

The difference being that in (1), β is interpreted as affecting the hazard rate, while in (2) γ is interpreted as affecting the log of duration. Weibull yields to both PHM and AFT specifications, while Cox only admits the PHM specification. In case of Weibull, the error term $\varepsilon_i = \ln(\sigma u_i)$. This leads to ε_i having an extreme value distribution whose variance σ is to be estimated.

PHM models also allow for controls for unobserved heterogeneity (similar to random effect models in regression). In particular, in continuous time PHM models, data could be dispersed and not controlling for such heterogeneity may produce incorrect estimates. To incorporate unobserved heterogeneity, we modify (1) such that

$$h_1(t_i, X) = h_0(t_i) \exp(X_i \beta + v) \tag{3}$$

where v is gamma distributed with mean 0 and variance σ^2 which can be estimated.

Data Set

We used the same data as described earlier. Thus our Billboard Chart data includes all weekly data over the periods 1995–1997 and 2000–2002, the pre- and post-change periods in the markets. In addition, we collected data on the survival model explanatory variables (X_i) which we operationalize as follows.

Survival: Number of weeks an album appears on the Billboard top 100 charts. On occasion, an album may drop off for some weeks and reappear again on the chart. Each album is continuously tracked till its final drop-off. As noted earlier, our data does not suffer from left or right data censoring issues, as we track each album from its chart debut (birth) until its final drop off (death) from the charts. Note that the drop-off may occur well beyond the 34 weeks of each time segment.

Debut rank: The rank at which an album debuts on the Billboard top 100 chart. Numerically higher ranked albums are less popular.

Debut post-TS: This is an indicator variable which is 0 for albums that debut from 1995 to 1997 and 1 for albums that debut from 2000 to 2002. This dummy captures the effect of technological changes on album survival.

Superstar: A binary variable denoting the reputation of the artist. If a given album's artist has previously appeared on the Billboard top 100 charts for at least 100 weeks (on or after January 1, 1991) prior to the current album's debut, then the variable is set to 1, otherwise 0.

Minor label: A binary variable that is set to 0 if the distributing label for a given album is one of Universal Music, EMI, Warner, or SONY-BMG. A value of 1 denotes independent and smaller music labels.

Solo male: A binary variable that denotes if an album's artist is a solo male (e.g., Eric Clapton).

Solo female: A binary variable that denotes if an album's artist is a solo female (e.g., Britney Spears).

Group: A binary variable that denotes if an album's artist is a group (male or female) (e.g., U2, The Bangles).

Holiday month debut: To control for the holiday effect (or "Christmas effect"), we include an indicator variable for December, which is 1 if album debuted in that month and 0 otherwise.

Number of albums released per year: Album survival may depend on the number of albums released per year.

Estimation and Results

We estimate model (3) using Weibull distribution and gamma frailty. The results are consistent with Cox Models as well.

Table 8.6 Estimates for Album Survival

Parameter	Weibull PHM (Hazard Ratio)
Debut rank	1.09** (14.8)
Debut post-TS	2.80** (5.7)
No of albums released	1.00 (1.3)
Superstar	0.20** (7.81)
Minor label	1.75** (3.03)
Solo male	3.07** (4.45)
Group	4.80** (6.22)
Holiday month debut	0.52** (2.83)
Frailty variance σ	3.52** (14.6)
Weibull shape parameter	3.62** (21.3)
	LL = -2014

We report hazard ratios that are easier to interpret. A hazard ratio >1 indicates that the variable increases the hazard rate and vice-versa. Thus a hazard ratio of 1.09 for debut rank means that each increase in debut rank, on average, increases the hazard rate by 9%. Thus an album debuting at higher numerical rank will exit the charts faster than the album debuting at lower numerical rank. Except the no_of_albums variable, all other variables are significant and in expected direction. Notice that in the post period, the hazard rate has gone up by as much as 180%. We can interpret the hazard ratios to affect the total duration as well (recall that Weibull model yields to both PHM and AFT specifications). Thus, we can calculate that in the post period, albums' survival, on average, has decreased by 42%. Thus they survive only 5.8 weeks now if they survived for 10 weeks earlier.

Superstar effect is also quite strong. Controlling for debut, superstars tend to survive longer on charts than otherwise. In particular, at any time, non-superstars' hazard of exiting the charts is 80% higher than superstars.

Minor labels do worse than major labels and surprisingly, both males and groups perform worse than females on Billboard 100 charts (at least in terms of survival). Albums debuting in the month of December tend to survive longer.

High frailty variance (variance of gamma distribution) indicates the importance of including unobserved heterogeneity.

We plot the hazard rate and survival rate for albums in post and pre period. Similarly, we plot the hazard rate and survival rate for albums with superstar to get more insight.

In Fig. 8.1a, we plot estimated hazard function for before and after data. Similarly, in Fig. 8.1b, we plot predicted hazard function for superstar and non-superstar. First note that hazard function is non-monotonic. As we saw in the previous section, the hazard is very high during the first 2–3 weeks (In short, many albums exit the Billboard chart within couple of weeks). However, past 3 weeks, hazard is decreasing. Thus once the album survives the first few weeks, it has a lower probability of exiting (or high probability of surviving longer). Also, note that the hazard functions are not proportional. It is because of the unobserved heterogeneity (gamma distribution) we introduced.

As our results indicated, hazard rate has increased significantly for albums in the post period (2000–2002) compared to pre period (1997–1999). Similarly, superstars have less hazard of exiting the Billboard 100.

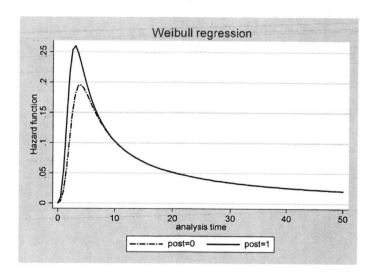

Fig. 8.1a Hazard rate in the Pre and Post periods

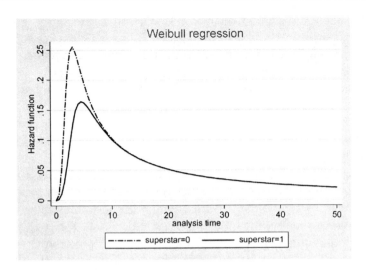

Fig. 8.1b Hazard rates for superstars and non-superstars

Similarly, in Fig. 8.2, we plot the predicted survival conditioned on exogenous factors (namely pre and post period and superstar or non-superstar). Notice that there is less than 20% chance of an album surviving beyond 10 weeks and once the albums survive 10 weeks, its survival rate more or less remains unchanged. Also, as the hazard graph indicated, survival rate is higher for superstars and survival rate in the post period has gone down significantly.

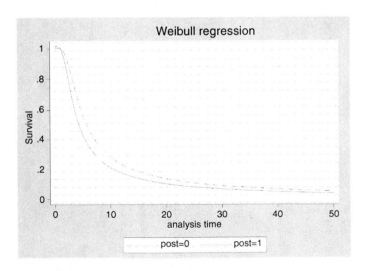

Fig. 8.2a Survival rates for albums in Pre and Post Period

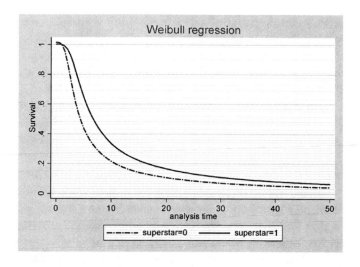

Fig. 8.2a Survival rates for superstars and non-superstars

Discussion and Conclusion

Technological advances can have significant impacts on economic markets. We have analyzed the impacts of the technological innovations of MP3 and online file-sharing on the music industry landscape. Our initial analysis focused on the development of a robust stochastic model to capture the overall dynamics of the music album life cycle on the Billboard Chart. The subsequent analysis focused on the exogenous album-related factors that impact the survivability of the Billboard Chart. In both analyses, the overall objective was to discern whether and how the recent technological innovations have fundamentally altered the music industry.

Following earlier work related to the markets for artists, we developed a stochastic process model of the life cycle of albums. Brute-force estimation yielded excellent fits for all years. The nature of the estimated models indicates a shift after the technological innovations of MP3 and online file-sharing that occurred over the 1998–1999 period. The 2000–2002 period is characterized by a much shorter life cycle. We find that music as a digital good has been significantly impacted by market changes brought about by easier information dissemination and product access to potential consumers. While overall album survival has decreased in the 2000–2002 period, the chances of survival increase dramatically after an album has survived beyond the first week during this period. This indicates a pattern that the "good" albums survive more. This also suggests that the new environment brought on by technological and other market innovations is not conducive to lower quality music albums. Easier sampling and information dissemination hurts the lower quality albums. In general, the life cycle of lower quality products will tend to diminish faster under this new environment. The analysis also suggests that albums face a shorter life cycle overall. Even with significant "churn" in the music market and related environment between the 1995–1997 and 2000–2002 periods, our simple yet robust model effectively captures the stochastic component of the chart life cycle process.

Our subsequent analysis sheds light on the exogenous factors that impact album survival and the shifts in the patterns of impact since the technological changes. We find that albums' survival has decreased significantly in post-period. We also find that superstar effect is quite strong. Superstars' albums tend to survive longer. Albums promoted by major labels and by females survive longer. Similarly, albums released in the month of December tend to survive longer.

In the face of file sharing networks that enable widespread sharing and downloading of music in digital forms, music companies have felt pressured to take steps to simultaneously safeguard their digital products and bolster their market performance. Their strategic decisions and actions have thus far focused on incorporating security mechanisms in the digital products themselves and on legal threats and actions against both operators of file sharing networks and individual file sharers (Bhattacharjee et al. 2006a,b). As illustrated by the Sony BMG situation earlier, embedded security measures can frustrate consumers and have significant negative impacts. Further, no security measure used by the entertainment industry so far has been foolproof. As Bhattacharjee et al. (2006a,b) detail, legal threats and actions have reduced sharing by individuals, but significant piracy opportunities remain. Further, such actions have been industry actions rather than individual firm actions.

Our focus has been on modeling life cycle on the charts and how it has been affected by significant changes in the landscape of the music market. A key finding is that the market landscape has shifted and that life cycle has shortened with lowered probabilities of surviving for each subsequent week on the chart. The significantly shorter shelf life of digital music calls for accelerated tactical and operational decision-making on resource allocations, in particular marketing and promotional efforts that target potential winners. In the latter period (2000–2002), the likelihood of surviving another week falls below one-half by the fifth week while this doesn't occur until the eighth week in the earlier period (1995–1997). Hence music companies may well opt to move promotional efforts earlier in the cycle. Interestingly, while the landscape has shifted, the underlying drivers that govern the life cycle process appear to have remained steady. That is, even with significant "churn" in the music market and related environment between the 1995–1997 and 2000–2002 periods, our underlying model form is robust and succinctly captures the life cycle process for the entire duration. Thus the same underlying decision models, where the parameters are constantly monitored and re-estimated, would provide a music firm with a reliable benchmark to gauge and assess their suite of the music albums in the marketplace, and make better decisions in an uncertain environment.[6]

Appendix: Steady State Characterization of the Stochastic Process

T_k, the total number of music albums that have appeared on the chart at the end of week k, can be expressed as

$$T_k = \sum_{m=1}^{k} C_{m,1} \tag{4}$$

$TD_{k,w}$, the total number of albums that were on the chart for exactly w weeks before falling off the charts at the end of week k, can be expressed recursively as

$$TD_{k,w} = TD_{k-1,w} + (1 - p_w)C_{k,w} \tag{5}$$

Note that $TD_{w,w-j} = 0 \;\; \forall j \geq 1$. Therefore (5) can be expressed as

$$TD_{k,w} = (1 - p_w)\sum_{m=1}^{k-w} C_{m+w,w} + TD_{w,w} \tag{6}$$

Further, we have

$$TD_{w,w} = (1 - p_w)C_{1,1}\prod_{j=1}^{w-1} p_j \tag{7}$$

$$C_{m+w,w} = C_{m+1,1}\prod_{j=1}^{w-1} p_j \tag{8}$$

Using (7) and (8), (6) can be expressed as

$$TD_{k,w} = (1 - p_w)\prod_{j=1}^{w-1} p_j \sum_{m=1}^{k-w} C_{m+1,1} + (1 - p_w)\prod_{j=1}^{w-1} p_j C_{1,1} \tag{9}$$

Simplifying, we obtain

$$TD_{k,w} = (1 - p_w)\prod_{j=1}^{w-1} p_j \sum_{m=1}^{k-w+1} C_{m,1} \tag{10}$$

From (4) and (10), we have

$$\frac{TD_{k,w}}{T_k} = (1 - p_w) \prod_{j=1}^{w-1} p_j \left(\frac{\sum\limits_{m=1}^{k-w+1} C_{m,1}}{\sum\limits_{m=1}^{k} C_{m,1}} \right) \tag{11}$$

For finite values of w,

$$\lim_{k \to \infty} \left(\frac{TD_{k,w}}{T_k} \right) = (1 - p_w) \prod_{j=1}^{w-1} p_j \tag{12}$$

which is independent of k, thus yielding our steady state.

Notes

The authors gratefully acknowledge the Treibick Family Endowed Chair, the Treibick Electronic Commerce Initiative, the XEROX CITI Endowment Fund, the GE Endowed Professor Fund, The Center for Internet Data and Research Intelligence Services (CIDRIS), and the Gladstein Endowed MIS Research Lab for support that made this work possible. Rahul Telang acknowledges the generous financial support of the National Science Foundation (NSF) through the CAREER award CNS-0546009.

1. MP3 is a commonly used audio compression technology.
2. Recently, legal threats from RIAA may be changing the landscape a bit (e.g., see Bhattacharjee et al. (2006)).
3. The top 100 albums per week are available free at http://www.billboard.com/ bbcom/charts/chart_display.jsp?f=The+Billboard+200&pageNumber=Top+1-10&g=Albums
4. Our empirical data show that the probability of an album re-appearing on the chart is minimal.
5. This also avoided the inclusion of periods with expected frequencies less than 5, a consideration when we analyze the appropriateness of our stochastic model.
6. Sudip Bhattacharjee is an Associate Professor and Ackerman Scholar in the Department of Operations and Information Management in the School of Business, University of Connecticut. Email: Sudip.Bhattacharjee@ business.uconn.edu. Ram D. Gopal is GE Endowed Professor of Business in the Department of Operations and Information Management in the School of Business, University of Connecticut. Email: Ram.Gopal@business.uconn.edu. James R. Marsden is the Treibick Family Endowed Chair in e-Business and Board of Trustees Distinguished Professor. Email: Jim.Marsden@ business.uconn.edu. Rahul Telang is an Assistant Professor of Information Systems and Management at the Heinz School, Carnegie Mellon University. Email: rtelang@andrew.cmu.edu.

References

Adler, Moshe, "Stardom and Talent," *American Economic Review*. 75 (March 1985) 208–212.

Albert, Steven, "Movie Stars and the Distribution of Financially Successful Films in the Motion Picture Industry," *Journal of Cultural Economics*. 22 (1998) 249–270.

Associated Press, "Norwegian hacker cracks iTunes code," *CNN*, November 27, 2003, http://www.cnn.com/2003/TECH/internet/11/27/itunes.code.ap/index.html

Bergstein, B., "Copy Protection Still a Work in Progress," *Associated Press*, http://news.yahoo.com/s/ap/20051119/ap_on_hi_te/music_copy_protection;_y lt=ArOQdPcARo.I0hnGv20mpcdk24cA;_ylu=X3oDMTBidHQxYjh2BHNlY wN5bnN0b3J5, Nov 18, 2005.

Bhattacharjee, S., R.D. Gopal, K. Lertwachara, and J.R. Marsden, "Impact of Legal Threats on Individual Behavior: An Analysis of Music Industry Actions and Online Music Sharing," *Journal of Law and Economics*. 49 (1) (April 2006) 91–114.

Bhattacharjee, S., R.D. Gopal, K. Lertwachara, and J.R. Marsden, "Whatever Happened To Payola? An Empirical Analysis of Online Music Sharing," *Decision Support Systems*. 42 (1) (2006) 104–120.

Bradley, M., "Sony Aims at Pirates – and Hits Users," *Christian Science Monitor*, Nov 9, 2005, http://www.csmonitor.com/2005/1109/p14s01-stct.html

Bradlow, Eric T. and Peter S. Fader, "A Bayesian Lifetime Model for the Hot 100 Billboard Songs," *The Journal of the American Statistical Association*. 96 (2001) 368–381.

Chung, Kee H. and Raymond A.K. Cox, "A Stochastic Model of Superstardom: An Application of the Yule Distribution," *Review of Economics and Statistics*. 76 (4) (November 1994) 771–775.

Clarke, G., "DVD Jon Hacks Media Player File Encryption," *The Register*, September 2, 2005, http://www.theregister.co.uk/2005/09/02/dvd_jon_ mediaplayer/

Cox, A.K. and Kee H. Chung, "Patterns of Research Output and Author Concentration in the Economics Literature," *Review of Economics and Statistics*. 73 (4) (Nov. 1991) 740–747.

Cox, D.R., "Regression Models and Life Tables," *Journal of the Royal Statistical Society Series B*. 34 (1972) 187–220.

Craver, S.A., Min Wu, Bede Liu, Adam Stubblefield, Ben Swartzlander, Dan W. Wallach, Drew Dean, and Edward W. Felten, "Reading Between the Lines: Lessons from the SDMI Challenge," *Proc. of 10th USENIX Security Sym_ posium* (August 2001).

Felten, E.W., "A Skeptical View of DRM and Fair Use," *Communications of the ACM*. 46 (4) (April 2003) 56–61.

Felten, E.W., "Inside RISKS: DRM and Public Policy," *Communications of the ACM*. 48 (7) (July 2005) 112.

Goodley, S., "Disharmony over music pirates on the Internet," *The Telegraph*, January 9, 2003, http://www.telegraph.co.uk

Halderman, J.A., "Evaluating New Copy-Prevention Techniques for Audio CDs," *Proc. ACM Workshop on Digital Rights Management*, Washington, DC, November 2002.

Levene, Mark, Trevor Fenner, Geroge Loizou, and Richard Wheeldon, "A Stochastic Model for the Evolution of the Web," *Computer Networks*. 39 (2002) 277–287.

Patrizio, A., "Why the DVD Hack Was a Cinch," *Wired News*, November 2, 1999, http://www.wired.com/news/technology/0,1282,32263,00.html

Reuters, "CD Crack: Magic Marker Indeed," May 20, 2002, http://www.wired.com/news/technology/0,1282,52665,00.html

Reuters, "Sony Tests Technology to Limit CD Burning," *CNET News.* June 1, 2005, http://news.cnet.co.uk/digitalmusic/0,39029666,39189658,00.htm

Rosen, Sherwin, "The Economics of Superstars," *American Economic Review.* 71 (December 1981) 845–858.

Russinovich, M., "Sony, Rootkits and Digital Rights Management Gone Too Far," http://www.sysinternals.com/blog/2005/10/sony-rootkits-and-digital-rights.html, *Mark's Sysinternals Blog*, October 31, 2005.

Schneier, B., *Secrets and Lies: Digital Security in a Networked World.* John Wiley & Sons, Inc., New York, 2000.

Simon, Herbert A., "On a Class of Skew Distribution Functions," *Biometrika.* 42 (1955) 425–440.

Smith, E., "Sony BMG Faces Civil Complaint Over CD Software," http://online.wsj.com/article/SB113259581938503230.html?mod=mm_hs_entertainment, *The Wall Street Journal.* (November 22, 2005).

Yule, G. Udny, "A Mathematical Theory of Evolution, based on the Conclusions of Dr. J.C. Willis, F.R.S.," *Philosophical Transactions of the Royal Society B.* 213 (1924) 21–87.

Ziemann, George, "RIAA's Statistics Don't Add Up to Piracy," December 11, 2002, http://www.azoz.com/music/features/0008.htm

9

Characteristics and Potentials of YouTube: A Measurement Study

Xu Cheng, Cameron Dale, Jiangchuan Liu

Simon Fraser University

Introduction

Established in 2005, YouTube is one of the fastest-growing websites, and has become one of the most accessed sites in the Internet. It has a significant impact on the Internet traffic distribution, but itself is suffering from severe scalability constraints. Understanding the features of YouTube and similar video sharing sites is thus crucial to network traffic engineering and to sustainable development of this new generation of services.

In this paper, we present an in-depth and systematic measurement study on the characteristics of YouTube videos. We crawled the YouTube site for a 3-month period in early 2007, and obtained more than 2 million distinct videos. This constitutes a significant portion of the entire YouTube video repository. Using this collection of datasets, we find that YouTube videos have noticeably different statistics from traditional streaming videos, such as video length.

We also look closely at the social networking aspect of YouTube, as this is a key driving force toward the success of YouTube and similar sites. In particular, we find that the links to related videos generated by uploaders' choices form a small-world network. This suggests that the videos have strong correlations with each other, and creates opportunities for developing novel Peer-to-Peer distribution schemes to efficiently deliver videos to end users.

E.M. Noam and L.M. Pupillo (eds.), *Peer-to-Peer Video*, doi: 10.1007/978-0-387-76450-4_9,
© Springer Science + Business Media, LLC 2008

The rest of the paper is organized as follows. Next is a section presenting some background information and other related work. Following is a section which first describes our method of gathering information about YouTube videos, which is then analyzed generally, while the social networking aspects are analyzed separately in the subsequent section. The last section discusses the implications of the results, and suggests ways that the YouTube service could be improved. Finally, we draw our conclusions.

Background and Related Work

Internet Video Sharing

Online videos existed long before YouTube entered the scene. However, uploading videos, managing, sharing, and watching them was very cumbersome due to a lack of an easy-to-use integrated platform. More importantly, the videos distributed by traditional media servers and Peer-to-Peer file downloads like BitTorrent were standalone units of content. Each single video was not connected in any way to other related video clips, for example, to other episodes of a show that the user had just watched. Also, there was very little in the way of content reviews or ratings.

The new generation of video sharing sites, formed by YouTube and its competitors, has overcome these problems as they allow content suppliers to upload videos effortlessly, automatically converting them from many different formats, and to tag uploaded videos with keywords. Users can easily share videos by mailing links to them, or embedding them on web pages or in blogs. Users can also rate and comment videos, bringing new social aspects to the viewing of videos. Consequently, popular videos can rise to the top in a very organized fashion.

The social network existing in YouTube further enables the development of communities and groups. Videos are no longer independent from each other, and neither are users. This has substantially contributed to the success of YouTube and similar sites.

Workload Measurement of Media Servers

There has been a significant research effort into understanding the workloads of traditional media servers, looking at, for example, the video popularity and access locality [2][8]. We have found that, while sharing similar features, many of the video statistics of these traditional media servers are quite different from those of YouTube; for example, the video length distribution. More importantly, these traditional studies lack a social network among the videos.

A similar work to ours is the study by Huang et al. [5]. They analyzed a 9-month trace of MSN Video, Microsoft's VoD service, examining the user behavior and popularity distribution of videos. This analysis led to a peer-assisted VoD design for reducing the server's bandwidth costs. The difference to our work is that MSN Video is a more traditional video service, with far less videos, most of which are also longer than YouTube videos. MSN Video also has no listings of related videos or user information, and thus no social networking aspect.

We have seen simultaneous works investigating social networks in popular Web 2.0 sites, including Flicker, Orkut, and LiveJournal [7]. While YouTube is also one of the targeted sites in their studies, a thorough understanding of the unique characteristics of short video sharing has yet to be gained, particularly considering that YouTube has a much higher impact. Recently, a YouTube traffic analysis was presented which tracks YouTube transactions in a campus network [4]. The research focus was on deriving video access patterns from the network edge perspective. Our work complements it by crawling a much larger set of the videos and thus being able to accurately measure their global properties, and in particular, the social networks.

Characteristics of YouTube Video

In this paper, we focus on the access patterns and social networks in YouTube. To this end, we crawled the YouTube site for a 3-month period and obtained information on its videos through a combination of the YouTube API and scrapes of YouTube video web pages. The results offer a series of representative partial snapshots of the YouTube video repository.

Methodology of Measurement

Video Meta-data

YouTube randomly assigns each video an 11-digit ID. Each video contains the following intuitive meta-data: user who uploaded it, date when it was uploaded, category, length, number of views, number of ratings, number of comments, and a list of "related videos." The related videos are links to other videos that have a similar title, description, or related tags, all of which are chosen by the uploader. A video can have hundreds of related videos, but the webpage only shows at most 20 at once, so we limit our scrape to these top 20 related videos. A typical example of the meta-data is shown in Table 9.1.

Table 9.1 Meta-data of a YouTube video

ID	2AYAY2TLves
Uploader	GrimSanto
Added Date	May 19, 2007
Category	Gadgets & Games
Video Length	268 seconds
Number of Views	185,615
Number of Ratings	546
Number of Comments	588
Related Videos	aUXoekeDIW8, Sog2k6s7xVQ, ...

YouTube Crawler

We consider all the YouTube videos to form a directed graph, where each video is represented by a node in the graph. If video b is in the related video list (only among the first 20) of video a, then there is a directed edge from a to b. Our crawler uses a breadth-first search to find videos in the graph.

Our first crawl was carried out on February 22, 2007, and found approximately 750 thousand videos in about 5 days. In the following weeks we ran the crawler every two to three days. On average, the crawl found 80,000 distinct videos each time. We also crawled other statistics such as the file size and bitrate information. By the end of April 2007, we had obtained 27 datasets totaling 2,676,388 distinct videos. This constitutes a significant portion of the entire YouTube video repository.[1] Also, because most of these videos can be accessed from the YouTube homepage in less than 10 clicks, they are generally active and thus representative for measuring characteristics of the repository.

Video Category

One of twelve categories is selected by the user when uploading the video. Table 9.2 lists the count numbers and percentages of all the categories. In our entire dataset we note that distribution is highly skewed: the most popular category is "Music", at about 22.9%; the second is "Entertainment", at about 17.8%; and the third is "Comedy", at about 12.1%.

Table 9.2 List of YouTube video categories

Category	Count	%
Autos and Vehicles	66,878	2.5
Comedy	323,814	12.1
Entertainment	475,821	17.8
Film and Animation	225,817	8.4
Gadgets and Games	196,026	7.3
Howto and DIY	53,291	2.0
Music	613,754	22.9
News and Politics	116,153	4.3
People and Blogs	199,014	7.4
Pets and Animals	50,092	1.9
Sports	258,375	9.7
Travel and Places	58,678	2.2
Unavailable	24,068	0.9
Removed	14,607	0.5

In the table, we also list two other categories. "Unavailable" are the videos set to private, or videos that have been flagged as inappropriate, which the crawler can only get information for from the YouTube API, whilst "Removed" are videos that have been deleted by the uploader, or by a YouTube moderator (due to the violation of the terms of use), but are still linked to by other videos.

Video Length

The length of YouTube videos is the principal difference from traditional media content servers. Whereas most traditional servers contain a small to medium number of long videos, typically 1–2 h movies (e.g., HPLabs Media Server [8]), YouTube is mostly comprised of short video clips.

In our entire dataset, 97.8% of the videos last less than 600 s, and 99.1% are under 700 s. This is mainly due to the limit of 10 min imposed by YouTube on uploads by regular users. We do find videos longer than this limit though, as the limit was only established in March 2006, and also the YouTube Director Program allows a small group of authorized users to upload videos that are longer than 10 min.[2]

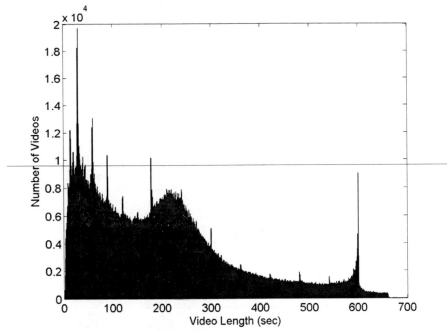

Fig. 9.1 Distribution of video length

Figure 9.1 shows the distribution of YouTube videos' lengths of less than 700 s, which exhibits three peaks. The first peak is for videos that last less than a minute, and contains more than 20% of all videos, which clearly demonstrates that YouTube is primarily a site for very short videos. The second peak is between 3 and 4 min, and contains about 16.7% of the videos. This peak is mainly caused by the large number of videos in the "Music" category. "Music" is the most popular category for YouTube, and the typical length of a music video is often within this range. The third peak is close to the maximum of 10 min, and is caused by the limit on the length of uploaded videos. This encourages some users to circumvent the length restriction by dividing long videos into several parts, each being near the limit of 10 min.

File Size and Bitrate

We retrieved the file size of nearly 190,000 videos. In our crawled data, 98.8% of the videos are smaller than 30 MB size. Not surprisingly, we find that the distribution of video sizes is very similar to the distribution of video lengths. We calculate an average video file size to be about 8.4 MB.

Considering there are over 42.5 million YouTube videos, the total disk space required to store all the videos is more than 357 terabytes! Smart storage management is thus quite demanding for such an ultra-huge and still growing site, which we discuss in another paper [3].

We found that the videos' bitrate has three clear peaks. Most videos have a bitrate around 330 kbps, with two other peaks at around 285 kbps and 200 kbps. This implies that YouTube videos have a moderate bitrate that balances quality and bandwidth.

Date Added – Growth Trend of Uploading

During our crawl we recorded the date that each video was uploaded, so that we could study the growth trend of YouTube. Figure 9.2 shows the number of new videos added every 2 weeks in our entire crawled dataset.

February 15, 2005 is the day that YouTube was established. Our first crawl was on February 22, 2007; this meant that we could only find early videos if they were still very popular videos or are linked to by other videos we crawled. We can see there is a slow start, the earliest video we crawled was uploaded on April 27, 2005. Six months after YouTube's establishment, the number of uploaded videos increases steeply.

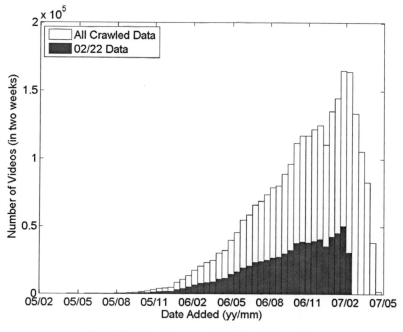

Fig. 9.2 Uploading trend of YouTube videos

Views – User Access Pattern

The number of views a video has had is the most important characteristic we measured, as it reflects the popularity and access patterns of the videos. We use a single dataset containing more than 100,000, which is considered to be relatively static.

Figure 9.3 shows the number of views as a function of the rank of the video by its number of views. The plot has a long tail on the linear scale (not shown), which means there are a few videos that have been watched millions of times, and there are also a great number of videos that are seldom watched. However, unlike website visitors distribution, web caching and Peer-to-Peer file sharing workload, the access pattern does not follow a Zipf distribution, which should be a straight line on a log–log scale. The figure shows that the beginning of the curve is linear on a log–log scale, but the tail (after the 2×103 video) decreases tremendously, indicating there are not so many less popular videos as Zipf's law predicts.

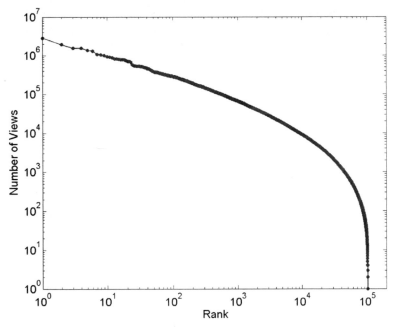

Fig. 9.3 YouTube videos rank ordered by popularity

The Social Network in YouTube

YouTube is a prominent social media application: there are communities and groups in YouTube, there are statistics and awards for videos and personal channels. Videos are no longer independent from each other, and neither are the users. It is therefore important to understand the social network characteristics of YouTube. We next examine the social network among YouTube users and videos, which is a unique and interesting aspect of this kind of video sharing sites, as compared to traditional media services.

Small-World Phenomenon

The small-world network phenomenon is probably the most interesting characteristic for social networks, and has been found in various real-world situations, such as URL links in the Web [1].

The concept of a small-world was first introduced by Milgram to refer to the principle that people are linked to all others by short chains of acquaintances (popularly known as six degrees of separation) [6]. This formulation was used by Watts and Strogatz to describe networks that are neither completely random, nor completely regular, but possess character-istics of both [9]. They introduce a measure of one of these characteristics, the cliquishness of a typical neighborhood, as the *clustering coefficient* of the graph. They define a small-world graph as one in which the clustering coefficient is still large, as in regular graphs, but the measure of the average distance between nodes (the *characteristic path length*) is small, as in random graphs.

The Small-World in YouTube

We measured the graph topology for all the YouTube data gathered, by using the related links in YouTube pages to form directed edges in a video graph for the entire dataset. For comparison, we also generate random graph with the same number of nodes and average node degree of the crawled dataset.

We found that the clustering coefficient of our YouTube dataset is quite high, about 0.3, and is especially large in comparison to the random graphs, which are nearly 0. We also found that the characteristic path length is about 8, which is only slightly larger than that of the corresponding random graph. This is quite good, considering the still large clustering coefficient of these datasets.

The network formed by YouTube's related videos list has definite small-world characteristics. The clustering coefficient is very large compared to a similar sized random graph, while the characteristic path length is approaching the short path lengths measured in the random graphs. This finding is expected, due to the user-generated nature of the tags, title, and description of the videos that is used by YouTube to find related ones.

These results are similar to other real-world user-generated graphs, yet their parameters can be quite different. For example, the graph formed by URL links in the World Wide Web exhibits a much longer characteristic path length of 18.59 [1]. This could possibly be due to the larger number of nodes (8×108 in the web), but it may also indicate that the YouTube network of videos is a much closer group.

Further Discussions

Can Peer-to-Peer Save YouTube?

Short video sharing and Peer-to-Peer streaming have been widely cited as two key driving forces to Internet video distribution, yet their development remains largely separated. The Peer-to-Peer technology has been quite successful in supporting large-scale live video streaming (e.g., TV programs like PPLive and CoolStreaming) and even on-demand streaming (e.g., GridCast). Since each peer contributes its bandwidth to serve others, a Peer-to-Peer overlay scales extremely well with larger user bases. YouTube and similar sites still use the traditional client-server architecture, restricting their scalability.

Unfortunately, our YouTube measurement results suggest that using Peer-to-Peer delivery for YouTube could be quite challenging. In particular, the length of a YouTube video is quite short (many are shorter than the typical connection time in a Peer-to-Peer overlay), and a user often quickly loads another video when finishing a previous one, so the overlay will suffer from an extremely high churn rate. Moreover, there is a large number of videos, so the Peer-to-Peer overlays will appear very small.

Our social network findings again could be exploited by considering a group of related videos as a single large video, with each video in the group being a portion of the large one. Therefore, the overlay would be much larger and more stable. Although a user may only watch one video from the group, he/she can download the other portions of the large video from the server when there is enough bandwidth and space, and upload those downloaded portions to other clients who are interested in them. This behavior can significantly reduce the bandwidth consumption from the server and greatly increase the scalability of the system.

Finally, another benefit of using a Peer-to-Peer model is to avoid single-point of failures and enhance data availability. While this is in general attractive, it is worth noting that timely removal of videos that violate the terms of use (e.g., copyright-protected or illegal content, referred to by the "Removed" category above) have constantly been one of the most annoying issues for YouTube and similar sites. Peer-to-Peer delivery will clearly make the situation even worse, which must be well addressed before we shift such sites to the Peer-to-Peer communication paradigm.

A Peer-to-Peer SImulation

Our ongoing work is to design a Peer-to-Peer structured short video sharing system. In this system, peers are responsible for redistributing the videos they have already downloaded. Therefore, the workload traffic of the server is significantly reduced. We conduct a simulation and plot the results in Fig. 9.4.

In Fig. 9.4, the topmost line represents the server bandwidth in client-server structure; the lowest line represents the server bandwidth in optimal Peer-to-Peer structure, in which the peer has unlimited uploading bandwidth, unlimited storage to store all the downloaded video, and exists all the time. The optimal situation is impossible to implement, thus we limit the peer's uploading bandwidth, storage, and existing time. In this case, the server bandwidth is represented by the second lowest line, and the total peer uploading bandwidth is represented by the second highest line. From the figure, we can easily find out that the server bandwidth is greatly reduced in Peer-to-Peer structure, amounting to approximately 39.8% of that in the client-server structure; the contribution of all the peers is more than that of the server.

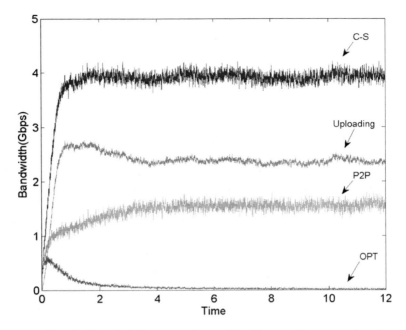

Fig. 9.4 Bandwidth comparison of the Peer-to-Peer experiment

Conclusion

This paper has presented a detailed investigation of the characteristics of YouTube, the most popular Internet short video sharing site to date. Through examining massive amounts of data collected in a 3-month period, we have demonstrated that, while sharing certain similar features with traditional video repositories, YouTube exhibits many unique characteristics, especially in length distribution. These characteristics introduce novel challenges and opportunities for optimizing the performance of short video sharing services.

We have also investigated the social network among YouTube videos, which is probably its most unique and interesting aspect, and has substantially contributed to the success of this new generation of services. We have found that the networks of related videos, which are chosen based on user-generated content, have both small-world characteristics of a large clustering coefficient indicating the grouping of videos, and a short characteristic path length linking any two videos. We have suggested that these features can be exploited to facilitate the design of novel Peer-to-Peer strategies for short video sharing.[3]

Notes

1. There are an estimated 42.5 million videos on YouTube: http://googlesystem.blogspot.com/2007/06/google-videos-new-frame.html
2. YouTube Blog: http://youtube.com/blog
3. Xu Cheng is a Ph.D. student in the School of Computing Science at Simon Fraser University, British Columbia, Canada. Email: xuc@sfu.ca. Cameron Dale is a M.Sc. student in the School of Computing Science Simon Fraser University. Email: camerond@cs.sfu.ca. Jiangchuan Liu is Assistant Professor in the School of Computing Science, Simon Fraser University, British Columbia, Canada. Email: jcliu@cs.sfu.ca.

References

Albert R., Jeong H., and Barabasi A. The Diameter of the World Wide Web. Nature, vol. 401, pp. 130, 1999.

Almeida J.M., Krueger J., Eager D.L., and Vernon M.K. Analysis of Educational Media Server Workloads. In Proc. of NOSSDAV, 2001.

Cheng X., Dale C., and Liu J. Statistics and Social Network of YouTube Videos. In Proc. of IWQoS, 2008.

Gill P., Arlitt M., Li Z., and Mahanti A. YouTube Traffic Characterization: A View From the Edge. In Proc. of IMC, 2007.

Huang C., Li J., and Ross K.W. Can Internet Video-on-Demand be Profitable? In Proc. of SIGCOMM'07.

Milgram S. The Small World Problem. Psychology Today, vol. 2, no. 1, pp. 60–67, 1967.

Mislove A., Marcon M.,. Gummadi K.P, Dreschel P., and Bhattacharjee B. Measurement and Analysis of Online Social Networks. In Proc. of IMC, 2007.

Tang W., Fu Y., Cherkasova L., and Vahdat A. Long-term Streaming Media Server Workload Analysis and Modeling. Technical report, HP Labs, 2003.

Watts D. and Strogatz S. Collective Dynamics of "Small-World" Networks. Nature, vol. 393, no. 6684, pp. 440–442, 1998.

10

YouTube and Its Mobile Distributing Consumer Media Venturing

Min Hang

Jönköping University and Tsinghua University

On Christmas Day in 2007, Queen Elizabeth II posted her traditional Christmas message on YouTube for the first time through a special royal channel on this popular Peer-to-Peer video-sharing website.[1]

"The queen always keeps abreast with new ways of communicating with people," Buckingham Palace said in a statement. "This will make the Christmas message more accessible to younger people and those in other countries."[2]

The Royal Channel in YouTube features a regal homepage illustrated with a photograph of Buckingham Palace in London flanked by guards in bearskin hats and red tunics. Therein, viewers can watch past Christmas messages as well as archive and contemporary footage of Britain's royal family. The footage of the queen's 1957 Christmas TV broadcast in the YouTube Royal Channel may remind viewers that TV once was as groundbreaking a creation as Internet is today.

"I very much hope that this new medium will make my Christmas message more personal and direct. That it is possible for some of you to see me today is just another example of the speed at which things are changing all around us," the queen said in television at the time.[3]

Just a half century later, today, the media landscape has changed with an even greater speed. The increasing use of broadband Internet connection and advances in streaming technology create tremendous possibilities to deliver media content over the Net. Among others, the emergence of Peer-to-Peer media devices and the striking example of a flourishing YouTube are representative of the most recent new media trends and movements.

E.M. Noam and L.M. Pupillo (eds.), *Peer-to-Peer Video*, doi: 10.1007/978-0-387-76450-4_10,
© Springer Science + Business Media, LLC 2008

This chapter will focus on the emerging Peer-to-Peer video sharing company YouTube. The author will introduce the emergence and development of YouTube as a fast growing consumer media company. The analysis of the company will be made from the perspective of its mobile distributing consumer media venturing – a major business venturing activity inside the company that is aiming at adding more mobility to its Peer-to-Peer video sharing services. The empirical findings presented in this chapter are extracted from a doctoral research project that investigates global media companies' organizational choices on the architecture for new media business venturing. Therefore, implications for YouTube to develop mobile media business will also be discussed in this chapter.

YouTube: The Emergence and Development

YouTube is a young but fast growing consumer media company that emerged only a couple of years ago. It grew from a website, YouTube.com, that was created for people to watch and to share video content through. Now it has become one of the most popular media entertainment websites worldwide with millions of people visiting it every day.

YouTube.com was founded by Chad Hurley, Steve Chen, and Jawed Karim in 2005. All three founders of the company were early employees of PayPal. After a dinner party in January 2005, they found it was hard to find a proper site through which they could share the video they'd taken during the party with their friends. So they came up with the idea of creating a website for video uploading and downloading.[4] "YouTube.com" was activated on February 15, 2005; the website was developed quickly over the following months. The founders offered the public a preview of the site in May 2005, and, 6 months later, YouTube made its official debut.[5]

In a similar way as many other technology start-ups, YouTube was started as a small enterprise in an inexpensive garage. In November 2005, a venture capital firm Sequoia Capital invested an initial $3.5 million in YouTube. Additionally, Roelof Botha, partner of the firm and former CFO of PayPal, joined the YouTube board of directors. In April 2006, Sequoia put an additional $8 million into the company, and YouTube immediately witnessed a boom of popularity and growth in just its first few months of operation.[6]

To make its business grow and also to protect the company from the threat of copyright-infringement[7] YouTube started to form strategic alliances with big content production media companies. In April 2006, YouTube allied with G4 to bring entertaining video content to their audiences. The alliance brought, for example, G4's interactive series "Star Trek 2.0" to YouTube, using the stop-motion animation.

In June 2006, YouTube allied with NBC to promote NBC's Fall program lineup and other preferred shows over the next year.[8] The alliance agreement included a cross-promotional advertising relationship on the YouTube service and on-air promotion provided by NBC. Under the terms of the agreement, NBC would create an official NBC Channel on YouTube to house its Fall Preview area with exclusive clips to promote NBC's content. In addition, over the next year, NBC was to upload several video presentations per week to the NBC Channel on YouTube. YouTube will also promote NBC's videos throughout its site.

In September 2006, YouTube and Warner Music Group (WMG) announced an agreement to distribute its library of music videos through YouTube. In the arrangement, YouTube users could incorporate music from WMG's recorded music catalog into the videos they created and uploaded onto YouTube. WMG became the first music company to harness YouTube's video entertainment service to commercially distribute its music video catalog. WMG also became the first global media company to embrace the user generated content.

In October 2006, YouTube and Universal Music Group announced an agreement offering YouTube and its users access to UMG's roster of artists covering every genre of music. In addition, under this agreement, UMG embraced the user-generated content, allowing users to incorporate music from UMG's recorded music catalog into the videos they create and upload onto YouTube.[9]

During the same month, YouTube announced another deal with Sony BMG to make available a wide variety of video content to the YouTube community. In addition, SONY BMG and YouTube agreed to work together to develop new opportunities which would allow users to include certain SONY BMG sound recordings in their own uploads.

In addition, YouTube signed a strategic content and advertising partnership agreement with CBS Corporation. The deal called for the CBS Television Network, its premium television service provider, Showtime Networks Inc., as well as its basic cable/digital media service, CSTV Networks, Inc., to offer the YouTube community a wide variety of short-form video programming from its news, sports, and entertainment divisions on a daily basis, beginning that month. Meanwhile, CBS was the first TV network to test YouTube's new content identification architecture and reporting system which would allow CBS to protect its intellectual property by identifying and locating copyrighted CBS content on YouTube. CBS would then have the opportunity to either remove it from the site or, at CBS's sole discretion, allow it to remain. If CBS allowed the content to remain on the site, CBS would share in any revenue from advertisements placed adjacent to the content.[10]

Through these agreements and alliances, YouTube has largely reduced the risks of possible lawsuits, and also strengthened its overall content and distribution capabilities. The incredibly fast growth of YouTube made this new company quickly become the target for many media and technology giants. Big media conglomerates, such as Google, Microsoft, Yahoo, the News Corporate, and Viacom all visited YouTube's headquarters in San Mateo to inquire about buying the company. Finally, on October 9, 2006, an announcement was made that YouTube would be purchased by Google for US$1.65 billion in stock. According to the purchase, YouTube would continue to operate independently, and the company's 67 employees and its co-founders would continue working with the company. The deal to acquire YouTube was closed on November 13, and became Google's biggest purchase to date.

Today, YouTube is one of the most booming websites on the World Wide Web, and the speed of its growth has even outpaced that of MySpace. According to a 2006 survey in the USA, 100 million clips are viewed daily on YouTube, with an additional 65,000 new videos uploaded every 24 hours. The site has almost 20 million visitors each month, according to Nielsen/NetRatings, where around 44% are female, 56% male, and the 12- to 17-year-old age group is dominant.[11] According to Hitswise.com, YouTube commands up to 64% of the UK online video market. These successes show that YouTube has achieved exciting performance in the online video market.

The Mobile Distributing Consumer Media Venturing in YouTube

To maintain its fast development, and to expand the scope of its business services, YouTube has been staying innovative and creative. Growing from a new venture providing video content on the web, recently the company has started to venture into another new arena – delivering video content to mobile users.

"Everybody carries a phone with them, but they may not have a computer," said Steve Chen, chief technology officer and co-founder of YouTube. With the mobile platform, people can take the phone out of their pocket while waiting for the bus and watch a video" he added.[12]

YouTube's move to mobile started in May 2006. In that month, YouTube launched a service that allowed people to upload videos directly from their mobile phones and PDAs to the YouTube Web site. Six months later, YouTube moved a step further to ally with mobile operators to deliver video content to mobile devices.[13]

In November 2006, YouTube announced that they would make the mobile phone debut, allying with Verizon Wireless. While its YouTube.com website is free, as it is based totally on an advertising model, YouTube's phone-based business requires a $15-a-month subscription to a Verizon Wireless service called VCast. Instead of choosing what to watch from a vast library of clips, VCast users will be limited to an unspecified number of videos selected and approved by the company. YouTube editors will select short videos from their library for the Verizon Wireless service.

Though there have been over thousands of mobile video titles already available to Cingular, Sprint, and Verizon Wireless Subscribers, YouTube is still the first to offer user-generated content. However, this new mobile service is not without problems. Many people doubt whether the limited selection of videos on the service will undermine the basic appeal of YouTube, which has grown popular in the past because users decide what they want to watch.[14] In addition, how far a subscription model can go is surrounded by uncertainty.

Nevertheless, there are also many people who believe that the YouTube online content could translate well to the mobile phone. And this new business will bring more opportunities for the company to promote their business in a larger arena.

"Our new mobile service is the first of many," said Kelly Liang, senior director of business development for YouTube. Ms. Liang said the company planned to introduce other such deals within the coming year.

"We are excited to launch our new mobile service and to partner with Verizon Wireless to bring YouTube videos to a new audience," said Steve Chen. "People want to be entertained in a way that fits their individual lifestyle. This service offers our community and Verizon Wireless subscribers a new opportunity to connect and engage with their favorite videos.

We will continue to roll out more exciting partnerships and features for the mobile user over the coming year."[15]

New business venturing is certain to happen in an innovative and young firm like YouTube. As many of the other new business initiatives, the starting of the new mobile distributing consumer media venturing in YouTube is associated with explicit and implicit organizational choices. The author of this chapter has conducted a doctoral research to examine these organizational choices, especially the choice concerning the organizational structure to accommodate the new mobile media distributing business.[16] The following text will give a brief summary of this research: the theories applied, empirical findings, and implications for the YouTube mobile distributing consumer media venturing.

Theories and Empirical Findings

The purpose of this research is to examine the organizational structural choice for new media venturing. There are basically two structural options for new business venturing. A common assumption is that the new business creation occurs within a hierarchical framework – namely, the new entities start up and develop within an existing organizational architecture. The other assumption is that new business can be developed through market modes, by allying with other companies on a cooperative base, or setting up a new entity outside the organizational architecture. Usually, the hierarchical modes and market modes represent two ends of the spectrum of viable organizational choices; thus, the challenge facing the companies is: which direction should they take?

To answer such a question, two theories can provide helpful guidance: the Industrial Organizational Theories (IO) – the traditional industrial economics theories – seek to give explanation to the new businesses development from an economics perspective. They tend to explain new business venturing as economic activities that aim to minimize costs. The Resource-based View (RBV) – a more recent internal resource/competence-based theory – seeks to give explanation to new business development from the resource perspective, by focusing on the resource/capability development of the new business.

The IO developed from the structure–conduct–performance (SCP) paradigm proposed by Bain (1968) for explaining industry structure and behavior, competition, etc. It was later popularized with a strategic flavor by Porter (1985). According to the IO, the choice of an organization to carry out any economic activity is a function of the transaction costs and agency costs in carrying out that activity. Thus, if the company does not own or control all the resources necessary to pursue an opportunity, they must deal with other resource controllers in order to have access to all required resources. The pursuit of opportunities can be organized in many alternative ways, and, if other things are equal, the firm will choose the way that minimizes the transaction costs and agency costs in the process of pursuing the opportunities.

In accordance with the IO, firms need to consider transaction costs and agency costs for rational organizational choices. IO further suggests that if certain "economic conditions" that include the level of transaction costs (mainly measured by the level of uncertainty and the level of specificity of investment) and the level of agency costs are high, it is more likely that firms will venture for new business internally with hierarchical modes; otherwise, firms will choose to develop new business with market modes, e.g., allying with external partners.

The Resource-based View suggests that a firm is best viewed as a collection of sticky and imperfectly imitable resources or capabilities that enable it to successfully compete against other firms.[17] Barney[18] referred to the resource "include all assets, capabilities, organizational processes, firm attributes, information, knowledge, etc; controlled by a firm that enable the firm to conceive of all implement strategies that improve its efficiency and effectiveness." In addition to the term "resource," researchers from the resource perspective have also been trying to explain firm behavior and competitiveness in terms and concepts such as capability[19] and competence.[20]

According to the RBV, when a company develops a new business, it must consider certain "resource conditions" that include, for instance, the managerial capabilities for resource recombination, new business production capabilities, and new business distribution capabilities. If such "resource conditions" are high, it is more likely that the firm will create new business internally; otherwise, the firm will develop new business externally, e.g., through allying with external partners.

To find empirical evidence for the above theoretical propositions, the author conducted case studies in several global media companies. In You-Tube, the author interviewed the business director and editors. In addition, company archives were reviewed, and relevant information was retrieved from the company's website and related publications. Table 10.1 presents a summary of the empirical findings.

Table 10.1 Empirical Findings

Economic conditions	There was a huge market potential to develop mobile related business, and YouTube was the first company to provide the user-generated content via mobile. The increasing popularity of YouTube brought huge brand benefits to its mobile services. The content delivered to mobile was selected by the company, which protected the new business from potential risks of legal infringement. There was no high specific investment in this case: as the content was user-generated and YouTube allied with network operators for content delivery, high transaction costs and agency costs were avoided. Therefore, the general level of "economic conditions" was relatively low.
Resource conditions	The company was young, lacked experiences in resource recombination. The company called itself "learning through doing," and the capabilities in resource recombination was not high in general. The company did not have its own distribution channel for mobile services,thus had to ally with wireless operators. Therefore, the general level of "resource conditions" was relatively low as well.
Structural choice for new media venturing	YouTube allied with external partners, and mobile media venturing activities were organized mostly with the market mode.

Summary and Implications

To sum up, for the YouTube mobile business venturing, the overall "economic conditions" that include the "level of uncertainty, the specificity of investment, and the level of agency costs" were relatively low, due to the huge market potential to develop mobile distributing business. In addition, the increasing popularity of YouTube brought positive brand benefits to the company's mobile services. The content delivered to mobile devices was selective in order to protect the new business from potential risks of legal infringement. Meanwhile, there was hardly any specific investment required by the new business, and, as the content was user-generated and YouTube allied with network operators for content delivery, high agency costs were avoided. Thus, the level of the "economic conditions" for the new mobile distributing business was relatively low.

In addition, the level of "resource conditions" that include the "managerial capabilities for resource recombination, new media production capabilities, and new media distribution capabilities" was also relatively low, as a consequence of the company's lack of experiences in resource recombination. Moreover, the company did not possess its own distribution channel for mobile services.

Constrained by the low "economic and resource conditions," the organizational choice for YouTube to develop the new mobile distributing business was basically to ally with external partners, and venturing activities were organized mostly in the market mode. Such empirical evidences derived from, and can also be related to, the aforementioned theories – low "economic conditions and resource conditions" would suggest the market mode for new media business venturing.

In the case of YouTube, the partnership with Verizon is only the first step of YouTube's mobile business exploration. The company expects to reach similar alliances with other wireless carriers in the near future to expand its presence in the mobile market.

On the other hand mobile carriers, with the wireless market increasingly saturated, are trying to find new ways to attract customers and to wrest them away from rivals, while they also want to promote mobile Internet services as another way of boosting revenue. YouTube's alliances with wireless carriers seem to be a win-win strategic action that will benefit both sides of the partnership.[21]

However, such allied mobile consumer video distributing business is not without problems. For example, by offering YouTube videos, music downloads, and similar services, YouTube and Verizon are especially targeting young audiences. Yet young customers tend to be more uncertain than older ones. Most young people already have cell phones, but many tend to be price-sensitive because of limited income.[22] So a subscription model designed for this mobile service will face challenges.[23]

Meanwhile, Verizon customers will be able to view the "selected" video content and post videos from this service, but analyses show that "the beauty of YouTube is that it is organic,"[24] thus the approved content will also present challenges. It is still unknown what strategic actions YouTube and its partners will take to tackle these issues, but it is clear that the above study will have some implications for the organizational decisions, and a further new media business strategy shift will be better guided with a good awareness of the company's economic and resource conditions.[25]

Notes

1. The Royal Channel in YouTube: http://www.youtube.com/theroyalchannel
2. Thomas Wagner, Queen Elizabeth Launches on YouTube, Press Release, December 24, 2007: http://www.guardian.co.uk/worldlatest/story/0,-7175212,00.html
3. See from: http://www.youtube.com/watch?v=mBRP-o6Q85s
4. News of University of Illinois Department of Computer Science, YouTube: Sharing Digital Camera Videos, retrieved on July 3, 2006 from: http://www.cs.uiuc.edu
5. Graham (2005).
6. Nielsen Media Research (2006).
7. Veiga (2006).
8. Wallenstein (2006).
9. Facets included in this part are retrieved from: *YouTube News 2006*, Retrieved in January, 2006 from http://www.youtube.com/press_room
10. Facets included in this part are retrieved from: *YouTube Archives 2006*, Retrieved in January, 2006 from http://www.youtube.com/press_room.
11. Nielsen Media Research (2006).
12. Facets included in this part are retrieved from: *YouTube Archive 2006*, Retrieved in January, 2006 from http://www.youtube.com/press_room
13. Richtel (2006).
14. Bryant (2006).
15. Facets included in this part are retrieved from: *YouTube Archive 2006*, Retrieved in January, 2006 from http://www.youtube.com/press_room
16. More details of this research can be seen in Hang, M., "*Media Business Venturing*," Jonkoping International Business School, Sweden, 2007.
17. Wernerfelt (1984).
18. Barney (1991, p. 101).
19. Collis (1996).
20. Sanchez and Howard (1996).
21. Bartash (2006).
22. Bartash (2006).
23. Del Conte (2006).
24. Bryant, (2006).
25. Min Hang works for Tsinghua University, China and the Media Management and Transformation Center (MMTC) of Jönköping University, Sweden. Email: min.hang@ihh.hj.se.

References

Bain, J.S. (1968) Industrial Organization. (2nd ed.) New York: Wiley.
Barney, J.B. (1991) Firm resources and sustained competitive advantage. Journal of Management, 17 (1), 99–120.

Bartash, J. (2006) Verizon, YouTube See a Future for Mobile Video. November 2006, http://www.marketwatch.com/news/story/verizon-youtube-see-future-mobile/story.aspx?guid=%7B0E3D29F0-180C-408D-A45D-A0CB08199BD7%7D

Bryant, S. (2006) Google's YouTube Mobile Phone Service is Being Lose. http://oraclewatch.eweek.com/blogs/google_watch/archive/2006/11/28/14828. aspx, December 2006.

Collis, D. (1996) Organizational Capability as a Source of Profit in Organizational Learning and Competitive Advantage. Betrand Moingeon and Amy Edmondson (Eds.), pp. 139–163. London: Sage.

Del Conte, N. (2006) What Will YouTube Be Like On Your Mobile Phone? http://www.techcrunch.com/20p06/11/28/what-will-youtube-be-like-on-your-mobile-phone/, November 2006.

Graham, J. (2005) Video Website Pop-up. US Today, 2005-11-12.

Nielsen Media Resarch. (2006) YouTube US Web Traffic Grows 17 Percent Week over Week. http://www.nielsen-netratings.com, September 2006.

Porter, M.E. (1985) Competitive Advantage, New York: Free Press.

Richtel, M. (2006) YouTube Coming Soon to Cellphones. November 2006. http://www.nytimes.com/2006/11/28/technology/28tube.html?ex=1322370000&en=650dd49648ba275c&ei=5088&partner=rssnyt&emc=rss

Sanchez, R.A. and Howard, T. (Eds.). (1996) Dynamics of competence-based competition. New York: Pergamon.

Veiga, A. (2006) Anti-piracy System Could Hurt YouTube. http://www.msnbc.msn.com, October 2006.

Wallenstein, A. (2006) NBC Pressures Websites on Video Clips. http://www.backstage.com, October 2006.

Wenerfelt, B. (1984) A resource-based view of the firm. Strategic Management Journal, 5, 171–180.

PART III – Peer-to-Peer: Policy

11

Compulsory Licensing v. Private Negotiations in Peer-to-Peer File Sharing

Michael Botein[1] and Edward Samuels[2]

[1]New York Law School
[2]Intellectual Property Consultant

Introduction

Peer-to-Peer sharing of creative works over the Internet poses a particularly thorny issue for copyright law. On the one hand, full copyright liability may seem inappropriate in such an environment, since it might inhibit the broad dissemination of creative works promised by the new technology. On the other hand, carte blanche immunity from copyright liability might erode the commercial value of creative works.[1]

In an effort to chart a course between the two unsatisfactory extremes, some commentators have recently proposed a compulsory license to authorize and regulate the Peer-to-Peer distribution of copyrighted works, primarily over the Internet.[2] We are sympathetic with the goals of such a compromise, and believe that the issues need to be fully aired. Nevertheless, we remain skeptical about the feasibility of implementing such a system. To this end, we think it worthwhile to take a brief look at the history of compulsory copyright licenses in a number of different settings. As will be seen, compulsory licenses have been less than successful in implementing public policy goals.

Moreover, the general legal backdrop of the Peer-to-Peer issue has changed dramatically in the last few years. In June, 2005, the US Supreme Court's decision in *MGM v. Grokster*[3] made clear that Peer-to-Peer transfer of copyrighted material violated the Copyright Act in the absence of a copyright license.[4] The case thus increased the importance of negotiations between intellectual property owners and potential distributors – thus,

E.M. Noam and L.M. Pupillo (eds.), *Peer-to-Peer Video*, doi: 10.1007/978-0-387-76450-4_11,
© Springer Science + Business Media, LLC 2008

arguably reducing the potential role of compulsory copyright and other forms of government intervention. Even without Grokster's tilting of the scales towards private negotiations, compulsory copyrights generally have not functioned very effectively.

To begin with, compulsory licenses are not new to intellectual property. They have been invoked to resolve several troublesome technological issues, primarily in the past quarter of a century. Some compulsory licenses have been moderately successful, but their general track record has been disappointing. At best, these licenses should be viewed as interim accommodations to preserve a balance between the extremes of full and no liability during periods of technological or other change.[5] But such arrangements are not as successful as, and should yield as soon as possible to, private systems of compensation.

In traditional economic terms, privately negotiated contracts simply may be more efficient than governmental intervention. At least in theory, private arrangements should reflect better the changing realities of the marketplace. Even after 210 years of copyright law in this country and in the face of new technologies, the marketplace still best serves the public interest in encouraging both the creation and dissemination of new works.

As a backdrop for considering a new license in the Peer-to-Peer environment, this paper reviews existing compulsory licenses. We first discuss the audio compulsory licenses: the original compulsory license for mechanical reproduction of phonorecords, established in the Copyright Act of 1909 and preserved in section 115 of the current Act[6]; the jukebox compulsory license, enacted as section 116 of the 1976 Copyright Act, and repealed in 1993[7]; the digital audio home recording royalty, established in 1992 in chapter 10 of the Copyright Act[8]; and the digital performance right in sound recordings license, established in 1995, set out in section 114 of the current Act.[9]

Because the technology and the economics of the video market are different from those of the audio market, we will review separately the television compulsory licenses, primarily focusing upon the cable compulsory license, adopted as section 111 of the 1976 Act.[10] We also will consider briefly the public broadcasting license established in section 118[11]; the satellite retransmission license enacted in 1988, as set forth in section 119[12]; and the local-to-local retransmission license enacted in 1999 as section 122 of the current Act.[13]

We will conclude by considering other aspects of the copyright system that should be borne in mind as we contemplate the adoption of yet another compulsory licensing system.

Audio Compulsory Licenses

The Compulsory License for Making and Distributing Phonorecords

The most enduring compulsory license is the original one, adopted in the Copyright Act of 1909. The elaborate scheme was Congress's response to the Supreme Court's decision in *White-Smith v. Apollo*[14] holding that piano rolls, and, by extension, phonorecords, were not "copies" of the musical works they recorded. That holding meant that the creators of phonorecords or other mechanical reproductions of musical works did not have to pay the owners of copyrights in the songs they reproduced.

In 1909, Congress legislatively overruled the *White-Smith* case by providing that the making of phonorecords or other mechanical versions of songs was subject to copyright protection. Congress created the phonorecord compulsory license to protect against the monopolization of music by the sound recording industry, and to assure that performers would have access to any songs they wanted to "cover" by making their own recordings at a reasonable price.[15] The provision has stood the test of time, increasing from 2 cents per song in 1909 to 9.1 cents per song (or 1.75 cents per minute of playing time) in 2006.[16]

The success of this original compulsory license may have inspired Congress to adopt other compulsory licenses in the 1976 Copyright Act. But the phonorecord license arose in a context significantly different from any of the other compulsory licenses, and particularly the Peer-to-Peer environment. The phonorecord compulsory license does not involve the "pooling" of funds, but rather the direct payment by a user/performer (or the performer's recording company) to the owner of copyright in the underlying musical work (or payments made through the Harry Fox Agency as a designated intermediary).

The phonorecord license thus is simpler to administer than the later, more complicated compulsory licensing schemes. It also tracks more closely the private contract negotiation that would have occurred in the absence of the compulsory license.[17]

At least part of the justification for interfering with the normal market in musical works was the fact that the users – the performers and record companies involved in making new versions of older works – also contributed creatively to the pool of available versions of songs. This is not the case in the typical Peer-to-Peer transaction, which usually involves the simple multiplication (and potential displacement) of copies of works that are already available through commercial channels. A different situation might pertain if file sharing produced a large number of derivative works, through sophisticated digital editing and manipulation. But this has not been the case to date.[18]

The story of the first compulsory license, however, is not finished. As electronic dissemination of musical works displaces the traditional sale of phonorecords and CDs, any compulsory license pegged only to the old technology soon would be doomed to failure. In 1995, Congress updated section 115 to compensate music copyright owners for the digital delivery of works authorized under the compulsory license, as well as the sale of old-fashioned "phonorecords" (defined broadly enough to include CDs).[19]

The Jukebox Compulsory License

Under the 1909 Act, copyright did not extend to playing music on jukeboxes, because Congress adopted a specific exception in favor of the jukebox industry.[20] Although the exception was potentially justified by the assumption that jukebox play of music promoted record sales, this unusual free ride by an industry that made a lot of money from copyrighted works seemed inconsistent with the general principles of copyright.

To some extent, the reasoning behind the jukebox free ride is analogous to the reasoning of some creators today who choose to make their works available for download without a license or fee; for a new entrant, it may very well be an excellent form of marketing, ultimately creating a demand for paid performances – such as bookings and recordings. In a market-based system, creators are of course free to make whatever arrangements they want for the cheap or free distribution of some of their works. We believe, however, that such a choice should be up to the individual copyright owners, not imposed across the board by a compulsory licensing system.

In 1976, Congress responded to this free ride problem by adopting a compromise – a compulsory license for the playing of music "by means of coin-operated phonorecord players."[21] The initial fee was set at $8 per jukebox. Through periodic adjustments, the fees climbed to almost 8 times that amount within a decade.[22] In a two-step set of amendments in 1988 and 1993, Congress replaced the fees with "negotiated licenses" agreed to by the affected industries.[23] The current fees have been negotiated at $275 for the first jukebox by any particular operator, $55 for the second through tenth jukeboxes, and $48 for each additional jukebox.[24]

It would be tempting to suggest that Congress viewed the compulsory license as a temporary fix, and that the shift to a marketplace alternative was a natural and anticipated evolution in the treatment of the jukebox industry – from exception to compulsory license to (relatively) free market. Congress's action was prompted primarily by concerns that the jukebox compulsory licensing system violated US obligations under the Berne Convention, particularly Article 11(1); this assures copyright owners the exclusive right in the public performance of their works.[25] Perhaps the more important lesson of this history is to underscore the international context of the copyright system, which we will consider in the last but one section, below.

The Digital Audio Home Recording Royalty

Prior to 1992, it was unclear whether the home tape recording of music was a copyright violation. On the one hand, manufacturers argued that they were not liable under the principles applied to video recorders in the *Betamax* case,[26] and rights against home users were, as a practical matter, unenforceable. On the other hand, some arguably distinguishing features made the audio market different from the video market of 1984. Of particular importance was the emergence of digital audio tape ("DAT") as a near-perfect method of making copies.

In 1992, in response to the issues raised by the new digital technologies, Congress passed the Audio Home Recording Act.[27] Among other things, the Act provided for a statutory fee to be charged on the sale of digital audio recorders (generally 2% of the manufacturer's or importer's price, with a minimum of $1 and a maximum of $8) and digital audio media (generally 3%). The proceeds were to be distributed to the owners of copyright in music and sound recordings, based upon estimated shares of the market.

The DAT experience might seem to be a good precedent for a Peer-to-Peer compulsory licensing system, with fees under the new system based upon the price of MP3 recorders and memory devices. The problem is that the DAT technology was a non-starter. The fees never have amounted to much more than $4 million per year, and the aggravation in collecting and disseminating the funds has been disproportionately large.[28] Perhaps more than any other, this license has resulted in "spending dollars to chase dimes." It is hardly a model for future legislation.

The Digital Performance Right in Sound Recordings License

Prior to 1995, though there was an exclusive performance right in the underlying music, there was no exclusive performance right in sound recordings as such. In 1995, however, Congress created such a right. It was limited to the digital performance or transmission of such works with lots of exceptions that nullified much of the potential impact of the new right.[29] As part of the package, Congress created a compulsory license that applied to some non-interactive digital transmission services. Such a compulsory license might seem relatively easy to set up, since it involves a relatively finite number of webcasters, who do or could operate their websites for profit, and who presumably are in a position to absorb reasonable performance fees.

After Congress adopted the complicated new right and incorporated the compulsory license into section 114 of the Act, observers waited to see how the compulsory license would work out. Even before any fees had been collected under the license, however, it became obvious that the statutory language was unclear. Did it apply to "streaming audio"? No one knew. By 1998, as part of the Digital Millennium Copyright Act, Congress revised the language to clear up some of the ambiguities.[30] A Copyright Arbitration Royalty Panel was established to recommend the initial rates for the compulsory license[31]; it came up with a proposed rate of 0.14 cents for each song streamed on an Internet-only webcast, and 0.07 cents for each song included as part of an AM or FM radio retransmission. After much public discussion and complaint, the Librarian of Congress adopted a compromise rate of 0.07 cents for each song delivered, whether by AM, FM, or Internet-only transmission.

Many people thought that the rates were outrageous, and that smaller operators could not afford them. Congress intervened by passing the Small Webcaster Settlement Act of 2002.[32] Currently, the webcasting royalty rates are divided into nine categories of digital audio services, depending upon such factors as whether the service is commercial or noncommercial. Fees range from as low as $200 for noncommercial webcasters devoted primarily to news, talk, and sports, to 10% of gross proceeds for such commercial services as XM Satellite Radio and SIRIUS Satellite Radio.

Since its rocky start, the compulsory license has begun generating at least a moderate flow of revenue, reaching as high as $35 million in 2005.[33] While the fees might seem to bode well as a model for a Peer-to-Peer compulsory license, the comparison is misleading. Much of the revenues generated by the new digital performance right are attributable to commercial satellite radio services such as XM and SIRIUS. Most Peer-to-Peer exchanges on the Internet, by contrast, will presumably be in a noncommercial setting, where revenues are not likely to be generated, and funds will not likely be available for distribution.

Video Compulsory Licenses

The Cable Compulsory License

For almost two decades, the broadcast and cable industries fought over whether and how much cable systems should pay rights holders for cable systems' retransmission of programs broadcast by television stations. As a first step to establish a bargaining advantage, television broadcast networks and producers sued to establish that cable use of copyrighted broadcast programming was a copyright infringement. Partly out of fear of strangling the then-emerging cable industry, the Supreme Court twice flatly held that this type of use was "passive" in nature, and thus created no liability.[34]

After the Teleprompter decision, the broadcast and production interests got the message that no judicial relief was in sight, and turned their attention to the decades-old Congressional fight over cable fees. The result was a compulsory license in section 111 of the 1976 Copyright Revision Act, which went into effect in 1978. This hideously complicated provision provided that cable operators could carry both local and distant broadcast television signals for a fee mandated by the Act, subject to periodic adjustments by the Copyright Royalty Tribunal. (Later, upon the abolition of the Tribunal, Copyright Arbitration Royalty Panels were appointed by the Librarian of Congress. Most recently, in November 2004, the panels were themselves replaced by a new system of Copyright Royalty Judges, to be phased in gradually.) The fee was based upon the number of "distant signal equivalents" ("DSEs") that a cable system imported, counting a distant independent station as one and a network-affiliated station or educational station as 1/4. The number of DSEs was multiplied by a figure initially set by Congress and later adjusted by the Tribunal, to establish the percentage of their gross revenues charged for importing distant television signals.[35] The revenues collected by the licensing system then were divided among the copyright owners, after elaborate hearings that typically held up distributions for many years. The big winners in this process generally were broadcast programming and sports rightsholders.[36]

The percentage of gross revenues charged for each DSE has increased over the years.[37] Similarly, the total gross revenues of cable systems have increased steadily every year. (See Table 11.1, reproduced at the end of this article, showing an increase from just over $1 billion in revenues when the Copyright Act was first passed, to almost $30 billion in 2002). But the total payment under the cable compulsory license actually has decreased in the last decade. After peaking near $200 million in 1989, it has gone down to only about $120 million in the last few years. (In part, this is offset by an increase in the compulsory licensing fees for satellite distribution systems under section 119, described below, which in 2002 amounted to almost $69 million.[38])

Why have the royalties under the compulsory license decreased? Quite simply, cable systems do not import as many distant signals as in the early days. Today, viewers are interested not in distant signals, but rather in satellite networks – free, per-channel, or pay-per-view – for which cable operators negotiate fees in a free marketplace. Indeed, cable subscribers today get more than half of their programming from non-broadcast sources, and the percentage seems to be increasing steadily.

Even in its infancy, the cable compulsory license system was implemented against the backdrop of FCC regulations that severely limited the number of DSEs a cable system could import.[39] While the FCC long ago repealed the limitation, the section 111 fees effectively continue the cap on distant signals, by pricing the importation of a DSE that would have been barred by the earlier FCC rules at 3.75% of gross revenue.[40] Cable operators thus do not view distant signal importation as a useful market strategy.

Broadcasters and cable operators also have fought over the rebroadcast of local over-the-air channels on cable systems within the same viewing area. Under the FCC's rules in the 1970s, cable systems were required to carry local programming under "must carry" rules.[41] Presumably, the local station operators did not lose money by this arrangement: broadcasters kept their local viewers – by being carried on cable systems – and were able to charge advertisers for them. Indeed, broadcasters actually may gain viewers in their local areas, since their signals often do not reach areas which they theoretically cover, because of terrain or other problems; this is particularly true in urban areas like New York, where tall buildings block reception by a large part of the potential audience.

The cable compulsory license did not compensate for the retransmission of local stations, since the cable operators were required to carry these signals in any event, and the local broadcasters wanted it that way; the DSE figure was based totally upon the importation of signals from outside the viewing area, and not upon retransmission of local television signals.

Most cable subscribers today watch satellite-delivered non-broadcast programming, for which the copyright model is not a compulsory license, but rather a negotiated contract. The broadcasters quickly began to figure out that the real money was in non-broadcast satellite networks.

With the decrease in carriage of distant signals, payments under section 111 naturally went down. The statute explicitly requires payments only for signals carried beyond their normal licensed area – that is, distant signals.[42]

Congress's theory quite reasonably seems to have been that broadcasters benefited from cable carriage of their signals; if the cable operators had any incentive not to carry local signals, broadcasters naturally would lose viewers – and hence advertising revenues – in their home markets. There was and is no need to impose a compulsory copyright scheme on local signals. Indeed, in many cases broadcasters assist local systems in receiving high-quality signals, by building direct fiberoptic or microwave connections to cable operators.

After the widespread development of satellite cable channels in the late 1980s, cable operators had a declining need to import distant signals.[43] And since systems do not pay for local signals, it was inevitable that copyright payments would fall – as discussed and as set forth in Table 11.1.

Although beyond the scope of this paper, the change in compulsory copyright's significance is a good illustration of the government's inability to predict rapid changes in market forces. In the decade after section 111's enactment, market changes reduced its importance significantly. Although satellite transmission existed at the time of the 1976 Copyright Revision Act, Congressional drafters simply did not foresee its effect upon the relevance of signal importation and hence of a compulsory copyright scheme oriented around distant signals.

At the same time that section 111 was becoming less relevant, broadcasters and cable operators were moving to a system of private negotiations. To accommodate the shift, Congress, in the Cable Television Consumer Protection and Copyright Act of 1992, provided for "retransmission consent" ("RTC") as an alternative to must-carry and effectively a supplement to section 111 royalties.[44] (Section 111 applies to owners of copyright in the individual programs; RTC extends rights to the broadcasters themselves, based upon their broadcast signal, and without regard to the ownership of any copyrights.)

Effective in 1993, section 325(b)(3) of the Communications Act allowed broadcasters and rights holders to negotiate for permission to carry their signals. This approach carries with it a risk under section 325(b)(4); if a broadcaster is unable to reach a retransmission consent ("RTC") agreement with a cable operator, it gives up its right to cable carriage locally under the current version of the "must carry" rules. But broadcasters appear to have sought such arrangements quite eagerly.

Instead of competing for relatively small slices of the compulsory copyright pie, after 1993 broadcasters seem to have preferred using the RTC option to negotiate for compensation. This apparently has not resulted in any purely financial windfalls. Instead, to the extent that the results of these negotiations are visible, they seem to reflect an increased reliance upon a form of barter.

Because the RTC deals are proprietary in nature, their details are never disclosed. Aside from the contracts' private nature, cable operators naturally fear that if they make a highly favorable deal with one popular local broadcaster, others will demand the same terms. Nevertheless, discussions with cable industry executives indicate some broad outlines of RTC agreements.

According to an industry trade association representative,[45] RTC deals never include outright monetary compensation. In the early days of RTC, a few broadcasters demanded cash and met instant rejection.[46] Instead, these arrangements generally involve reciprocal dealings. For example, it was not an accident that shortly after the major broadcast networks shifted to retransmission consent negotiations, most of them struck industry-wide cable agreements to create new cable networks with a network "brand" – e.g., CNBC, MSNBC, FNC. The broadcasters were anxious to expand into new video media, which resulted in new network-run cable channels. In some cases, cable operators received favorable terms under these agreements – for example, carriage rights to both a broadcast and a cable network for less than the cost of the former alone.

The key to these transactions was that the cable industry could give the networks something more valuable than small cash payments – that is, national coverage. (In some cases, these arrangements also exist between cable operators and strong non-network group-owned stations). Cable operators claim that they do not agree to or continue to carry cable networks with little audience interest. And some networks have had little success in launching new cable networks, even with the help of RTC agreements.

The general counsel at a major cable company indicated that other types of deals also are customary.[47] Since systems generally have excess advertising time on cable satellite channels, they often give or sell it at nominal rates to local network affiliates for running promotional material for upcoming network programs. Alternatively, an RTC agreement may commit cable operators to buy promotional time from local stations, at relatively low rates. Or broadcasters and cable operators may agree to share unused production time in their studios, for nominal payments.

This combination of carrying broadcasters' cable networks, giving excess advertising time to broadcasters, and sharing production capacity may or may not have real economic value. As the cable general counsel above noted, "It's the principle rather than the economic value. No one wants to admit paying cash. There would be network carriage and advertising agreements in any event, but the existence of RTC encourages and increases it."

While the compulsory licensing system may have represented an unhappy truce in the 1970s, it has been replaced to a large extent by negotiated agreements between the broadcasters and owners of programming, and the cable as well as satellite operators who control access to most viewers. Like the jukebox compulsory license that eventually yielded to industry negotiations, perhaps the best compulsory licenses are the ones that fade away – which section 111 basically began to do after its first decade.

The Other Television Compulsory Licenses

The Satellite Home Viewer Act of 1994 created a compulsory license to do for direct broadcast satellite (DBS) operators the same thing as section 111 did for cable systems. Although the systems vary in significant ways (for example, section 119 bases the fees upon a certain price per subscriber, instead of a percentage of gross revenues), the lesson for other compulsory licenses is the same. A compulsory license can work, but is not simple, and may require an administratively burdensome set of regulations.

The treatment of other evolving retransmission systems, such as systems delivered over fiber-optic phone cables, is under review. A 1997 Copyright Office Report favored extending a compulsory license to cover telephone companies that retransmit broadcast signals.[48] This may yet become a real issue in the future, if the major local telephone companies are able to implement "fiber to the premises" broadband service – Verizon's "FIOS" and AT&T's "Lightspeed."[49]

The public broadcasting or "noncommercial broadcasting" license fees set up pursuant to section 118 of the Copyright Act[50] should be considered sui generis. Under that section, fees have been set for the performance of musical compositions (providing lump-sum payments of several million dollars to ASCAP and BMI by PBS and NPR, and a few hundred dollars by college or university public broadcasting entities) and for pictorial, graphic, and sculptural works (generally in the tens of dollars per use).

In 1999, Congress added section 122 to the Copyright Act.[51] It granted satellite carriers the right to retransmit broadcast signals within the intended local market of a television broadcast station, ostensibly putting them more on par with cable operators. The license is royalty-free, on the assumption that the original broadcaster benefits by reaching viewers in its service area. As such, the provision is more an exemption from copyright liability than a traditional compulsory licensing system. The primary feature is that the satellite carrier must provide a list identifying all subscribers to whom the satellite carrier retransmits.

Even as it has held open the possibility of extending compulsory licenses in the context of cable and telephone communications, the Copyright Office has voiced skepticism about compulsory licensing systems on the Internet. As concluded by the Copyright Office, "it would be inappropriate for Congress to grant Internet retransmitters the benefits of compulsory licensing. The primary argument against an Internet compulsory license is the vast technological and regulatory differences between Internet retransmitters and the cable systems and satellite carriers that now enjoy compulsory licensing. The instantaneous worldwide dissemination of broadcast signals via the Internet poses major issues regarding the national and international licensing of the signals that have not been fully addressed by federal and international policymakers, and it would be premature for Congress to legislate a copyright compulsory license to benefit Internet retransmitters."[52]

Other Considerations

In considering the treatment of new technologies within the overall framework of copyright, it is important to remember that copyright is not necessarily, or even principally, a barrier to the dissemination of creative works. As stated by the Supreme Court in *Harper & Row Publishers, Inc. v. Nation Enterprises*[53]: "it should not be forgotten that the Framers intended copyright itself to be the engine of free expression. By establishing a marketable right to the use of one's expression, copyright supplies the economic incentive to create and disseminate ideas..."

For example, ASCAP, perhaps the best existing model for a collective rights organization, was not created by a compulsory license set by the Congress, but resulted from collective bargaining among the various parties, with periodic oversight by the courts through the lens of antitrust law,[54] and periodic adjustments of rights by the Congress (as in the so-called "Fairness in Music Licensing Act of 1998"[55]).

An initial determination that a use is covered by copyright gives a copyright owner considerable leverage in setting the fees for distribution or performance of such works, of course, but the copyright owner makes no money if there are no distributions. And an initial determination that copyright does not extend to a particular use, such as in the case of jukeboxes, cable, or the Betamax, will shift the bargaining power in favor of the users in any later consideration of a compulsory license.

On the other hand, a compulsory license is not the only means of placing limitations upon the rights of copyright owners. There are dozens of specific exceptions and limitations to the rights of copyright, including several in section 110[56] (covering certain "nonprofit" uses), and limitations resulting from basic principles of copyright, such as fair use, the idea–expression distinction, and the limitations upon copyright in works of utility. Many socially beneficial uses of copyrighted works on the Internet, even by people not owning the copyright, will be protected by these doctrines.

Although much maligned in the Internet community, the Digital Millennium Copyright Act (DMCA)[57] gives owners of works the right to control their works through copy protection systems and the use of copy management information systems. Anyone seriously considering a compulsory license will have to work through the interplay between such a license and the workings of the DMCA.

For example, would the existence of a compulsory license to disseminate works on the Internet trump the DMCA? Presumably not, unless we essentially want to dismantle the DMCA and require that copyright owners unlock their copyright protection systems. If the existence of a compulsory license lessened the economic value of copyrighted works, particularly those initially supplied in digital form, the net effect of a compulsory license might be to convince many copyright owners to adopt more technically intrusive copy protection systems – a result that would presumably undermine the whole purpose behind such a compulsory license.

One also must keep in mind the increasing international role in deciding copyright policy. Take, for example, the recently proposed "Public Domain Enhancement Act,"[58] introduced in Congress in 2003, that would impose a maintenance fee for continuing copyright beyond 50 years from first publication. Whatever the merits of such a requirement, it seems to fly directly in the face of the Berne Convention,[59] which prohibits such formalities as a limitation on copyright. It was only in 1988 that the United States finally did away with the requirement of copyright notice and registration, as a condition to joining Berne in the first place.[60]

Another recent international development of considerable relevance is the updating of the General Agreement on Tariffs and Trade to include intellectual property rights, under the new structure of the World Trade Organization. In a recent decision,[61] a WTO panel held the US exemption of certain restaurants and business establishments for retransmission of musical works received over the airwaves (section 110(5)) to be in violation of Berne obligations. The panel disapproved of national exceptions or limitations that "conflict with a normal exploitation of the work." It is quite possible that too broad a compulsory license also would be in violation of Berne obligations, triggering possible retaliatory sanctions in the WTO.

Conclusion

This discussion is not intended to preempt or forestall consideration of a new compulsory licensing system to balance competing interests in the emerging Peer-to-Peer environment. But the track record of prior compulsory licenses, the differences between those licenses and a Peer-to-Peer license, and other copyright as well as international considerations suggest that caution is in order before jumping headlong into any quick fix.

Table 11.1 Fees Compared to Gross Basic Industry Revenues 1978–2002

Year	Cable Royalty Fees*	Basic Cable Revenue**
1978	$ 12,910,027	$ 1,147,000,000
1979	$ 15,889,793	$ 1,332,000,000
1980	$ 20,044,492	$ 1,615,000,000
1981	$ 30,886,119	$ 2,023,000,000
1982	$ 41,156,873	$ 2,515,000,000
1983	$ 72,774,961	$ 3,041,000,000
1984	$ 92,272,898	$ 3,534,000,000
1985	$ 104,777,269	$ 4,138,000,000
1986	$ 124,725,475	$ 4,887,000,000
1987	$ 163,163,192	$ 6,016,000,000
1988	$ 193,103,897	$ 7,345,000,000
1989	$ 208,126,070	$ 8,670,000,000
1990	$ 170,335,290	$ 10,174,000,000
1991	$ 180,755,077	$ 11,418,000,000
1992	$ 188,537,115	$ 12,433,000,000
1993	$ 185,359,636	$ 13,528,000,000
1994	$ 161,271,446	$ 15,164,000,000
1995	$ 165,867,789	$ 16,860,000,000
1996	$ 177,604,829	$ 18,395,000,000
1997	$ 154,389,741	$ 20,383,000,000
1998	$ 108,244,085	$ 21,830,000,000
1999	$ 108,240,071	$ 23,135,000,000
2000	$ 120,177,595	$ 24,729,000,000
2001	$ 121,845,046	$ 27,031,000,000
2002	$ 120,795,554	$ 28,492,000,000***

*Source: US Copyright Office, July 2003.
**Source: US Census Bureau, Statistical Abstract of the United States: 2002.
***Kagan, World Media, a PRIMEDIA Company, Broadband Cable Financial Databook, 2002.

Notes

Michael Botein is Professor of Law and Director of the Media Center at New York Law School in New York City. Email: mbotein@nyls.edu. Edward Samuels is an intellectual property consultant in New York. Email: esamuels@ edwardsamuels.com.

A prior version of this article appeared in 30 Southern Illinois University Law Journal, 69 (2005).

1. Immunity could undermine the primary purpose of copyright law, which is to foster the creation of new works by granting authors exclusive rights in their works.
2. Neil Weinstock Netanel, Impose a Noncommercial Use Levy to Allow Free Peer-to-Peer File Sharing, 17 Harv. J.L. & Tech. 1 (2003).
3. 545 U.S., 125 S. Ct. 2764 (2005).
4. The Court refused to apply the reasoning of the Betamax case, which had held that the private use of video recorders to "time shift" the viewing of works distributed for free over the public airwaves was a fair use under copyright law. See discussion in text at n. 26 infra.
5. As discussed below, for example, the cable television compulsory copyright license filled a gap by resolving disputes between copyright owners and cable operators for a little more than a decade while the multichannel industry was developing. As soon as relations between broadcasters and cable operators stabilized, however, the industries migrated to a private law system of nego-tiated settlements under "retransmission consent" statutory provisions. As discussed below, although the old compulsory licensing provisions remain in effect, the industry players largely have migrated to negotiated arrangements. See discussion in text at n. 34 infra.
6. 17 U.S.C. § 1(e) (1909); 17 U.S.C. § 115 (2000).
7. 17 U.S.C. § 116 (2000) (Former 17 U.S.C. § 116 repealed and replaced by this new § 116, December 17, 1993, 107 Stat. 2309).
8. 17 U.S.C. §§ 1003–07 (2000).
9. 17 U.S.C. § 114(d)–(h) (2000).
10. See infra § II(A).
11. 17 U.S.C. § 118 (2000).
12. 17 U.S.C. § 119 (2000).
13. 17 U.S.C. § 122 (2000).
14. 209 U.S. 1 (1908).
15. See generally H.R. 2222, 60th Cong. (2d Sess. 1909).
16. See 17 U.S.C. § 1(e) (1909); 37 C.F.R. § 255.3(m) (1998).
17. To this extent, it thus resembles the system of retransmission consent in the cable industry. See discussion infra § II (A), beginning at text at n. 44.

18. If the proposed compulsory license was limited to the making of derivative works, then the "value added" by the user would indeed be a relevant factor. But the currently proposed compulsory license is to reproduce or display or perform a work generally, whether or not value is added in the form of the creation of a new work.

19. 17 U.S.C. § 101 (2000); 17 U.S.C. § 115(d) (2000).

20. 17 U.S.C. § 1(e), para. 3 (1909) (now superseded).

21. 17 U.S.C. § 116 (1976) (now superseded).

22. 37 C.F.R. § 254.3 (2003).

23. 17 U.S.C. § 116A (1988); 17 U.S.C. § 116 (1993).

24. Robert A. Gorman and Jane C. Ginsberg, Copyright; Cases and Materials 608 (6th ed., 2002).

25. The Berne Convention for the Protection of Literary and Artistic Works, art. 11 (1), Paris revision, July 24, 1971.

26. *Sony Corp. of America v. Universal City Studios, Inc.*, 464 U.S. 417 (1984).

27. 17 U.S.C. §§ 1001–10 (2000).

28. US Copyright Office, The Annual Report of the Register of Copyrights, available at http://www.copyright.gov/reports/index.html. The Annual Reports of the Register of Copyrights for 2001, 2002, and 2003 state that AHRA fees were $3.32 million in 2000, $4.124 million in 2001, and $3.448 million in 2002.

29. 17 U.S.C. § 114(d) (2000).

30. Digital Millennium Copyright Act, Pub. L. No. 105–304, § 405(a)(1)–(4), 112 Stat. 2890 (1998).

31. 17 U.S.C. § 114(f)(1) (2000).

32. Small Webcaster Settlement Act of 2002, Pub. L. No. 107–321, 116 Stat. 2780 (2002).

33. See Ben Sisario, Old Songs Generate New Cash for Artists, N.Y. Times, Dec. 28, 2004. § E, at 1. For current information, see the website run by Sound-Exchange, the organization assigned the task of collecting and distributing the compulsory fees, at http://www.soundexchange.com.

34. *Fortnightly Corp. v. United Artists, Inc.*, 392 U.S. 390 (1968) and *Teleprompter Corp. v. Columbia Broadcasting Sys., Inc.*, 415 U.S. 394 (1974).

35. The relevant gross revenues for the computation do not include payments from "on-demand" channels, but rather only on "basic" tiers with broadcast signals. *Cablevision Systems Dev. Co. v. Motion Picture Ass'n of Am. Inc.*, 836 F. 2d 599 (D.C. Cir.), cert. denied, 487 U.S. 1235 (1988). This creates a bit of a problem when a cable system includes distant signals in a higher or "enhanced" tier – which is uncommon. Since attempting to apportion a system's revenues between broadcast and non-broadcast revenues would produce major transactional costs, however, first the Copyright Royalty Tribunal and now the Copyright Office have chosen simply to ignore these rare cases.

36. Daniel L. Brenner, Monroe E. Price, and Michael Meyerson, Cable Television and Other Nonbroadcast Video: Law and Policy § 9.19 (Clark Boardman Callaghan) (1986).

37. In the 1976 Act, the fees ranged from 0.2 to 0.675 of 1% of gross receipts for each DSE. 17 U.S.C. §111(d)(1)(B). As of 1985, the fees were raised to a range of 0.265 to 0.893 of 1% of gross receipts for each DSE. In 1990, an additional 0.089 to 0.599 of 1% of gross receipts was added for each DSE, depending upon the number of DSEs, for cable systems in the top 50 or second 50 television markets. 37 C.F.R. §256.2(a) and (c).
38. See infra § II B.
39. Brenner, Price, and Meyerson, supra note 36, at § 9.19.
40. 37 C.F.R. §256.2(c).
41. The FCC's "must carry" rules were codified by Congress in the 1992 Cable Television Consumer Protection and Competition Act, 47 U.S.C. §§ 534–35. The statute and its implementation were upheld by the Supreme Court in *Turner Broadcasting System, Inc. v. FCC*, 512 U.S. 622 (1994) and *Turner Broadcasting Sys., Inc. v. FCC*, 520 U.S. 180 (1997).
42. 17 U.S.C. § 111(d)(1)(B)(1) (2000). See, e.g., Brenner, Price & Meyerson, supra note 36, at § 9:15; Ferris & Lloyd, Telecommunications Regulation: Cable, Broadcasting, Satellite, and the Internet, § 7.12(1) (LexisNexis 2004).
43. Distant signals still are important in some circumstances, where a station in one market is particularly attractive in another – because of program content, language, or the like. For example, cable systems in Puerto Rico carry several New York City signals; because many Puerto Rican residents have friends or relatives in New York City, developments there naturally are of interest.
44. 47 U.S.C. § 325(b) (2000).
45. Confidential interview with senior management, cable trade association, December 14, 2004.
46. Confidential interview with chief executive officer, cable multiple systems operator, November 18, 2004. In recent years, there has been an increasing but small number of situations in which broadcasters have publicly demanded payments for carriage of their signals. The outcome of these isolated incidents is difficult to estimate, since these negotiations too are treated by the broadcast and cable industries as proprietary. There are no reports as to actual financial agreements.
47. Confidential interview with general counsel of cable multiple systems operator, December 17, 2004.
48. See A Review of the Copyright Licensing Regimes Covering Retransmission of Broadcast Signals (August 1997), http://www.copyright.gov/reports/study.pdf, especially Executive Summary, http://www.copyright.gov/reports/exsum.pdf.
49. Leslie Ellis, Verizon Designs Data "Gusher," Multichannel News, November 28, 2005, at 31.
50. 17 U.S.C. § 118 (2000).
51. 17 U.S.C. § 122 (2000).
52. See A Review of the Copyright Licensing Regimes Covering Retransmission of Broadcast Signals (August 1997), http://www.copyright.gov/reports/study.pdf, Executive Summary, http://www.copyright.gov/reports/exsum.pdf, at 13
53. 471 U.S. 539, 558 (1985).

54. For example, *Broadcast Music, Inc. v. Columbia Broadcasting Sys. Inc.*, 441 U.S. 1 (1979).
55. Codified, in part, as 17 U.S.C. § 110(5)(B) (2000).
56. 17 U.S.C. § 110.
57. 17 U.S.C. §§ 1201–05 (2000).
58. Introduced as H.R. 2601, 108th Cong. (2003).
59. Berne Convention, supra note 25, art. 5(2).
60. 17 U.S.C. § 411 (2000).
61. Panel Report, United States – Section 110(5) of the U.S. Copyright Act, WT/DS160/R (June 15, 2000).

12

Crouching Tiger, Hidden Dragon: Proxy Battles over Peer-to-Peer Movie Sharing

Viktor Mayer-Schönberger

Harvard University

In the words of Jack Valenti, Peer-to-Peer video sharing engages the movie industry in a "furious battle" in which "file stealers" threaten to annihilate America's "greatest trade export and an awesome engine of growth, nourishing the American economy."[1] To an extent, Internet digerati agree.[2] Peer-to-Peer, they suggest, has changed the landscape of information control and ownership. The genie – Peer-to-Peer technology – is out of the bottle; and the content industry, as we know it, seems beyond help.

As is often the case in heated public debates over core governance challenges in a networked world, both sides paint the picture almost exclusively in black and white. They have strong incentives to do so. Stark contrast, binary choices, and extreme alternatives will best energize one's support base and reach out and draw in the vast majority of the public that does not yet mind or care.[3]

For all the rhetoric though, Valenti's "furious battle" is a battle over proxies, and it is sharing this quality with a number of other core arguments over Peer-to-Peer and video. In the following, these proxy battles provide the red thread to analyze the Peer-to-Peer and video debate.

Agency: Who is to Blame?

In principle the Internet provides bootleggers with a global distribution mechanism that is difficult to control. Peer-to-Peer offers an added service layer that makes – again in principle – locating infringers hard and searching

E.M. Noam and L.M. Pupillo (eds.), *Peer-to-Peer Video*, doi: 10.1007/978-0-387-76450-4_12, for and downloading movie files easy. In practice, however, sharing video files on the Internet is more difficult. First, DVD quality movies are around 3–4 GB in size. Downloading such a file is next to impossible for the 14% of current Internet users in the USA who are still utilizing dial-up connections.[4] Users with a broadband connection, just over 86% of US households by December 2007, need 1–10 hours (depending on the speed of their broadband connection) to complete the file transfer. Looking 3 years into the future, average broadband speeds to homes in urban areas will have reached 20 Mbit/s in cable and DSL networks, possibly reducing download times to an hour.[5] As bandwidth increases, however, so does the amount of data that needs to be transferred if consumers desire to download movies in next generation high definition quality.[6]

Second, most broadband connections provide asymmetric bandwidth for upload and download. Thus, a typical broadband user may be able to download at 3 Mbit/s, but as a peer of a Peer-to-Peer network only is able to offer her files to others at a significantly lower speed of 1 Mbit/s. Because of network topologies, asymmetric bandwidth is unlikely to go away soon, especially in cable networks. This triples minimum download times.

Third, these calculations presuppose perfect uptimes of the server from which the file is downloaded, servers having high capacity broadband connectivity and overall minimal network congestion. None of these conditions are present in current Peer-to-Peer networks. Despite some changes to the underlying file sharing protocols to make sharing of large files easier, as best exemplified by the BitTorrent protocol, such files take longer to download and thus are more vulnerable to peer servers going offline.

Fourth, it is currently very hard to differentiate between high quality and low quality, between playable and corrupt movie files when searching on Peer-to-Peer networks. The movie industry could use this to its advantage, only following the music industry successful lead: Joining Peer-to-Peer networks, rights holders have swamped networks with thousands of low quality or non-playable files.[7] This defensive move may not be popular among downloaders, but is – if used appropriately[8] – perfectly legal. It could easily be employed by the movie industry as well. By diluting the ratio of high quality movie files among the sea of useless bits on Peer-to-Peer networks, improvements in Peer-to-Peer download speeds can thus be offset. As long as identifying and eliminating decoys is more costly than producing them, the strategy pays off. And as long as Peer-to-Peer networks maintain their own openness for users to join, they also remain vulnerable to such flooding strategies.

In sum, downloading video files through Peer-to-Peer networks currently is time-consuming and requires repeated human intervention. Bandwidth will have to increase by orders of magnitude and Peer-to-Peer networks will have to find better ways to identify file quality and to improve download integrity before Peer-to-Peer may turn into a suitable consumer distribution channel for video content that rivals movie theatres, video stores, or nascent legal download services in terms of ease, convenience, and overall transaction cost.

Why then is Jack Valenti talking about an epic battle that is fought over video Peer-to-Peer? Why is not only he predicting doom and gloom, but why is the entire movie industry taking Peer-to-Peer so seriously? After all, being confronted with new technologies is not a novel situation. Technologies have challenged copyright holders in the past. Neither is it the movie industry's only piracy worry. Millions of bootleg DVDs are offered at Moscow's Red Square, Bangkok's Pantip Plaza, and Seoul's Namdemeung night market. Bootleg factories churn out tens of thousands of pirated high quality DVDs every day. Still, for the movie industry, these illegal markets in developing countries may not be worth their effort. But why is Peer-to-Peer?

Perhaps it is the fear of the slippery slope, the angst that the genie of Peer-to-Peer once out of the bottle cannot be controlled. Perhaps it is the painful memory of recent battles lost. Or perhaps it is the perceived ill fate of the music industry caused by Peer-to-Peer and a sense that video is next that keeps the adrenaline pumping. Whatever it is, it entices the Motion Picture Industry Association (MPIA) to fight this battle against a proxy without a sustained analysis of whether it in fact is the agent of change or at least provides – from the perspective of rights holders – a suitable chokepoint to stop or slow change.

Yet, stopping Peer-to-Peer networks is neither the only nor necessarily, as we have seen, the most effective (let alone efficient) chokepoint to interdict digital piracy. Other technologies are equally useful tools in reconfiguring the dissemination of information – from PCs and hard disks, to camcorders, DVD players and analog-to-digital converters.[9]

Perhaps it is not even technology that is the culprit. Philip Evans and Thomas Wuerster have described how in our networked times elements of existing value chains are eliminated or reconfigured,[10] but for them the agent of change is not technology. Only technological determinists[11] would imbue technology with a capacity to change society. Rather, Evans and Wuerster see digital technology as having facilitated (but not originated) the creation of a specific digital mindset, of a sense of "being digital,"[12] requiring from businesses a fundamental reevaluation of existing business models and value chains. This mindset accepts and embraces user's ability to acquire, process, and store massive amounts of information at low cost. It encourages in John Seely Brown's terms information *bricolage*, the re-combination by users of information elements into something new, and their ensuing dissemination.[13] Thanks to this digital mindset, technical developments have lowered some barriers of information creation and distribution, while other limitations of a Habermasian renaissance of public discourse remain largely unaffected.[14] This is not technology's fault, but the result of the digital mindset interacting with technology, and forming its very unique social reality.[15] Thus it is dangerous to attribute causality and agency too quickly, to look for simplistic reasons, and easy solutions, especially ones that give preference to engineering fixes over organizational, structural, or societal adaptation.

Hollywood is not the first sector to be transformed by the consequences of the digital mindset. Licensing online download services after resisting for years, the music industry may have finally understood that fundamental changes are necessary. Instead of glitzy High Street shops and elaborate distribution structures, digitized music available for legal downloaded eliminates the need for costly intermediaries. The music industry's new mantra is permitting limited sharing in return for a relatively weak protection against wider distribution. It required undoing a cornerstone of the music industry's past success: the album as a relatively arbitrary bundle of songs. Individual high quality songs at an affordable price rather than expensive albums provide a legal, easy to use one-stop alternative to illegal Peer-to-Peer downloads. By reconfiguring their value proposition, the music industry took a significant risk in offering songs individually rather than providing them in a prefab bundle. So far, it seems to pay off.

The movie industry will have to be similarly innovative. Their product, however, is not one that can be easily unbundled. Perhaps the opposite strategy might hold potential. Bakos and Brynjolfsson have shown that owners of large amounts of content rights – Hollywood's majors for example – can improve their competitive position by massively bundling products.[16] With hard disk storage prizes plummeting, a disk filled with 300 movies – either blockbusters or certain genres – may turn out to be the movie majors "next big thing." A decade ago, John Malone's hard disk jukebox for movies on demand was ahead of its time. Today it might be reborn as a consumer product. Customers could gain immediate access 24/7 to a sizeable movie library without having to either search endlessly in Peer-to-Peer networks, or run to the closest video rental store.

These and similar ideas are ways for the movie industry to survive – not the simple battle against a proxy, but the far more complex one of the digital mindset. For Hollywood, to reduce the issue to one over a particular technology (Peer-to-Peer) is to wage battle against a proxy – and not a very convincing one – and to show a blind eye to arguably more pertinent challenges it faces.

Object: What's to Tax?

Illegally sharing movies online will, economists tell us, persist as long as the overall cost – cost of the good itself plus associated transaction cost – involved in legally obtaining a movie is higher than the cost of getting a high quality copy of the same movie through Peer-to-Peer networks. Ronald Coase has famously emphasized the importance of transactional costs.[17] As the cost of a movie on Peer-to-Peer networks for consumers approaches zero, three levers remain: to lower the cost of obtaining the movie legally, to reduce the associated transaction cost, and to increase the transaction cost of getting the movie illegally. Of these three potential strategies, the main focus in the public debate has been on the transaction cost components.[18]

IP rights holders have long argued for increasing the cost of bootlegging through stricter enforcement and tougher punishment through criminal and civil action. Legal academics like Mark Lemley and Anthony Reese[19] have similarly suggested that more frequent criminal prosecution of Peer-to-Peer participants may result in the desired deterrent effect.[20] Lemley and Reese also suggest setting up a "quick, cheap arbitration system" that would permit rights holders to get "limited relief against abusers"[21] and point to the mandatory arbitration system for domain names under the UDRP[22] as an example of such a quick, cheap, and limited system.[23]

Technically, the cost of illegal sharing of files can be increased by making it more error-prone, time-consuming, and inconvenient. For example, offering significant numbers of decoys over Peer-to-Peer networks can be combined with bogus download requests that consume bandwidth of Peer-to-Peer servers. Charles Nesson suggests a mix of both better enforcement and such technical "speed bumps."[24] Digital rights management (DRM) technologies similarly promise to stem piracy. In their weak form, they make copying harder for the average user. While not dissuading the determined expert hacker (or simply the knowledgeable power user), they make it more time-consuming for typical users to share protected digital information with others, and thus serve the purpose of increasing transaction costs of illegal activity. Some have suggested strong DRM systems, in which even a master hacker could not unlock copyrighted information. Rights holders have lobbied for such systems. Even bills have been introduced to Congress mandating the use of DRM technology; a scenario Jonathan Zittrain has labeled "total control."[25]

Yet, perfect DRM remains an illusive target, both for technical and political reasons. Technically, any digital information will need to be transformed into analog form in order to be experienced by human beings:

it has to be displayed on a screen, for example. At what Eugene Volokh has termed the "unencrypted moment"[26] digital information protected by DRM has to be decrypted before being displayed or converted into audible sound. At that moment it is vulnerable to be copied in unencrypted, unprotected form.[27] Once content has been taken out of the protected confines of DRM it is once again open for anybody to use and share. Politically, the challenge is strong DRM's linkage to user surveillance: DRM needs to continuously check and evaluate user activity. Such an invasion of privacy is difficult to sell to consumers, at least as long as they have a choice when buying equipment on the market place. On the other hand, a legal mandate for DRM built into technical equipment may sound too much like Orwellian total surveillance to be politically feasible.[28]

This suggests that the best strategy of regulation is one narrowly tailored to the individual act of copying (or consumption). It ensures that free riding and other undesired spillovers of copyright protection regimes are kept at a minimum. Users of copyrighted information – and only they – should pay. But "narrow-tailoring" entails knowing a lot about each and every individual transaction. As with strong DRM, this may not only be problematic in terms of privacy, it also increases the required transactional overhead, thus potentially defeating its own purpose. In other words, the narrower a copyright regime is tailored to avoid over and under-inclusiveness, and thus to reduce overall transaction cost, the smaller the individual transaction. Reducing the transactional value increases the relative share of transactional cost associated with that transaction if the transaction costs do not decrease proportionally as well, which is unlikely. The problem is that our copyright regime requires us to know much about what is hard to know: how, when, and by whom information goods are used. This being a fundamental feature of the system, there is no easy way around.

Recently, commentators in the USA have suggested an alternative approach. Instead of purchasing a particular information good (actually consumers often buy a license to use), consumers would pay for information media (blank media) and access (bandwidth). In return, they would gain the right to access through the network and store on the media whatever copyrighted information they like. This is a distant relative of Lawrence Lessig's information commons.[29] Information goods would not become unprotected parts of the great information commons, as they do when copyright expires. Neither is it an extension of fair use. Fair use permits some specific use of protected information goods based on overall societal welfare. Instead, the suggested alternative systems are premised on the continuous protection of information goods. Consumers still pay for using information goods, only the mechanisms of payment changes: Consumers are not charged for the use of the information itself, but rather for a proxy they utilize to experience information goods. Such systems are simply, as proponents concede, mandatory license schemes.

Lemley and Reese among others have written about such a system of levies. Terry Fisher and Neil Netanel are eloquent advocates of similar systems. Netanel calls for a "non-commercial use levy,"[30] Fisher for an "alternative compensation system."[31] Each of them suggests a robust revenue stream for rights holders, and promises it to be easier to administer for rights holders and more transparent to consumers than systems using information goods to charge users. The idea to tax a surrogate like blank media and access rather than pay for copying an information good itself is not new. Continental European nations, like Germany, have had such systems for decades. Netanel suggests that the Europeans have not gone far enough.[32] Fisher, too, suggests a much more comprehensive system. The beauty of such a system is that the levy is placed on something that can be easily tracked, counted, and assessed – access and media for example – at comparatively low transaction cost. On the other hand, these systems have to address at least two important questions.

First, collecting a levy is only a first step. The collected monies then need to be disbursed to the rights holders, but using what formula? Continental European schemes use survey data and statistical methods to calculate appropriate shares for rights holders. Quite obviously such methods work best for the most popular information goods, for which useful tracking data is available. They do not work well for infrequently used information goods, for which survey data is lacking. As the use of information goods often is following a power log distribution function, most of the levy is allocated to the rights holders of the most popular information goods. The remainder – called the "long tail"[33] – cannot be distributed that easily and such schemes have to be augmented with a method for disbursing some monies to the vast majority of rights holders of rarely used information goods.

Given this lack of precision, clearly resulting in over- and under-inclusiveness, it is not surprising that advocates of such alternative systems have suggested elaborate tracking systems for information goods – not to calculate the levy but the amount to be disbursed to individual rights holders. However, if such an elaborate tracking system is created, with all the transactional cost involved, to offer precise disbursement of license fees, why not use it to collect the fee in the first place? It would eliminate the imprecision of collection. The result would be a system very similar to DRM described above. Proponents of an alternative levy system may suggest that users still prefer flat fee and subscription models to paying for individual transactions. If that is the case (and it implies some consumer irrationality), markets will offer it and there would be no need to mandate such a system through regulation.[34] The core issue, however, remains and proponents of alternative mechanisms would have to address how to disburse the monies collected, yet avoid mandating a more costly and less efficient DRM surrogate.

Second, any system that uses a proxy by definition is imprecise when collecting fees. The effect may not be severe, though, as long as the surrogate that is taxed tracks usage of information goods by individual consumers fairly well.[35] Taxing blank media, for example, will penalize those that use it to backup their own data on it. Yet, consumers buying blank media most extensively, arguably, are the ones that use them to store music, video, and other information goods on it. Similarly, with bandwidth, the faster a user's connection to the Internet, the more copyrighted information she will arguably be receiving. The issue is to identify the most appropriate proxy to collect the levy. Implementing any regime that will add a levy onto a good or service will be resisted by the affected businesses. They will argue that their products are penalized to pay a third party – the rights holders. Because of the inherent re-distributional effect, such systems are politically difficult to enact, at least in the United States.

More than 200 years ago, Fichte's idea of authorship prompted continental Europeans to shift value from the medium to the content.[36] Under Netanel's and Fisher's alternative systems authors upstream would still be paid for their creations (thus leaving Fichte's idea in place) but downstream consumers shift back to paying for the medium. In an odd turn of events, should these alternative systems take hold, future policy battles would focus less on protecting creations and more on taxing proxies.

Aim: Copyright's Utility?

When searching for a policy lever to protect video, we first turned to Peer-to-Peer networks, only to learn that the challenge may not simply be the technology of Peer-to-Peer (or any other technology), but the more fundamental mindset of digitalization. This prompts a change of societal structures stemming from the analog world – of business models as well as regulatory frameworks. The suggested switch from charging for information goods to taxing surrogate products and services brings into play a different set of proxies – not the agent of change, but the object onto which we pin copyrights. The goal – ostensibly – is still to protect the rights holders. What needs to be done, Lemley and Reese write, is "to reduce piracy enough that [the rights holders] can make a return on their invest-ment."[37] Technology may change, agency may shift, rights may be altered and reshaped, but the overall aim making rights holders reap profits seems like the fixed star in this constellation.

Copyright's aim has been to foster and facilitate the artistic creations. It does so by protecting those that invest in creativity, whether authors who spend time and energy to create, or investors who spend money to finance creators. Influenced by Locke's theory of labor copyright differs funda-mentally from continental European author's rights.[38] Unlike copyright, continental European author's rights are seen as society's recognition of the creative genius and acknowledge that the author and his/her creations are connected through an immutable band.[39] This band contains a com-mercial and a personal strand: authors may license others to use their creations, thus commercializing them. They also retain a bundle of personal (or often called "moral") rights, including to be named as author. Very much like other personal rights, these author's rights are not transferable.[40]

Copyright contrast has always been seen as a tool, as a means to an end, not an end in itself. Like property it can be traded and transferred at will. Lawrence Lessig said famously that copyright is a "creation of the state." Enacted to foster creativity and innovation – even the US. Constitution explicitly mentions the utility of copyright[41] – , Congress can alter and change copyright with great, albeit not complete latitude.[42] Hence, copyright itself turns out to be a proxy, a tool to a larger end: to maximize the utility of creativity by both fostering society's creative pro-duction and facilitating its use.

The issue, therefore, may be not just to discover the accurate agency and find the appropriate object to link copyright to. Instead, what may be neces-sary is to re-evaluate copyright and ask: Does it still fulfill its function sufficiently well? What alternative models to foster creativity and inno-vation and to facilitate their use can be conceived of, and how would such alternatives fare when compared with the existing regime? What would happen, for example, if copyright would be abolished? At first blush, one might think that rights holders would lose the ability to protect their creations from use, while free riders could use whatever information good they want. Yet, trademark law would still be in place. Disney Corporation could enjoin others from sharing information that would violate any of Disney's trademarks. The movie Pocahontas could be shared freely on Peer-to-Peer networks or burnt on DVDs and given out by anybody, but nobody except the Disney Corporation could call it Pocahontas. Descriptive terms would have to be used by third parties, which in turn increase the transaction cost (both for adding such a description on the supply side and for searching on the demand side), while the Disney Corporation and its licensees could offer downloads using the well-known brand names protected by trademark law. The higher the transaction cost to find information without its brand name, the higher the price former rights holders could extract from consumers to use their information legally.

Or, to suggest another example, one could imagine Europeans abolish the commercial side of author's rights, but keep moral rights in place. Like in the trademark hypothetical, consumers could share information goods, but not claim authorship or change its content. Using information goods would thus still be constrained.

Each of these alternatives offers different constraints and different incentives for consumers: in the first scenario, users are free to combine information goods, to create new information bricolage, which could then be offered under a different label. In this important aspect, it may even encourage creative activity on the consumer rather than professional end of the spectrum. At the same token, professional content producers, like Hollywood's majors, may continue to protect their information goods through trademark law – at least to an extent. The moral rights scenario, on the other hand, incentivizes diffusion and use of information goods, while it hinders creative combinations and information bricolage.

The importance of these scenarios is not to present working alternatives to the existing copyright regime, rather they exemplify that alternative mechanisms are conceivable and – at least to an extent – may act as possible intellectual property surrogates. To be sure, each one of these alternatives comes with its own baggage of constraints and limitations, providing incentives for some activity, and discouraging other. It is important, though, to recognize that alternatives exist. Such alternative mechanisms *may* work better. Perhaps copyright itself can be reinvented and reshaped as its utility may have suffered by a change in technical and societal context. Fundamentally, copyright is but a mechanism, a proxy to achieve a bigger goal.

After the proxy battles over change agency and regulatory object, this is the third such battle and the most significant one. It is the battle over identifying and implementing the best proxy mechanism to further the societal aim of fostering the creation and diffusion of information goods. And as with the other two proxy battles it's most important for us to understand that the proxy itself isn't exclusive, we simply have a choice.[43]

Notes

1. All quotes from Statement of Jack Valenti, "Privacy & Piracy: The Paradox of Illegal File Sharing on Peer-to-Peer Networks and the Impact of Technology on the Entertainment Industry" before the Senate Committee on Government Affairs, September 30, 2003.
2. See Dan Hunter, Culture War, http://ssrn.com/abstract=586463 August 10, 2004.
3. For another binary cyberlaw debate, see Viktor Mayer-Schönberger, The Shape of Governance: Analyzing the World of Internet Regulation, 43 Virginia Journal of International Law 605 (2003).
4. Even at top modem speeds of 56 kbit/s, a single feature length movie would take 140 h to download; the numbers on US broadband users are from Broadband Growth Trends in the US (citing Nielsen Online), Web Site Optimization LLC, December 2007.
5. This situation may be different in advanced broadband nations like South Korea or Japan, where broadband speeds have reached 10 Mbit/s in 2004 and may reach 100 Mbit/s before the end of the decade. Often it is argued that users of Peer-to-Peer networks will perceive downloads as instantaneous if download time does not exceed the movie's playing time. In such cases, users could start watching the movie right away, while it is still being downloaded. This presupposes that downloaded times do not vary much, and that any slowdown that does occur can be overcome through buffering. In practice, Peer-to-Peer networks even at very fast connections show vastly varying download speeds. As Peer-to-Peer networks do not guarantee a certain level of service, users will have to expect interruptions while watching movies. Moreover, users will never know if the movie they download is in fact complete, and will download in its entirety.
6. For example, to download a high definition movie encoded with a modern compression engine in real time, i.e., the time it takes to watch the movie, a bandwidth of 17.5 Mbit/s and higher may be required.
7. Keith Ross has recently suggested that up to 70% of music files on Peer-to-Peer networks are not working, and many of them the result of decoys sent into the networks by the music industry; see Keith Ross, Pollution in Peer-to-Peer File Sharing, Presentation at CITI Peer-to-Peer Video conference, September 10, 2004.
8. See the recent case of *Altnet v. RIAA*, alleging patent infringement for automatized seeding of decoy files, http://www.infoworld.com/article/04/09/09/HNPeer-to-Peerpartner_1.html
9. See e.g., Kevin Zhu, Internet-Based Distribution of Digital Videos: The Economic Impacts of Digitization on the Motion Picture Industry, Electronic Markets, 11 (4), 273–280.
10. Philip Evans and Thomas Wuerster, Blown to Bits, HBS Press (1999).
11. Cf. Stephen Kern, The Culture of Time and Space 1880–1918, Harvard University Press. (2003); Joshua Meyerowitz, No Sense of Place: The Impact of Electronic Media on Social Behavior, Oxford University Press (1985).

12. Nicholas Negroponte, Being Digital, Knopf (1995).
13. John Seely Brown and Paul Duguid, The Social Life of Information, HBS Press (2000); for a more personal take, see Michael Schrage, The Debriefing: John Seely Brown, Wired Issue 8.08 (August 2000).
14. For an analysis of why see Viktor Mayer-Schönberger, The Authority of Law in Times of Cyberspace, 2001 University of Illinois Journal of Law, Technology & Policy 1; for a complementary view see A. Michael Froomkin, Habermas@ discourse.net: Toward a Critical Theory of Cyberspace, 116 Harvard Law Review 749 (2003); Habermas famously chronicled the advent and formalization of public discourse in Jürgen Habermas, Der Strukturwandel der Öffentlichkeit, Suhrkamp (1990); in English Jürgen Habermas, The Structural Transformation of the Public Sphere: An Inquiry into a Category of Bourgeois Society, MIT Press (1989).
15. This is following Wiebe Bijker, Thomas Hughes, and Trevor Pinch (eds), The Social Construction of Technological Systems, MIT Press (1987); see also Wiebe Bijker, Of Bicycles, Bakelites, and Bulbs, MIT Press (1997); Claude S. Fischer, America Calling, University of California Press (1992).
16. See e.g., Yannis Bakos and Erik Brynjolfsson, Bundling and Competition on the Internet, Marketing Science, 19 (1) (Winter 2000) 63–82.
17. No article it seems these days can do without citing Coase; this one is no exception: Ronald H. Coase, The Nature of the Firm, 4 Economica 386 (1937); Ronald Coase, The Problem of Social Cost, 2 Journal of Law and Economics 1 (1960).
18. It is understandable that rights holders do not want to lower the price of their informational goods. More surprising is that few voices in the public debate have suggested a lowering of the price of movies as one component of rebalancing the cost equation. To be sure, given negligible transaction costs, one would have to lower the price of movies to zero to compete with free downloads via Peer-to-Peer. Transaction costs, however, do play a significant role. Price reductions may hence be potentially sufficient to rebalance the cost equation.
19. Mark Lemley and R. Anthony Reese, Reducing Digital Copyright Infringement Without Restricting Innovation, 56 Stanford Law Review 1345 (2004).
20. For a review of the general debate on how much of a threat is required, see Viktor Mayer-Schönberger, The Shape of Governance, p. 614 et seq.
21. Lemley and Reese, Reducing Digital Copyright Infringement, supra note 18, at 1351.
22. Uniform Dispute Resolution Policy, http://www.icann.org/; whether the UDRP is in fact effective, efficient, and just is the subject of an intense academic debate; see Michael Geist, Fair.Com?: An Examination of the Allegations of Systemic Unfairness in the ICANN UDRP, 27 Brooklyn Journal of International Law 903 (2002); Annette Kur, UDRP, http://www.intellecprop.mpg.de/Online-Publikationen/2002/UDRP-study-final-02.pdf
23. Lemley and Reese, supra note 18, at 1411 et seq.
24. See http://cyber.law.harvard.edu/events/Speedbumps/Speed-bumps_conference.html

25. See Elaine McArdle, Up on Downloading, Harvard Law Bulletin, Summer 2004, p. 17 at 18.
26. Volokh attributes the term to David Post; see Eugene Volokh, "Paper Books? They're So 20th Century," The Wall Street Journal, May 30, 2000, at A26, online at http://www1.law.ucla.edu/~volokh/ebook.htm
27. This is not the only technical problem. Interoparability issues pose another challenge as different flavors of DRM in different equipment will have to work together flawlessly and without user intervention.
28. A legal mandate for a particular DRM standard poses another challenge. It creates a huge incentive for hackers to break the DRM (and thus have the entire system crumble like a deck of cards).
29. Lawrence Lessig, The Future of Ideas: The Fate of the Commons in a Connected World, Vintage Books (2002).
30. Neil Weinstock Netanel, Impose a Noncommercial Use Levy to Allow Free Peer-to-Peer File-Sharing, 17 Harv. J. Law & Tec 1 (2003).
31. William W. Fisher, Promises to Keep: Technology, Law, and the Future of Entertainment, Stanford University Press (2004).
32. Netanel, supra note 29, at 32.
33. Chris Anderson, The Long Tail: Why the Future of Business Is Selling Less of More, Hyperion (2006).
34. It is different if one were to suggest a voluntary system; see Fred von Lohmann, Voluntary Collective Licensing for Music File Sharing, Communications of the ACM, 47 (10) (October 2004) 21.
35. This is, as Netanel comments, the undeniable advantages of his proposal over government reward systems to replace copyright.
36. Johann Gottlieb Fichte, Beweis der Unrechtmäßigkeit des Büchernachdrucks, Berliner Monatsschriften 1793, p. 443.
37. Lemley & Reese, Supra Note 18, at 1351.
38. For an exhaustive analysis, see Julia Ellins, Copyright Law, Urheberrecht, und Ihre Harmonisierung in der Europäischen Gemeinschaft, Duncker & Humblot (1997).
39. An analysis of this band is the central theme in Viktor Mayer-Schönberger, Information und Recht, Springer (2001), p. 66 et seq.
40. See only Jane C. Ginsburg, Have Moral Rights come of (Digital) Age in the United States?, 19 Cardozo Arts & Ent LJ 9 (2001), Natalie C. Suhl, Moral Rights Protection in the United States Under the Berne Convention: A Fictional Work?, 12 Fordham Intell. Prop. Media & Ent. L.J. 1203 (2002); Henry Hansmann & Marina Santilli, Authors' and Artists' Moral Rights: A Comparative Legal and Economic Analysis, 26 J. Legal Stud. 95 (1997).
41. US Const. art. I § 8, cl. 8 "...to promote the Progress of Science and useful Arts..."
42. What Congress can do is limited by the US Constitution's guarantee of copyright protection; see Eldred v. Ashcroft, 5.
43. Viktor Mayer-Schönberger is Associate Professor of Public Policy at the John F. Kennedy School of Government, Harvard University. Email: viktor_mayer-schoenberger@harvard.edu.

13

Peer-to-Peer Network and the Distribution in the EU

Andrea Gavosto[1], Bruno Lamborghini[2], Stefano Lamborghini[3]

[1]*Fondazione Giovanni Agnelli*
[2]*Catholic University in Milan*
[3]*Telecom Italia*

Introduction

Broadband internet connections are growing rapidly throughout Europe: after a slow start, the old continent has caught up with the USA and other industrialized countries. The diffusion of broadband is a key factor to develop digital convergence between telecommunications and television, new Internet applications and services, and new online contents. Peer-to-Peer networks are becoming an increasingly important avenue to distribute such contents across broadband connections. In our work we will describe the working of Peer-to-Peer networks, its evolution towards legal business models, its regulatory challenges, and the role that they will play in a convergent world.

Through strong advancement in the DSL technology, broadband lines in the European Union have reached a world record of more than 58 million lines at the end of 2005 (+50% over the previous year), or one-third of the world total, vis–à–vis China with 29 million, the USA with 22 million ADSL (in the USA there are also 24 million cable modems which provide broadband connections). The European Union is expected to reach 120 million broadband lines by 2010.

In the mobile market, the European Union reached 700 million cellular lines at the end of 2005 (penetration rate: 150%), and is today moving rapidly to increasing bandwidth capacity through UMTS and HSPDA.

E.M. Noam and L.M. Pupillo (eds.), *Peer-to-Peer Video*, doi: 10.1007/978-0-387-76450-4_13,
© Springer Science + Business Media, LLC 2008

Content services are benefiting from the steady rise in the broadband subscriber base. The pioneer services that were launched before 2000 suffered from a lack of bandwidth, from the lack of cooperation between content providers, online distributors and ISPs, and from difficulties in establishing business models. But most of these obstacles have been lifted as bitrates increase, thus improving the quality of the services. Other contributing factors include a more open attitude from content providers, the impetus provided by new entrants coming from other industries such as Consumer Electronics (CE) and the growth of online advertising, along with the growth of the online audience. Some services have proven that it is in fact possible to market paid content via the web.

The online content market (video, music, publishing, games, and adult content) is expected to increase more than double in the next 4 years, thus increasing from close to €1 billion in 2006 to €2.2 billion in 2009.

The European Union of 25 Member countries thus appears to be a major area for the development of new Internet applications, of new online contents, and also of new Peer-to-Peer industry-based content and services. Many Peer-to-Peer developments – such as KaZaA or Skype – have been originated by European initiatives. More than 20 million European computers are using Peer-to-Peer software and this figure is expected to double in four years' time.

Peer-to-Peer technologies are defined as a communication structure in which individuals interact directly, without necessarily going through a centralized system or hierarchy. Users can share information, make files available, contribute to shared projects, or transfer files.[1]

The most notable feature of Peer-to-Peer networks is that each computer belonging to a community, i.e., a network, is simultaneously a digital content client (demander and downloader), and a supplier and uploader. By combining a search engine and communication tools, Peer-to-Peer becomes a community tool for exchanging and sharing digital resources.

There are two types of Peer-to-Peer architecture. The first is *centralized*, such as the one used by Napster, iMesh, and SoulSeek. Centralized Peer-to-Peer is characterized by the presence of a central server that opens users' access to a network of peers, which references all peers and collects information on the data that are stored for exchange. The second type of architecture is *distributed*. A distributed service is characterized by the absence of a central server. Users do not connect to a server but rather to another user. The information transits in Peer-to-Peer mode, in the same fashion as files are exchanged.

A distinction has to be made between Peer-to-Peer software, Peer-to-Peer protocol, and Peer-to-Peer networks.

Peer-to-Peer software is the application which, once it has been installed on the peer's computer, provides access to the network, and allows community members to perform searches on other peers' computers for content which is available for download. Around the middle of August 2005, close to 1,400 Peer-to-Peer open source file sharing software projects were under development.

A Peer-to-Peer network is formed by a group of servers which are connected simultaneously to one another through the Peer-to-Peer application.

Peer-to-Peer protocol is the set of specifications that describes the rules and agreements adhered to during a Peer-to-Peer data exchange. Each network has a proprietary protocol. Protocols too can be open – like the applications – and so can be reused by other applications.

A number of companies focusing on business segments – which are more restricted than the content distribution and consumer services segments – are evolving within the sphere of Peer-to-Peer.

As initial Peer-to-Peer exchanges often occurred in breach of legal rules on content rights, Peer-to-Peer networks are now attempting to create a market within a legal framework where data sharing can be controlled. Aware of the fact that it will be harder to win customers' trust than it has been for most, these solutions publishers have been careful to ensure the legality of their activities, and the legal implications of the transfers and exchanges they enable.

Peer-to-Peer software publishers offer audio, video, image, and text file exchange applications, along with applications built around this strategy of legality, and are now entering the stage where they seek to establish their legitimacy with the content industries. This stage will involve signing partnership agreements with content providers and making the transition to a paid and approved model.

Broadband as Peer-To-Peer Technology Enabler

Broadband access for all

The number of people in Europe who access the Internet via broadband is increasing at a steady rate, even if the percentage of connected households still varies largely from one region, or one country, to the next. The European Commission estimates that the number of connections in EU25 will increase from the current 60 million to twice as much by 2009.

Indeed, progress made by DSL technologies has brought about not only an enlargement of the geographic area served by broadband, but also a marked increase of the bitrate. In some countries, operators have made a concerted effort to upgrade their cable networks, or to deploy networks using technologies that allow them to deliver telecommunication services such as Internet access and IP telephony (Tables 13.1–13.18).

Table 13.1 Broadband subscribers in million[2]

	2002	2005	2006	2010
France	1.7	9.7	12.0	17.6
Germany	3.1	9.7	12.6	22.4
Italy	1.1	6.8	9.1	15.4
Spain	1.3	5.0	6.4	10.0
Total EU 25	12.8	58.4	75.8	119.5
USA	18.3	45.8	56.5	84.1

The bitrates on offer are constantly increasing

Table 13.2 Peak bitrates and monthly subscription costs for residential customers, selection of European ISPs, Oct. 2005

Country	ISP	Network	Maximum bandwidth (Mbps)	€/month
France	France Telecom	ADSL	18	39.90
	Telecom Italia	ADSL	18	29.95
	Free	ADSL	20	29.99
	NC Numericâble	Cable	20	39.90
Germany	T-Online	ADSL	6	29.95
	AOL	ADSL	6	29.90
	Hansenet	ADSL	6	n.a.
	Ish	Cable	5	59.90
Italy	Telecom Italia	ADSL	4	36.95
	Wind	ADSL	4	n.a.
	Fastweb	ADSL	6	40.00
	Fastweb	FTTH	10	40.00
Spain	Telefonica	ADSL	4	39.07
	Wanadoo	ADSL	2	39.00
	Jazztel	ADSL	20	29.95
	AunaCable	Cable	2	42.00
United Kingdom	BT	ADSL	2	32.95
	Tiscali	ADSL	2	32.95
	Wanadoo	ADSL	2	32.95
	NTL	Cable	10	55.90

Development and Diffusion of Peer-to-Peer in Europe

Peer-to-Peer's Reach

The penetration rate for Peer-to-Peer software in households equipped with a broadband Internet connection varies between 15% in Poland and nearly 34% in Germany. Given the continuous increase of the installed broadband subscriber's base, as projected by the European Commission and by several information providers, the number of Peer-to-Peer users, therefore, is set to continue to grow.

The average length of the active use of Peer-to-Peer also varies across countries. A French household equipped with at least one Peer-to-Peer application uses[3] it for an average of 8 h and 30 min a month, while a German household uses it, on average, for only 3 h and 45 min.

Table 13.3 Peer-to-Peer's reach

	France	Germany	Italy	Poland	Spain	Sweden	UK	Rest of EU 25	USA
Broadband subscribers in millions	9.7	9.7	6.8	2.0	5.0	1.8	10.1	1.3	52.4
Peer-to-Peer penetration rate in %	31	34	25*	15*	20*	30*	18	15*	26
No. of peers in millions	3.0	3.3	1.7	0.3	1.0	0.5	1.8	0.2	13.5
Active Peer-to-Peer duration per month (hh:mm:ss)	08:32:35	03: 47:32	n.a.	n.a.	n.a.	n.a.	05:01:20	n.a.	04:24:42

* IDATE estimate. Source: Nielsen//NetRatings – Service MegaPanel 2005

Peer Profile

Whilst in France, the UK, and Germany over 60% of Peer-to-Peer users are men, in the USA there are far more female than male peers.

Although most peers belong to the 35- to 64-year-old category, which reflects the population in general, 15- to 24-year-olds are – unsurprisingly – over-represented amongst Peer-to-Peer users.

Table 13.4 Peers by gender in %

	France	Germany	UK	USA[4]
Men	63.5	69.6	65.8	33.6
Women	36.5	30.4	34.2	66.4

Source: Nielsen//NetRatings – Service MegaPanel 2005

Table 13.5 Penetration of Peer-to-Peer based on age, in %

	France	Germany	UK	USA
15–24	58	38	37	33
25–34	44	20	18	16
35–49	38	17	19	13
50–64	32	16	15	7
65+	19	10	6	3

Source: Nielsen//NetRatings – Service MegaPanel 2005

Peer-to-Peer penetration is higher among students, but file-sharing is used by all age categories.

Number of Peer-to-Peer Applications Used

Peer-to-Peer households use up to five different applications, but 95% of them use only two; this implies a certain expertise among file-sharers.

Table 13.6 Number of applications used, in %

No. of applications used	France	Germany	UK	USA
1	76.8	80.7	81.4	86.0
2	18.0	14.6	15.0	12.0
3	3.9	4.1	3.2	1.4
4	0.8	0.3	0.3	0.3
5 or more	0.5	0.3	0.1	0.2

Source: Nielsen//NetRatings – Service MegaPanel 2005

Peer-to-Peer Software and Network Penetration

Twenty applications constitute the base of the most commonly-used Peer-to-Peer applications. In most of the countries surveyed, however, usage was concentrated on five applications in particular.

"Community" Peer-to-Peer networks such as **eMule, eDonkey, WinMX** and **Freenet** are among the most popular. Interestingly, German peers use more "Community" Peer-to-Peer software than users in other countries. eDonkey and WiMX are no longer being developed and their upgrades have ceased, following an agreement with the major music providers. Nevertheless, users continue to use the latest versions available.

In all countries, **KaZaA** is one of the most widely-used applications (ranking first in Germany, second in the UK and France, and third in the USA). KaZaA is the most widely known, which would explain its high penetration level. Music and adult content form the bulk of file exchanges on KaZaA. KaZaA too is no longer being developed.

LimeWire is also present in all of the surveyed countries, and is ranked number one in the United States. LimeWire allows users to download all kinds of content.

WinMX is particularly popular in the UK, where it ranks as number one, and in the USA. It is an application with a strong community component, and involves negotiating with peers. In the same vein, eMule, an open source application, is particularly popular in France, where it is the most popular software, and in Germany. However, it does not even figure among the top five in the UK or the USA.

BitTorrent does not yet rank among the most widely-used Peer-to-Peer systems, even if it is perceived as highly efficient. One of the reasons for this lack of use is the difficulty in consolidating the many applications that use the BitTorrent protocol: there are close to 25 in all, including eMule. Moreover, BitTorrent is used primarily for downloading films, whereas most of the other applications enable all types of files to be exchanged. Another reason is that BitTorrent does not operate the same way as other Peer-to-Peer applications. The lack of a built-in search engine and the need to locate and register a link to the file that one intends to download, make it much less accessible than its counterparts. It is, however, by far the most efficient protocol.

Most Popular Software

Table 13.7 France, most popular software in 2005, in %

	Penetration in Internet households	Peer-to-Peer market penetration[5]
EMule	26	69
KaZaA	8	21
Shareaza	6	15
eDonkey	2	5
LimeWire	1	3

Source: Nielsen//NetRatings – Service MegaPanel 2005

Table 13.8 Germany, most popular software in 2005, in %

	Penetration in Internet households	Peer-to-Peer market penetration[6]
KaZaA	8	44
Emule	6	31
WinMX	2	11
Freenet	2	10
LimeWire	1	6

Source: Nielsen//NetRatings – Service MegaPanel 2005

Table 13.9 UK, most popular software in 2005, in %

	Penetration in Internet households	Peer-to-Peer market penetration[7]
WinMX	5	34
KaZaA	5	29
LimeWire	4	22
BearShare	1	6
Ares Galaxy	1	6

Source: Nielsen//NetRatings – Service MegaPanel 2005

Table 13.10 USA, most popular software in 2005, in %

	Penetration in Internet households	Peer-to-Peer market penetration[8]
LimeWire	3	29
WinMX	2	23
KaZaA	2	18
BearShare	1	9
Ares Galaxy	1	7

Source: Nielsen//NetRatings – Service MegaPanel 2005

Most Popular Peer-to-Peer Networks

Table 13.11 France, most popular Peer-to-Peer networks in 2005, in %

	Penetration in Internet households	Peer-to-Peer market penetration
eDonkey	38	83
FastTrack	32	23
Gnutella	9	20
BitTorrent	8	17
OpenNap	7	3
Other Networks	1	4

Source: Nielsen//NetRatings – Service MegaPanel 2005

Table 13.12 Germany, most popular Peer-to-Peer networks in 2005, in %

	Penetration in Internet households	Peer-to-Peer market penetration
FastTrack	9	45
eDonkey	7	39
Gnutella	3	16
OpenNap	2	11
BitTorrent	1	7
Other Networks	2	12

Source: Nielsen//NetRatings – Service MegaPanel 2005

Table 13.13 UK, most popular Peer-to-Peer networks in 2005, in %

	Penetration in Internet households	Peer-to-Peer market penetration
Gnutella	6	38
FastTrack	6	35
OpenNap	5	33
eDonkey	2	14
BitTorrent	1	8
Other Networks	2	10

Source: Nielsen//NetRatings – Service MegaPanel 2005

Table 13.14 USA, most popular Peer-to-Peer networks in 2005, in %

	Penetration in Internet households	Peer-to-Peer market penetration
Gnutella	5	47
OpenNap	2	23
FastTrack	2	21
eDonkey	1	8
BitTorrent	1	5
Other Networks	2	20

Source: Nielsen//NetRatings – Service MegaPanel 2005

CacheLogic estimates that, in terms of traffic, the two most heavily used networks are eDonkey and BitTorrent. A compelling fact provided by CacheLogic is eDonkey's vast popularity in Latin American countries. It is also popular in Belgium, Germany, Israel, and South Korea.

What is Peer-to-Peer Used For?

Music Downloads

Music is the most widely downloaded type of content (in terms of number of files) in all of the countries surveyed. Video files rank second and images or photos third.

The United States is by far the country where music enjoys the highest popularity amongst Peer-to-Peer households. In France and the USA, video content ranks second after music while, in Germany and the UK, it is software that comes second.

Because of their size, which are often of several Giga bytes (GB), video games rank lower than other types of content. The same holds true for text files, books, and comic books, which are more accessible in their original format.

Table 13.15 Type of content downloaded via Peer-to-Peer, in %[9]

	France	Germany	UK	USA
Audio files	64.8	52.2	73.4	81.3
Video files	35.2	26.1	24.7	26.8
Written materials (books, documents, PDF documents, etc.)	17.6	26.6	15.2	13.2
Images or photos	26.8	22.8	20.3	15.3
Video games	15.1	17.9	18.4	15.3
Software	30.9	42.9	30.4	25.5

Source: Nielsen//NetRatings – Service MegaPanel 2005

In terms of traffic, the most commonly exchanged audio format are, unsurprisingly, MP3 files.

Close-up on Shared Video Content

In France, Germany, and the USA, more than 30% of Peer-to-Peer users download television programs. This is naturally fuelled by the volume of programs made available on the networks. To some extent, Peer-to-Peer is used by viewers as a PVR (personal video recorder), allowing them to access their TV programs whenever they want to. The software replaces the electronic program guide, and the computer's hard drive replaces the PVR.

Films on Digital Versatile Disks (DVD) are also very popular. Here, Peer-to-Peer acts like a video-on-demand service, and a substitute for rental. When compared to physically renting a film, the appeal of Peer-to-Peer lies in the fact of not having to go to the video shop or distributing machine. Compared to VoD, Peer-to-Peer's main appeal is that the films can be kept once they are downloaded, burned, transferred, and so on.

The interest in "screeners" (films shot by an audience member in the theatre) is far lower, no doubt due to their poor quality. It could have been thought that the appeal of viewing a newly-released film would have made this category popular, but apparently quality prevails over novelty.

Table 13.16 Breakdown of video content downloaded, in %

	France	Germany	UK	USA
Film trailers	8.6	10.4	11.8	9.6
Screeners	18.5	20.0	17.5	16.6
Films available on DVD	31.4	29.9	34.3	27.8
TV programs	33.9	31.0	27.6	36.2
Other audio-visual programs (collections, foreign series, etc.)	7.5	8.7	8.8	9.8

Source: Nielsen//NetRatings – Service MegaPanel 2005

Peers' Downloading is not Limited to Peer-to-Peer Networks

Among the countries surveyed, roughly 90% of Peer-to-Peer users also download content from web sites, in addition to using, albeit to a lesser extent, e-mail, Instant Messenger (IM), and File Transfer Protocol (FTP) to exchange files. Downloads via e-mail rank second, followed by IM, except in Germany where FTP ranks third.

Table 13.17 Downloading from sources other than Peer-to-Peer, in %

	France	Germany	UK	USA
Download via regular website	65.1	72.8	69.0	72.8
Download via a blog (someone else's website)	12.8	13.6	12.0	8.9
Download via FTP server	14.3	36.4	15.2	16.2
Download via e-mail	43.9	41.3	60.8	63.0
Download via an IM	35.2	22.8	29.1	23.4
Other	10.2	6.0	6.3	11.1

Source: Nielsen//NetRatings – Service MegaPanel 2005

These figures are corroborated by the data supplied by CacheLogic. In terms of traffic, the Peer-to-Peer phenomenon is gaining more momentum than FTP or classic web traffic. In late 2004, it accounted for close to 60% of all IP traffic, versus just over 40% for ordinary Internet traffic.

The Response of Content Providers: Business Models for Online Contents

A first generation of online content services was launched in the late 1990s. These included music and video services but, on the whole, were not overly popular for a number of reasons:

Lack of bandwidth: The available bitrates were too low and ill-suited for listening to music or watching videos. Live TV was not available and the downloading delays were not acceptable to customers.

Lack of cooperation between content providers, online distributors and ISPs: Initially, music publishers in particular adopted a vertical integration strategy, in an effort to keep control over the distribution of their products, a process which held little appeal for consumers who wanted access to the broadest possible selection. This led to a limited offer of digitally distributed music, which did not correspond either to web users' habits or to their needs.

Competition between online content shops and physical retailers: This is because the former puts pressure on rights' holders to maintain the same level of prices as offline distribution, without the consumer benefiting from the savings generated by digital distribution. Also, content owners refused to sell the rights on their most popular content as they didn't want to disrupt classic distribution systems or undermine their business models.

At the time, no entrenched business model for digital content distribution had emerged: Online content providers found that at the time consumers were only willing to pay for Internet access and not for additional content, except for some specific services such as adult content. A number of content providers, therefore, placed their bets on advertising revenues, but the advertising expenditures on the Internet grew more slowly than expected and were concentrated on a limited number of websites.

And, finally, the dotcom crash in 2001 created a rather hostile environment for investing in new services.

Most of these negative factors have now disappeared:

The rise in available bitrates enables shorter download times, and even real-time video viewing.

Content providers have rolled out more nuanced strategies. In the area of music, in particular, rights holders appear to have given up on trying to control their catalog's distribution, and are signing non-exclusive agreements with online vendors. Leaders in the video world are still resisting change. However, several major Hollywood studios having joined forces to create their own online distribution service called MovieLink.

At the same time, new operators have entered the fray as online digital content vendors. Such operators have a variety of backgrounds: computing (Apple/iTunes, Microsoft/MSN Music Club), CE (Sony/Connect), retail chains (Virgin), and new entrants (OD2/LoudEye). This shift is also taking place with video content, with the emergence of online distributors who are independent from the producers (e.g., MovieSystem, a subsidiary of French TV channel Canal+). In the long run, music and video distribution services are likely to merge.

The growth of the online advertising market is also expected to have a positive impact on content services. While music and video are always likely to depend on direct payment from consumers (per unit or via subscription), online news services depend largely on indirect financing from advertising.

iTunes' online music sales and the rise in the number of subscribers to certain online financial journals are both indicative of a degree of willingness amongst consumers to pay for content, when digital distribution offers appealing products which are affordable and easy to access. The reliability of a content pay-for-service, its security (from viruses), the assurance of being able to access authorized products, and the quality of image and sound alike are also key incentives for consumers to pay for content which could otherwise be obtained free of charge via Peer-to-Peer networks.

Appraising the Online Content Market

According to Jupiter, Western Europe's paid content market will increase from €0.7 billion in 2004 to €2.8 billion in 2009.

Adult entertainment is still the most popular form of online content, but its share of the market is decreasing steadily as demand for other types of content increases. Music and, to a lesser extent, video are likely to experience the highest growth rates in the coming years.

Table 13.18 Appraisal of paid online content revenues in Western Europe, 2006–2009[10]

€ million	2006	2007	2008	2009
Publishing	268	326	370	403
Video	88	133	186	244
Games	368	485	610	762
Music	269	452	652	836
Other[11]	448	487	518	540
Total content revenues	1441	1883	2336	2785

Source: JupiterResearch – European Paid Content and Services Forecast

Veterans and New Entrants – Impact on the Content Value Chain

The broadband content Internet market is not a reproduction of the offline market. Several different strategies are being deployed both by brick-and-mortar content companies and by pure Internet players.

Content publishers may seek to *by-pass their traditional distributors* and address customers directly. Examples of this include:

Films on demand (MovieLink, CinemaNow and Akimbo): studios (and Hollywood in particular) are creating their own video-on-demand (VoD) services which, in the short term, will be available only on PC. The volume of revenues generated by their longstanding clients, namely TV channels, prevents them from offering their service on the TV set.

Online game distribution (TryMedia and Boonty): these services offer digital distribution of PC games. New business models have been tested: download of a trial version of the game, renting games on a per-unit basis and flat fees for unlimited access to a catalog of games available for download.

Other players are leveraging their areas of expertise to enter the content market. Some CE manufacturers, for instance, are banking on combining their products with services to ensure the availability of appealing content and/or to occupy a larger portion of the value-added chain. Apple and Sony combine sales of MP3 players and online music distribution. RealAudio bundles games on its RealArcade player. Portable video player manufacturer Archos has signed agreements with EchoStar in the USA, and Canal+ in France, to distribute the two operators' TV programs.

New intermediaries, so called "search–find–obtain" companies (e.g., Google, eBay, Amazon, Yahoo!, Expedia, Meetic, and Yellow Pages) that enable users to search for information, people, products, and services, have become leading players in the Internet content and services market. The emergence of companies, whose business is to compile all of the available content and allow consumers to acquire it, appears a likely evolution of the Internet.

Following the acquisition of Skype by eBay, new entrants specialized in "search–find–obtain" business could invest in Peer-to-Peer solutions to reinforce their position of intermediaries along the value chain.

Content-generated revenues or indirect revenues?

For some operators, marketing online content is part of a larger objective. CE manufacturers use online music sales (and no doubt video in the future) as a means of increasing the sales of their audio and video equipment. Operators are allotted only a marginal portion of the revenues generated by online content sales, which are not their main source of profit.[12]

Advertising-based Financing or Subscriber Payment?

Pioneer illegal online content downloads sites sought to develop a financing model based on advertising, by having adverts displayed on their portal's homepage. When operating a legal business, it is conceivable that advertising can help finance a content distribution operation. Radio stations, for instance, are financed entirely by advertising, and contribute significantly to record companies' revenues. Although the online advertising market has been back on an upwards swing for the past two years, it is still limited by certain features:

The Internet's share of advertising is still well below its audience share in the media market. The Internet has roughly a 13% share of the audience in the USA, but only a 4% share of the advertising market. Advertisers' gradual cutbacks in spending on the number one advertising platform, i.e., television, are nevertheless expected to help reduce this gap.

Advertisers' investments are still highly concentrated on select sites. In 2004 in the USA, for instance, the top 10 sites alone accounted for a 71% share of the online advertising market, while the top 25 sites had the lion's share of 94%.[13]

The most common type of advertising found on the net now is the "paid search," in other words links to sites supplied by search engines. This form is more beneficial to "search–find–obtain" intermediaries than to pure content sites.

Subscription or Pay-as-you-go?

The first digital content distribution services opted for a replica of the tariff model used by physical retail vendors, offering content sales and rentals on a per-unit basis. Models based on subscriptions in exchange for limited access were also tested. The combination of subscriptions and per-unit sales may well be the best response, with the choice of the tariff model being a reflection of the content's appeal and commercial potential. Some VoD services offer both flat rate subscriptions for access to a catalog of programs, and a pay-per-view system.

Sale or Rental?

Contents can be made available using a sales model (whereby consumers acquire complete ownership of the content) or a rental model (whereby they have access either for a limited amount of time or for a limited number of viewings/plays). Both models now coexist.

Although these models are still uncertain, the market is populated by operators for whom offering content for free allows them either to market other products and services (players, Internet subscriptions), or to generate advertising revenues (search engines), while for others content marketing remains a profit center. For the latter, the fundamental choice lies between a model based on the principle of exclusivity and control over a program's distribution (as with TV programs), and a broad distribution model (as with music sales), widely available on the Internet. Because of this, intermediaries' and aggregators' (TV channels, shops) position is being threatened by a growing number of distribution channels, and on-demand TV viewing and radio listening.

Peer-To-Peer and the EU Regulatory Framework

In the European Union the regulatory approach towards Peer-to-Peer is considered within the general legislation for copyright and related rights in the online environment.

The EU Copyright Directive

The European Parliament and Council's directive 2001/29/EC, dated 22 May 2001, on the harmonization of certain aspects of copyright and related rights in the information society (Copyright Directive) aims to transpose and ensure the implementation of the World Intellectual Property Organization Treaty on Copyright and on Performance and Phonograms of December 1996.

The Copyright Directive harmonizes the legal protection granted to rightsholders for on-line uses of protected works and tries to balance rightsholders' exclusive rights with exceptions for consumers for specific legitimate uses (private copying). Moreover, it forbids the circumvention of anti-copying devices and provides exemption for network operators to obtain the rightsholders' authorization to make temporary copies of protected material for transmission purposes.

Right of Reproduction and Exceptions to the Exclusive Right

According to the Directive, any copy (permanent or temporary, direct or indirect) of protected material has to be authorized by the rightsholders and all of the exceptions provided cannot conflict with the normal use of the protected material; further, they cannot unreasonably prejudice the legitimate interests of the rightsholders. No authorization is required for making temporary copies of protected material if the copies are an "integral and essential part of a technological process"; if the sole purpose of the technological process is to "enable a transmission in a network between third parties by an intermediary or lawful use"; and if the copies have no "independent economic significance."

These exceptions cover copies made for browsing and caching purposes, and those which enable transmission systems to work efficiently, provided that the intermediary does not modify the information and does not interfere with the lawful use of technology – which is widely recognized and used by the industry – to obtain data on the use of the information.

Further, optional, exceptions to the authorization for the reproduction right include: copies made for private use, for the benefit of publicly accessible institutions such as libraries, museums or archives, educational and scientific purposes, for news reporting or quotation purposes, for use by people with disabilities, for public security uses, and for uses in administrative and judicial proceedings.

In the case of private copying, rightsholders must receive fair compensation determined by Member States.

Right of Communication to the Public

All communication to the public regarding protected material, including making it available on demand via the Internet, must be authorized by its rightsholders.

The provision of physical facilities for enabling or actually making communication does not constitute a "communication to the public" and intermediaries do not require the authorization of the rightsholders before transmitting protected material over communication networks. Some exemptions to the authorization are allowed for educational and scientific purposes, for news reporting or quotation purposes, for use by people with disabilities, for public security purposes, and in administrative and judicial proceedings.

Right of Distribution

Distribution to the public of protected material via a physical medium (e.g., DVDs) must be authorized by rightsholders.

Once protected material is marketed on a physical medium in the European Union by or with the consent of the rightsholder, the latter cannot oppose any subsequent resale. Parallel imports are therefore permitted provided that they originate from a Member State.

Protection of Anti-Copying Devices

The Copyright Directive provides protection against the circumvention of "effective technological measures," which are intended to protect intellectual property rights (DRM, digital rights management systems). It also establishes that Member States must provide adequate legal protection against any activity (including the manufacturing or distribution of devices, products, or components and the provision of services) carried out with the knowledge – or with reasonable grounds to know – which is "primarily designed, produced, adapted, or performed to enable or facilitate the circumvention of these technological measures," or has only limited commercially significant purpose or use other than circumvention, or is promoted, advertised, or marketed for the purpose of circumvention of these technological measures.

Member States must provide legal protection against the removal or alteration of electronic copyright management information and distribution, and the import and communication to the public of works from which rights management information has been removed or altered without authority.

Moreover, in order to make the exceptions to the exclusive rights possible, rightsholders must guarantee that the beneficiaries of some of the exceptions can indeed benefit from these exceptions. This provision only applies to off-line use and not to on-demand delivery of protected material under agreed contractual terms (in the case of a private copy of a legitimate CD-ROM, users should be able to make copies without authorization even if the CD-ROM is protected by an anti-copying device).

Liability of Intermediaries

The Copyright Directive does not regulate the conditions under which information society service providers can be held liable for third party illegal content when they act as "online intermediaries," but the Electronic Commerce Directive (European Parliament and Council Directive 2000/31/EC of June 8, 2000 "on certain legal aspects of information society services, in particular electronic commerce in the internal market") merely specifies that rightsholders must be entitled to apply for an injunction against intermediaries when their services are used by third parties to infringe intellectual property rights.

The Electronic Commerce Directive states, as a general principle, that Member States may not impose a general obligation on intermediaries to monitor third party information, which they transmit or store, and provides cases where liability limitations may be applied to all forms of illegal activities (including copyright and trademark infringements, defamation, misleading advertising, etc.).

Limitations to the Liability of Intermediaries: Mere Conduit

Service providers, whose role consists in the transmission of information originating from third parties and the provision of access through a communication network, cannot be held liable for third party illegal content if they do not initiate the transmission, do not select the receiver of the transmission, and do not select or modify the information transmitted (Mere conduit).

Limitations to the Liability of Intermediaries: Caching

Automatic, intermediate, and transient storage of information which takes place during the transmission of the information in order to carry out the transmission is covered by the exemption of liability.

Service providers cannot be held liable for third party illegal content when providing caching facilities if they do not modify the information, if they comply with the conditions on access to information and with the rules on the updating of the information, if they do not interfere with the "lawful use of technology" to obtain data on the use of the information, or if they act "expeditiously" to remove access to the information stored having been informed that the information has been removed from the network, when access to it has been disabled or when a responsible authority has ordered the removal (Caching).

Limitations to the Liability of Intermediaries: Hosting

Service providers who store information supplied by and at the request of a recipient of the service are not liable (for criminal liability) if they do not have "actual knowledge" that the information or the activity is illegal (for civil liability), if they are not aware of facts or circumstances which would make the illegal activity apparent, or if they "expeditiously" remove access to the information once informed of its illegality (Hosting).

Peer-to-Peer and National Legislation in Europe

The Copyright Directive has been transposed in internal legislation by the majority of the EU Member States and their national legislation towards Peer-to-Peer relates to the rules within the Copyright Directive.

France

France adopted a law on copyright and related rights in the information society in June 2006 which requires Internet users to implement the technical means of protection which Internet access providers must offer to their subscribers to ensure that the Internet is not used for non-authorized reproduction purposes.

The law foresees the creation of a new independent administrative authority, which is responsible for monitoring DRM and the identification of protected works that will take duties for settling disputes relating to the interoperability of digital rights management systems. The authority will also ensure that the exceptions to intellectual property rights can be effectively exercised and will establish the number of private copies that can be made under the private copy exemption.

The circumvention of technical protection measures that seek to prevent or limit non-authorized uses of protected works (other than software, videos, and sound recordings) – such as DRM systems – is prohibited by law.

According to the law, technical protection measures should not prevent interoperability, and providers of technical measures are to provide access to information required to ensure interoperability. Should access be refused, software editors, manufacturers of technical systems, and service providers may ask the administrative authority to adopt a decision within 2 months.

Unauthorized acts of reproduction and communication to the public of protected works that have been made available through a Peer-to-Peer file sharing software will be sanctioned by fines, and distributors and publishers of software intended for illegally making protected works available will be subject to penalties.

Germany

Germany began a reform of the copyright legislation in 2003 in order to fulfill the requirements of the information society. In March 2006, the Federal Cabinet adopted a decision that allows the analogue and digital copying of protected works for private purposes, but prohibits private copying if the copy is made from an "obviously illegal" copy or if it was "obviously illegally" made available to the public (e.g., films on the Internet or via Peer-to-Peer). The exception according to which illegal private copying would not be prosecuted where only a small number of protected works are illegally exploited and solely for private purposes was removed.

The circumvention of anti-copying devices was prohibited.

Italy

In Italy, the law (Legislative Decree 68, 2003) implementing the EU Copyright Directive aligns the rightsholders' exclusive rights of reproduction, communication to the public and distribution with the provisions of the EU and provides for exceptions and limitations to these rights and for the protection of technological measures.

Rightsholders have an exclusive right to authorize the reproduction, the communication to the public and the distribution of their protected works. Nevertheless, the Italian law provides some exceptions regarding the private reproduction of audio and visual materials, if made by natural persons for their own private use.

Criminal sanctions (administrative penalties and/or imprisonment) are envisaged for those who circumvent the rules on technological measures or abusively alter or remove the rights management information placed on the works.

Moreover, in 2004 the Italian Parliament adopted a law on "measures aimed at combating the abusive telecommunication diffusion of audio-visual materials and interventions for supporting the cinema and show-biz activities" (decree, 2004 no. 72 or "Peer-to-Peer law") which provided administrative sanctions for anyone who diffused (by means of telecommunication tools or file-sharing techniques) copyrighted films or similar works, and criminal sanctions for anyone who diffused copyrighted films to the public using file-sharing techniques, or promoted related activities. Finally, it foresaw the obligation for Internet service providers to inform public authorities when they were aware of illicit file-sharing activities. The Peer-to-Peer law was modified in 2005 by law n 43 that allows offences for illicit file-sharing of copyright works to be extinguished by the payment of an administrative fine and replaces the aim "for profit" with "for purpose of gain" for the application of criminal sanctions to activities which do not lead to a direct gain but to an indirect one.

Spain

Spain has adopted a law transposing the Copyright Directive but the final version of the law is not yet available.

The law contains a mechanism to set copyright levies on digital copying devices, whereby interested parties can propose a list of devices and the amount that should be levied on the cost of the device to the government. The government then makes a final decision on the levies to be paid (the law already contains provisional fees that will be valid until the final decision is adopted).

United Kingdom

In the UK, the Copyright Directive was implemented with the Copyright and Related Rights Regulations 2003. The British regulation relates to the right of communication to the public, including the broadcasting of the work and its being made making available to the public by electronic transmission in such a way that members of the public may access it from a place and at a time individually chosen by them, and to the right for intermediaries to make temporary copies of works that are transient or incidental, that are an integral and essential part of a technological process and the sole purpose of which is to enable a transmission of a work in a network between third parties.

The Copyright and Related Rights Regulations 2003 deals with the protection of technological measures (e.g., anti-copying devices) through the creation of the offence of manufacturing, importing, selling, letting, offering for sale or hire, advertising, possessing or distributing devices or services that are designed to circumvent technological measures. It also allows individuals to issue a complaint to the Secretary of State if an effective technological measure prevents a person from carrying out a permitted act, by providing the legal protection to the electronic rights management information and by enabling courts to grant injunctions against service providers if they have actual knowledge that other persons are using their services to infringe copyright.

The Future of Peer-to-Peer

Expected Developments in Peer-to-Peer Systems

Securing Distant Content Management

Some Peer-to-Peer applications offer the possibility of downloading information and statistics via mobile phones. The ability to configure a Peer-to-Peer application to access information on the ongoing operations (speed, completed downloads, etc.), and on the launch of a request over a mobile handset, opens the way to nomadic Peer-to-Peer use.

Ensuring the Continuity of the Peer-to-Peer Distribution Service

Continuity of service is now virtually guaranteed by the creation of de-centralized networks. This means that a decentralized network, which has been ordered to shut down, will continue to exist as long as there are peers using the software. Following a decision by the US Supreme Court in June 2005 against Grokster and Morpheus, many publishers elected to amend their services. Some are offering a new version of their software that requires a user ID and password, which are given after payment of a monthly or yearly subscription fee. Nevertheless, users who elect to connect to these networks by using an older version of the client software can still enjoy unrestricted access to the content. This means that unauthorized exchanges continue, but the publishers are protected from legal repercussions.

Securing Swaps in a Satisfactory Way for Rights Owners, Content Providers, and Publishers

Several initiatives have been conducted in order to incorporate a mechanism for collecting monies, sometimes referred to as tips, to be paid to copyright holders. Such a mechanism can involve a tool for identifying the content and continuous calculation of royalties to be paid out. Despite the technical complexity of the procedure and its implementation in a Peer-to-Peer environment, it now appears crucial for a legal offer – approved by the record companies – to emerge. More efficient solutions in this area appear to be coming from DRM systems that incorporate this feature – among others.

Availability on Mobile Devices

Mobile phones are enjoying an ever-increasing, and no doubt irreversible, popularity well beyond mere telephony. It is now technologically possible to implement a Peer-to-Peer kernel in a mobile phone. A number of telecom operators, service providers, and handset manufacturers are focusing their efforts in this direction.

Anonymous Use, Encrypted Exchanges, and Closed Networks

At a time when complaints against Peer-to-Peer software publishers and users are becoming louder, developers are proposing a new kind of Peer-to-Peer application, where peers remain anonymous. This implies that there is less risk for a user to be identified which in turn, encourages him or her to share content. In addition, exchanges are encrypted in such a way as to make it difficult to identify what content is exchanged. And, finally, some applications make it possible to create small Peer-to-Peer communities which are accessed using a login and password. The rise of this type of community could make the battle against unauthorized content swaps even more difficult. In addition, the exchange of encrypted contents could raise serious concerns about security.

Peer-to-Peer Technology for TV Broadcasting

Several applications use Peer-to-Peer technology for broadcasting TV programs in real time, without the broadcasters' approval. PPLive, Coolstreaming, QQLive, PPStream, Sopcast and TVants are all examples of software that enable access to a host of live TV channels picked up from a satellite, cable, or terrestrial network. The TV stream is captured by a peer and then streamed over the Peer-to-Peer network. Increases in the bitrates offered by broadband flat rates allow for steady and fluid play. TV broadcasting via Peer-to-Peer could represent a major economic stake in the coming years.

Expectations for the Future of Peer-to-Peer in Europe

The online content market (video, music, publishing, games, and adult content) is thus expected to more than double in 4 years, going from close to €1 billion in 2006 to €2.2 billion in 2009.

Business models nevertheless remain uncertain. For some operators, offering free content paves the way either to marketing other products and services (players, Internet subscriptions) or to generating advertising revenues (search engines). For others, content marketing remains a profit center even if online content models cannot replicate offline models exactly. With the exception of premium content, marketing music, videos and video games on a per-unit basis appears less suitable than flat rate subscription models.

The increase in the broadband user base does not only benefit online content distribution services. Peer-to-Peer networks and systems too are becoming more sophisticated, user-friendly, and efficient.

In the larger EU countries, between 15% and 34% of broadband Internet subscribers use at least one Peer-to-Peer application and most Peer-to-Peer households use two. eMule, BitTorrent, WinMX, LimeWire, Shareaza and KaZaA are the most popular. Noteworthy is the fact that 90% of Peer-to-Peer users state that they also download and exchange files using other sources such as websites, e-mail, IM, and FTP servers.

In France, the UK, and Germany, over 60% of Peer-to-Peer users are men with, unsurprisingly, an over representation of 15- to 24-year-olds and students. Music is the top-ranking type of content downloaded, followed by video, then images and photos. In the video content category, films rank number one, although TV programs account for roughly a third of downloaded videos.

The price for online content is by far the main incentive for using Peer-to-Peer networks, but users also cite diversity of content and ease of access as contributing factors.

In terms of traffic, the Peer-to-Peer phenomenon is gaining more momentum than FTP or classic web traffic. In late 2004, it accounted for close to 60% of all Internet Protocol (IP) traffic, versus just over 40% for ordinary Internet traffic.

The exploitation of intellectual property in digital form has required that the existing *legal framework* protecting copyright be amended. However the legal status of Peer-to-Peer systems remains largely undefined and the content industry has taken several legal steps against the unauthorized sharing of digital content files:

against Internet users, to establish a legal character for Peer-to-Peer,
against ISPs, to force them to divulge the identity of subscribers who use Peer-to-Peer services,
against advertisers who display adverts on Peer-to-Peer services, to deprive the services of their prime source of revenue,
against Peer-to-Peer software publishers, to establish their responsibility in illegal file sharing. In the United States, this strategy has proven most effective and led several Peer-to-Peer services either to shut down or to seek agreements with rights holders.

The gradual clarification of Peer-to-Peer's legal status and the obligation to respect copyright holders' rights are leading to the creation of *new business models*. The introduction of *payment systems* as part of Peer-to-Peer services is now the most commonly adopted path. It involves marking the content that is available on the Peer-to-Peer networks, and routing consumers to an e-commerce site to pay for the content rights. Another solution involves billing consumers for a *flat rate subscription* to access the Peer-to-Peer network. The success of these systems, nevertheless, supposes that the exchanged content be marked, and that network access can be confined to subscribers.

A third strategy for financing the content exchanged in Peer-to-Peer mode involves inserting *advertising* in the software. While some copyright holders have agreed to give limited authorization to this type of service, there is no guarantee that the advertising market is capable of generating sufficient revenues to pay royalties on the content.

Superdistribution of content represents a more innovative strategy. Here, each consumer can redistribute the content s/he acquired using a paid model, and earns a commission on distribution.

Peer-to-Peer's medium-term development will be fuelled by a series of positive factors in the areas of consumption (user-friendliness, community of peers, on-demand access), content (vast catalogs), technology (robustness of decentralized architectures, optimization of file distribution, interoperability and speed downloading), and costs (distribution of costs among users).

Three major uncertainties have prevented Peer-to-Peer from developing outside the margins of unauthorized content: a stabilized legal framework, efficient technical solutions to manage rights, and business models suited to the content industry.

A virtuous circle of the legal use of Peer-to-Peer networks could start in Europe in the near future:

The legal actions taken by the content industry, although not fully coherent, have severely limited Peer-to-Peer software publishers' ability to launch new services without signing agreements with the content industry.

DRM solutions can now be used in the context of Peer-to-Peer systems, both in terms of tracking file exchanges and of payment solutions.

Innovative business models are being tested, building on the specificity of the Peer-to-Peer systems.

As a result, some content companies (mostly in the field of music) have already made content available to Peer-to-Peer services, albeit still on a limited basis.

It is unlikely that these positive steps will fully eradicate unauthorized file sharing over the next 5 years. But the launch of content-industry backed, Peer-to-Peer-based services will increase the volume of authorized content on the Internet.

From a quantitative standpoint, the number of European peers could reach 44.5 million in 2010, with the number of files exchanged growing from 1.3 billion in 2005 to 110 billion in 2010. Audio files could account for half of the exchanged files, while video files (films and TV programs) for a quarter. Looking more specifically at online music, authorized Peer-to-Peer services could represent €0.3 billion in 2010, close to a third of the total market.

In the longer term (10–20 years), a further step would be the massive incorporation of file sharing in day-to-day communication processes. Advanced multimedia IM could be the future of file sharing, with Peer-to-Peer software integrated with IM devices and solutions. Today's major content distributors could lose their edge in the value-chain as producers and publishers would "inject" content into the networks, using DRM to monitor file sharing and invoicing via micro-payment mechanisms included in all communication systems, both fixed and mobile. In addition, superdistribution systems would reward peers who are influential in their community.

According to this view, it is no longer the "one-to-many" distribution model that drives the online circulation of content but the very "point-to-point" nature of the Internet.[14]

Notes

The present paper is based on the findings of the Special Study "The digital broadband value-added services industry and markets in Europe: Peer-to-Peer networks and markets" provided by IDATE in close cooperation with the EITO Task Force and published in the 2006 EITO Report.

1. Source: Minar and Hedlund: Peer-to-Peer, harnessing the benefits of a disruptive technology. Oram, A. (Ed). Beijing, O'Reilly.
2. 2002: actual, 2005: estimates, 2006 and 2010: forecasts.
3. Active use: all time spent to issue requests or monitor downloads.
4. A larger proportion of women answering the survey can account for the higher rate of women using Peer-to-Peer in the USA.
5. Share of households using a given Peer-to-Peer software in households using Peer-to-Peer software.
6. Share of households using specific Peer-to-Peer software in households using Peer-to-Peer software.
7. Share of households using specific Peer-to-Peer software in households using Peer-to-Peer software.
8. Share of households using specific Peer-to-Peer software in households using Peer-to-Peer software.
9. Multiple answers are available.
10. Paid content includes fee-based text, image, or audio information delivered digitally via a website, online service, or other interactive medium. Content fees must be paid directly by consumers on a subscription or an à la carte basis. This excludes any portion of access fees collected by Internet service providers for distribution to content providers for time spent by users on their sites. These figures do not include mobile phone-based content and therefore do not compare directly with the figures published in EITO 2005: "The Online content market and distribution in Europe."
11. Includes adult-oriented content.
12. More than 94% of revenues are redistributed to the music publishers and the other right owners, leaving the online music store with 6% of revenues. Other expenses amount to about 5% of revenues, therefore leaving a 1% margin on online music sales for the online store.
13. Source: PWC-IAB: Internet Advertising Revenue Report, 2004 Full Year Results.
14. Andrea Gavosto, Director Fondazione Giovanni Agnelli, formerly Cheif Economist, Telecom Italia.

About the Editors and Contributors

DR. ELI M. NOAM is professor of Finance and Economics at the Columbia University Graduate School of Business and Director of the Columbia Institute for Tele-Information. He has also served as Public Service Commissioner engaged in the telecommunications and energy regulation of New York State and on the White House's President's IT Advisory Committee. His publications include 27 books and over 400 articles on USA and international telecommunications, television, Internet, and regulation subjects. He served as a board member for the federal government's FTS-2000 telephone network, of the IRS' computer modernization project, and of the National Computer Lab. He is a member of the Council on Foreign Relations. Professor Noam received an A.B. (1970, Phi Beta Kappa), a Ph.D. in economics (1975), and a J.D. law degree (1975) from Harvard University. He is a member of the New York and Washington, D.C. bars, a licensed radio amateur Advanced Class, and a commercially rated pilot.

DR. LORENZO MARIA PUPILLO is an Executive Director in the Public Affairs Unit of Telecom Italia and Affiliated Researcher at Columbia Institute for Tele-Information. In Telecom Italia, he is in charge of Economics of Public Strategies. He is an economist by training and has worked in many areas of telecommunications demand and regulatory analysis, publishing papers in applied econometrics and industrial organization. He has also been Advisor to the Global Information and Communication Technologies Department of the World Bank in Washington. He has also been Adjunct Professor of Economics of ICTs at University of Rome, La Sapienza. Before joining Telecom Italia in 1992, he was member of technical staff at AT&T Bell Laboratories in Murray Hill, NJ. He earned a Ph.D. and an M.A. from University of Pennsylvania, an M.B.A. from Istituto Adriano Olivetti in Ancona, Italy, and an M.S. in Mathematics from University of Rome.

Contributors

SUDIP BHATTACHARJEE is an Associate Professor and Ackerman Scholar in the Department of Operations and Information Management in the School of Business, University of Connecticut. He received his Ph.D. in Management Science and Systems, with a minor in Industrial Engineering, from SUNY Buffalo. Dr. Bhattacharjee's research interests lie in distributed systems, multi-objective optimization, information systems economics and related issues of intellectual property rights, and supply chains. His research has been published or is forthcoming in various journals such as Management Science, INFORMS Journal on Computing, Journal of Management Information Systems, Journal of Business, Journal of Law and Economics, Communications of the ACM, IEEE Transactions, Decision Support Systems, and other journals and conference proceedings. He received the School of Business Innovation in teaching award in 2002, the Graduate teaching award in 2004, and the Best research paper award in 2005. His research has been highlighted in various media outlets such as Connecticut Public Television, Business Week, Washington Post, San Francisco Chronicle, Der Spiegel, Christian Science Monitor, slashdot.org, Business 2.0 Web Guide, and others.

MICHAEL BOTEIN is Professor of Law and Director of the Media Center at New York Law School in New York City. He holds a B.A. from Wesleyan University, and J.D. (law review) from Cornell University, as well as an LL.M. and J.S.D. (Ph.D. in Law) from Columbia University. He is the author/editor of more than 15 books, and has published more than 70 scholarly articles. He has been a visiting professor at Bond University, Australia, Columbia University, New York, Haifa University, Israel, Jerusalem University, Israel, Monash University, Australia, the University of Poitiers, France, and Wroclaw University, Poland. He has worked at the US Federal Communications Commission as well as National Telecommunications Administration, and is on the Board of the European Audiovisual Observatory, Council of Europe.

ALAIN BOURDEAU DE FONTENAY is a visiting scholar and Senior Affiliated Researcher with the Columbia Institute for Tele-Information (CITI), Columbia University, as well as Co-founder of the International Telecommunications Society (ITS) and Bellcore's (Telcordia) Distinguished Member of the Technical Staff. Alain Bourdeau de Fontenay's recent research activities include organizing an international research team on the economics of the "exchange commons" to better account for externalities and other interdependences, a research project on Internet peering in an age of convergence with telephony with applications in areas such as Internet backbone competition, Peer-to-Peer networks and vertical integration (http://www.citi.columbia.edu), and a study on economic growth, information and communications technologies (ICT), and inequality.

ERIC BOURDEAU DE FONTENAY is Manager of the Toronto-based "kaiso" band Kobo Town. Eric has spent his career steeped in what has been called the "digital revolution." In the 1990's, he worked on a variety of policy issues surrounding the communication and broadband sectors for telecommunication carriers and regulators across the world. With the emergence of the Internet, Eric established MusicDish (formerly Tag It) in 1997 as a new media firm utilizing emerging technologies and models to produce, package, and distribute original web-based content. Making an early bet the music sector, Eric launched what has grown into some of the leading voices in the growing debates challenging and shaping the industry through its trade e-publications MusicDish and Mi2N. Under his leadership, Music-Dish expanded into artist development through saturated marketing and online branding, using innovative strategies such as syndicated and relationship marketing, online street teams, and Peer-to-Peer viral distribution. Eric continues to be a frequent speaker at conferences worldwide.

JOHN CAREY is Professor of Communications and Media Industries at Fordham Business School and Director of Greystone Communications, a media research and planning firm. Previously, he taught at Columbia Business School and New York University. He has more than 25 years experience in conducting research about new media, consumer behavior, and telecommunication policy. Recently, he has conducted studies on consumer use of mobile video technologies, the impact of digital television on viewing behavior, the media habits of 18- to 34-year-olds, and the adoption of satellite radio. Clients have included A&E Television Networks, Cablevision, Corporation for Public Broadcasting, The Markle Foundation, NBC Universal, The New York Times, PBS, Primedia, Real Networks, and XM Satellite Radio, among others. John is a board member of the Donald McGannon Communication Research Center and on the Advisory Board of the Annenberg School for Communications. He has also served as a Commissioner on the Annenberg Press Commission and on the board of the Adult Literacy Media Alliance. He holds a Ph.D. from the Annenberg School for Communication at the University of Pennsylvania and has more than 100 publications about new technology adoption and consumer use of media.

XU CHENG is a graduate student and research assistant in the School of Computing Science at Simon Fraser University, British Columbia, Canada. He received a B.Sc. degree in computer science from Peking University, Beijing, China, in 2006. His research interests include Peer-to-Peer networks, video streaming, and sensor networks.

CAMERON DALE is a graduate student in Physics and Computing Science at Simon Fraser University. After 5 years of work experience, mostly in the Fiber Optics industry, he returned to Simon Fraser and is now working on completing his Master's in Computing Science. Cameron's interests are in Networking, in particular Peer-to-Peer and BitTorrent-related issues, and he is also active in the open source community.

GALI EINAV is currently the Director of Digital Technology Research at NBC Universal where she oversees strategic and consumer research across various digital technologies such as VOD, Mobile, and online media.

Building on her work at Columbia University's Interactive Design Lab, Gali specialized in researching the use and content of interactive media, focusing on the state of interactive television in the USA and the UK. She is the author of "Producing Interactive Television," and "The Content Landscape of Internet Television," published in "Television over the Internet: Network Infrastructure and Content Implications."

Gali has worked as a senior producer and journalist for the second television channel in Israel where she produced, researched, and brought to air numerous investigate reports, documentaries, and in-depth interviews. She also taught television and media studies at the New School of Communications in Tel-Aviv.

Gali holds an M.A. in Communications and Journalism from Hebrew University and a Ph.D. in Communications from Columbia University's School of Journalism. She is a member of NATAS and its New York Chapter Advanced Media Committee. Since 2003, she has been serving as Judge for the Advanced Media Technology Emmy Awards.

ANDREA GAVOSTO is Director of the Fondazione Giovanni Agnelli. Until last December he was Chief Economist of the Telecom Italia Group, where he worked on the main regulatory and strategic issues, such as the regulatory market analyses, network separation, and the future of the telecom markets. Beforehand he was Chief Economist of the Fiat Group and worked for both the Research Department of the Bank of Italy and the Research Department of Confindustria, the Italian employers' association. He holds a degree in Business and Economics from the University of Turin, and did his postgraduate work at the London School of Economics, where he obtained an M.Sc. in Economics. He was also Visiting Fellow at the National Bureau of Economic Research of Cambridge, Cambridge, MA. He is author of several publications on macroeconomic forecasting and applied labor and industrial economics.

RAM D. GOPAL is GE Endowed Professor of Business in the Department of Operations and Information Management in the School of Business, University of Connecticut. His current research interests are in the areas of data security, privacy and valuation, database management, intellectual property rights and economics of software and music piracy, online market design and performance evaluation, economics of online advertising, technology integration, and business impacts of technology. His research has appeared in Management Science, Operations Research, INFORMS Journal on Computing, Information Systems Research, Journal of Business, Journal of Law and Economics, Communications of the ACM, IEEE Transactions on Knowledge and Data Engineering, Journal of Management Information Systems, Decision Support Systems, and other journals and conference proceedings. He is the recipient of the School of Business Undergraduate teaching award in 2002 and the School of Business Graduate teaching award in 2003. He currently serves as the Ph.D. director for the department and is on the editorial board of Information Systems Research, Journal of Database Management, Information Systems Frontiers, and Journal of Management Sciences.

MIN HANG is currently working for Tsinghua University, China and the Media Management and Transformation Center (MMTC) of Jönköping University, Sweden. Hang obtained her Ph.D. degree in Business Administration from Jönköping University, Sweden. She also holds a Master Degree in European Business Administration and Business Law from Lund University, Sweden and a Master Degree in Management Science from Hohai University, China. Prior to joining the MMTC in Sweden, Hang was in charge of the International Cooperation Development Affairs in the Department of International Cooperation for the Ministry of Communications in China. Her research interests include cross-national management, strategy in the media companies and market differences in the media industries. Dr. Hang is the author of a number of books, book chapters, journal articles and conference papers on New Media Strategy, International Media Portfolios Management, Media Economics and Management, Media and Entrepreneurship, and Media Human Resources Management.

BRUNO LAMBORGHINI is Professor of Business Administration and Marketing at the Catholic University in Milan, since 2002. After receiving a degree in Economics summa cum laude, Bruno Lamborghini began his career as a consultant and journalist and afterwards joined Olivetti where he reached managerial responsibilities as Chief Economist, Director of the European Affairs Department, Chief Strategist and Member of the Executive Committee. In June 1996, he was nominated Vice-Chairman of Olivetti Telemedia, Olivetti's holding in the area of telecommunications and Board Member of Infostrada and Omnitel, the Olivetti telecommunications operating companies. In October 1996 he joined the Olivetti Board of Directors and in May 1997 was elected Chairman of Olivetti Lexikon (in 2001 renamed Olivetti Tecnost), the Olivetti operating company in the area of office automation until end of 2004. In 2005, he has been nominated Vice Chairman of Olivetti (formerly Olivetti Tecnost). Since its foundation, he is Chairman of the EITO, the European Information Technology Observatory. In 2001 he was elected Chairman of BIAC-OCDE until 2004 when he was nominated Vice Chairman of BIAC. An author of books and articles, Bruno Lamborghini is also a lecturer in Industrial Economics in various Italian Universities (Turin, Bologna, and Milan).

STEFANO LAMBORGHINI is Senior Economist at Telecom Italia, Strategy Unit, focusing on content, regulatory affairs and on technological, economical, and social impact analysis of new media. Always interested in technological, economical, and social impacts of innovation, after a graduation in International/UE Law with specialization in intellectual property rights, Stefano Lamborghini has always worked in telecommunications, internet and multimedia sectors. In the 1990s, he was a consultant for the main Italian multimedia industry and ISP services associations (Anee and AIIP) with duties and tasks concerning regulatory and institutional affairs, relationships with Italian and European authorities, and legal issues about the electronic publishing and internet service provider industry (copyright, fight against piracy and counterfeiting, privacy protection, on line publishing, and competition).

JIANGCHUAN LIU received the B.Eng. degree (cum laude) from Tsinghua University, Beijing, China, in 1999, and the Ph.D. degree from The Hong Kong University of Science and Technology in 2003, both in computer science. He is currently an Assistant Professor in the School of Computing Science, Simon Fraser University, British Columbia, Canada, and was an Assistant Professor at The Chinese University of Hong Kong from 2003 to 2004. He was a recipient of Microsoft Research Fellowship (2000), a recipient of the Hong Kong Young Scientist Award (2003), and a co-inventor of one European patent and two US patents. His research interests include Internet architecture and protocols, media streaming, wireless ad hoc networks, and service overlay networks. He serves as TPC member for many networking conferences, including IEEE INFOCOM and IWQoS.

He was TPC co-chair for The First IEEE International Workshop on Multimedia Systems and Networking (WMSN'05), Information System co-chair for IEEE INFOCOM '04, and guest-editors for ACM/Kluwer Journal of Mobile Networks and Applications (MONET), special issues on wireless sensor networking and wireless mesh networking. He is an editor of IEEE Communications Surveys and Tutorials. He is a member of the IEEE and Sigma Xi.

JAMES R. MARSDEN is the Treibick Family Endowed Chair in e-Business and Board of Trustees Distinguished Professor. He came to UConn in 1993 as Professor and Head of the Department of Operations and Information Management. Jim has overseen the growth of OPIM from 8 faculty members in 1993 to 27 today. Dr. Marsden also serves as Director of the OPIM/SBA MIS Research Lab and was a founding member of the Advisory Board and the Steering Committee of CIBER (Center for International Business Education and Research). Dr. Marsden has a lengthy publication record in market innovation and analyses, economics of information, artificial intelligence, and production theory. His research work has appeared or is forthcoming in numerous leading academic journals. Professor Marsden received his A.B. (Phi Beta Kappa, James Scholar, Evans Scholar) from the University of Illinois and his M.S. and Ph.D. from Purdue University. Having completed his J.D. while at the University of Kentucky, Jim has been admitted to both the Kentucky and Connecticut Bar. He is an Area Editor of Decision Support System, on the Editorial Board of Journal of Management Information Systems, editor of the Journal of Organization Computing and Electronic Commerce, and serves in a frequent external evaluator for major US and international universities. He has held visiting positions at the University of York (England), University of Arizona, Purdue University, and the University of North Carolina. Jim was an Invited Lecturer at two NATO Advanced Study Institutes on Decision Support Systems and has given keynote addresses and university seminars throughout North America, Europe, and Asia.

STEVEN ROSENBAUM is the CEO of Magnify Networks (http://www.Magnify.net). As the Founder and CEO of Magnify.net, Steven Rosenbaum has developed a worldwide reputation as a storyteller with a passion for person storytelling. His award-winning television, internet and film projects cover the range from reality based documentary and hard news coverage to narrative fiction. Rosenbaum has produced hours of primetime television for such outlets as A&E, CourtTV, Animal Planet, MSNBC, The History Channel, TLC, BBC, CBS, and CNN. He is best known for creating the groundbreaking series MTV News UNFILTERED. He went on to Direct "7 Days In September" a documentary feature that chronicled the days after 9/11. Rosenbaum's work has been acknowledged for excellence, with a recognition that includes 2 Emmy Awards, 6 New York Festival's World Medals, 4 CINE Golden Eagles, and 6 Telly awards. Today, Rosenbaum is the CEO of Magnify.net. Magnify provides a platform solution that allows web sites, niche communities, and publishers to easily empower their community to embrace User-Generated Video. Magnify powers more than 3000 channels of User-Generated Video, and is working closely with a wide variety of media makers, communities, and publishers who are evolving their content offerings to include content created by and sorted and reviewed by community members.

EDWARD SAMUELS is an intellectual property consultant in New York. Prior to that, he was for 25 years a Professor of Law at New York Law School. He has written dozens of articles on copyright law, and *The Illustrated Story of Copyright* (St. Martin's 2000). The book and other writings are available at his website, http://www.edwardsamuels.com.

VIKTOR MAYER-SCHÖNBERGER is Associate Professor of Public Policy at the John F. Kennedy School of Government, Harvard University. He has published seven books and is the author of over 80 articles and book chapters on the legal and political aspects of modern information and communication technologies. After successes in the International Physics Olympics and the Austrian Young Programmers Contest, Dr. Mayer-Schönberger studied law in Salzburg (Mag.iur, '88, Dr.iur '91), Cambridge (UK) and Harvard LL.M. '89. In 1992 he received an M.Sc. (Econ) from the London School of Economics, and in 2001 the venia docendi on (among others) information law. In 1986 he founded Ikarus Software, a company focusing on data security, and developed the Virus Utilities, which became the best-selling Austrian software product. The recipient of numerous awards for innovation and entrepreneurship, he was voted Top-5 Software Entrepreneur in Austria in 1991 and Person of the Year for the State of Salzburg in 2000. He is the cofounder of the SubTech conference and from 2003–2006 served on the ABA/AALS National Conference of Lawyers and Scientists. He chairs the Rueschlikon Conference on Information Policy and is on the academic advisory board for privacy of Microsoft's Trust worthy Computing Initiative.

W. EDWARD STEINMUELLER is Professor of Information and Communication Technology Policy at SPRU – Science and Technology Policy Research, University of Sussex. He received his Ph.D. in economics from Stanford University where he was Senior Research Associate and Deputy Director at Stanford Institute for Economic Policy Research. His works include industrial economics studies of software, integrated circuit and telecommunication industries and the book *Mobilizing the Information Society: Strategies for Growth and Opportunity*, Oxford University Press, 2000 (with R. Mansell). He also has written on science policy including co-editing (with A. Geuna and A Salter) of *Science and Innovation: Rethinking the Rationales for Funding and Governance*, Edward Elgar, 2003. His current areas of research include the economics of open source communities, purposive virtual communities such as Wikipedia, the economics of scientific knowledge production and distribution, and the relationships among social, organizational, and technological factors in the production and adoption of new Internet related technologies. He is internationally known for his work on the integrated circuit, computer, telecommunication, and software industries and is a policy consultant in areas of industrial policy and high technology competition such as intellectual property rights, competition policy and standardization.

RAHUL TELANG is an Assistant Professor of Information Systems and Management at the Heinz School, Carnegie Mellon University. He received his Ph.D. in Information Systems from the Tepper School of Business at Carnegie Mellon University in 2002. Dr Telang's key research field is in economics of Information security. He has done extensive empirical as well as analytical work on disclosure issues surrounding software vulnerabilities, software vendors' incentives to provide quality, mechanism designs for optimal security investments in a multi-unit firms, etc. His work on impact of vulnerability announcement on vendors' stock price has received wide media coverage. Dr Telang has received the prestigious National Science Foundation CAREER award for his research in economics of information security. He has also done extensive work on consumer usages of new technologies (like Peer-to-Peer networks) and impact of these technologies on market structure. His work on the used book market has been reported in The New York Times among other media outlets. His dissertation won the William W. Cooper Doctoral Dissertation Award. His research has been published in leading journals including Management Science, Information Systems Research, Journal of MIS, Journal of Marketing Research, etc. He is on the editorial board of Management Science and Information systems research, and has served as the co-chair of the International Conference on Electronic Commerce (ICEC 2003), Conference on Information Systems and Technology (CIST 2006), and Workshop on Economics of Information Security (WEIS 2007). He has been a visiting professor at the Indian School of Business.

KEVIN WERBACH is a leading expert on the business, policy, and social implications of emerging information and communications technologies. Werbach is an Assistant Professor of Legal Studies and Business Ethics at

The Wharton School, University of Pennsylvania. His research explores the legal and business issues generated by the Internet and other technological phenomena. Werbach is also the founder of the Supernova Group, a technology analysis and consulting firm, and organizer of Supernova <http://www.supernova2007.com>, a leading executive technology conference. He was formerly the Editor of Release 1.0, a renowned monthly technology report published by Esther Dyson. He served as Counsel for New Technology Policy at the Federal Communications Commission, where he helped develop the US Government's Internet and e-commerce policies. He is frequently quoted by leading media outlets, has testified before the US Senate and Federal Communications Commission, and is the author of numerous academic and popular publications.

Index